Praise for *On Rhetoric and Black Music*

"Scholar and musician Earl Brooks's *On Rhetoric and Black Music* marshals the author's scholarly curiosities and musical prowess into a unique, multisited study, impressive in its historical reach and capacious in its genre coverage. Excellent for teaching courses on Black music, American music, and cultural studies, this book takes on the spirituals, ragtime, jazz, and gospel and analyzes them with an original take. With this study, Brooks establishes a compelling multidisciplinary voice in several fields—one that readers will find accessible and illuminating."

—Guthrie P. Ramsey Jr., author of *Who Hears Here? On Black Music, Pasts and Present*

"Deeply imaginative, thoroughly researched, and theoretically sound, Earl Brooks's *On Rhetoric and Black Music* challenges conventional thinking about the discursive practices that underscored the ideology, movement, and activity that framed the larger historical span of the struggle for social change and racial reconciliation in America. Brooks offers new readings into how musical sound persuaded, informed, and motivated Black America during key historical periods by anchoring his theoretical framework in an examination of the cultural work of five key sound identities that were central to the progression of American music: Scott Joplin, Duke Ellington, Mary Lou Williams, John Coltrane, and Mahalia Jackson. This alone makes this work a must-read!"

—Tammy L. Kernodle, former president, Society for American Music

"Earl H. Brooks's *On Rhetoric and Black Music* offers a brilliant new way of thinking about the contributions of Black musical artists. He provides a rhetorical analysis of the musical artistry of Harriet Tubman, John Coltrane, Duke Ellington, Mary Lou Williams, and Mahalia Jackson. His analysis demonstrates that Black music is not just or only entertainment but a lifeline, a 'sonic lexicon' which articulates the feelings, emotions, and states of mind that have shaped Black people's cultural and political development."

—Geneva Smitherman, University Distinguished Professor Emerita, Michigan State University, and author of *My Soul Look Back in Wonder: Memories from a Life of Study, Struggle, and Doin Battle in the Language Wars*

"*On Rhetoric and Black Music* is a brilliant, resonant story of Black music and meaning-making, of Black sonic and social worlds. Earl Brooks invites us to hear the expressive force and persuasive power in our musical tradition. That power might manifest in a poignant lyric, a piano trill, a blue note, or a wordless moan—and in all the conversation, contemplation, inspiration, creation, and community that emerge with these sounds. Alongside the rhetorical quality of Black music, I am moved by the musical quality of Brooks's own rhetoric. He writes with great beauty, clarity, agility, and melody—a singing book."

—La Marr Jurelle Bruce, author of *How to Go Mad Without Losing Your Mind: Madness and Black Radical Creativity*

ON RHETORIC
AND
BLACK MUSIC

African American Life Series

A complete listing of the books in this series can be found online at wsupress.wayne.edu.

Series Editor
Melba Joyce Boyd
Department of Africana Studies, Wayne State University

ON RHETORIC AND BLACK MUSIC

Earl H. Brooks

WAYNE STATE UNIVERSITY PRESS
DETROIT

© 2024 by Wayne State University Press, Detroit, Michigan 48201. All rights reserved. No part of this book may be reproduced without formal permission.

ISBN 9780814346488 (paperback)
ISBN 9780814346471 (hardcover)
ISBN 9780814346495 (e-book)

Library of Congress Control Number: 2023942041

Cover images courtesy of the New York Public Library and Wikimedia Commons. Cover design by Kristle Marshall.

Wayne State University Press rests on Waawiyaataanong, also referred to as Detroit, the ancestral and contemporary homeland of the Three Fires Confederacy. These sovereign lands were granted by the Ojibwe, Odawa, Potawatomi, and Wyandot Nations, in 1807, through the Treaty of Detroit. Wayne State University Press affirms Indigenous sovereignty and honors all tribes with a connection to Detroit. With our Native neighbors, the press works to advance educational equity and promote a better future for the earth and all people.

Wayne State University Press
Leonard N. Simons Building
4809 Woodward Avenue
Detroit, Michigan 48201-1309

Visit us online at wsupress.wayne.edu.

Contents

Acknowledgments	ix
Introduction: Of Our Spiritual and Musical Strivings	1
1. Ragtime, Race, and Rhetoric	19
2. Duke Converses with the World	43
3. The Rhetoric of Mary Lou Williams	69
4. A (Rhetorical) Love Supreme	99
5. Move On Up: The Rhetorical Mastery of Mahalia Jackson	123
Conclusion: Shout Chorus	161
Notes	169
Bibliography	195
Index	213

Acknowledgments

I owe a debt of gratitude to Elizabeth Surles and the staff of the Rutgers Institute of Jazz Studies for all their support with the Mary Lou Williams collection. I also want to express my thanks to the staff of the Tulane University Special Collections for their assistance with the Mahalia Jackson collection. This book was completed with support received from the Dresher Center for the Humanities at the University of Maryland, Baltimore County (UMBC) and the Charles L. Blockson Collection of African-Americana and the African Diaspora at Penn State University.

    Two mentors who have been consistent supporters of my work include Keith Gilyard and Maryemma Graham. Thank you both for your wisdom and guidance. I am grateful for kind words of support from scholars Tony Bolden, Thabiti Lewis, John Edgar Tidwell, Jack Selzer, Debra Hawhee, Cheryl Glenn, Daniel Anderson, Jordynn Jack, Jenny Stoever, Guthrie Ramsey, Rich Furman, Robert Rodriguez, and Allyson Flaster. There are also many colleagues who have been important sources of affirmation and encouragement that I feel grateful to call friends. Many thanks to Mudiwa Pettus, Brandon Erby, Gabriel Green, D'Angelo Bridges, David Green, Ersula Ore, Adam Banks, Maria Durán, Gale Greenlee, Robert Birdwell, and Mark Villegas. To my UMBC colleagues Jessica Berman, Matt Belzer, Lindsay DiCuirci, Keegan Finberg, Drew Holladay, Lucille McCarthy, Kathryn McKinley, Emily Yoon, Jody Shipka, Orianne Smith, Raphael Falco, Carol Fitzpatrick, Elaine MacDougall, Tanya Olson, Michele Osherow, Marsha Scott, Jean Fernandez, and Sharon Tran, and Courtney Hobson, thank you for your camaraderie.

    My close friends and family were tremendous sources of inspiration. A very special thanks to my parents, Earl and Vanessa Brooks, my parents-in-love, Cecilia and Melanio Matos, my uncle Charles Holmes, cousins Sadie and Herman Davenport, and Jordan Brooks, as well as my siblings Troy Brooks, Lanae Towner, Jeremiah Brooks, Shanise Brooks, and David Brooks. To Adrian Carter, Jerome Tatum, Brandon Bayless, Chad Hughes, Walter Farabee, and Michael Kelly, thank you for your brotherhood. Finally, and most importantly, this book would not be possible without my moon and stars, Jessica and Kamarah, my beloved wife and daughter.

Introduction

Of Our Spiritual and Musical Strivings

On June 1, 1863, Harriet Tubman led a raid on Port Royal, South Carolina, near the Combahee River, as a scout for the Union Army under Colonel James Montgomery. She became the first woman to plan and lead an armed attack for the American armed forces. The raid was a tremendous success, and the number of liberated slaves exceeded expectations.[1] As the newly freed men, women, and children sought refuge on the boats carrying the Union forces, panic began to spread due to fears that the soldiers would leave them behind. Colonel Montgomery urged Tubman to calm their concerns in words that amounted to "speak to your people." Tubman was bewildered by the request at first, given that they were strangers to her as well. "I didn't know any more about them than he did," Tubman recalled. However, "I went when he called me on the gunboat, and they on the shore. They didn't know anything about me, and I didn't know what to say. I looked at them about two minutes, and then I sung to them."[2] Her medium was the spirituals. Those on the riverbanks began to join her in song, punctuating their responses with shouts of "Glory!" The effect of the singing brought composure to the crowds of people, leading to a safe evacuation.

The circumstances surrounding Tubman's use of spirituals point to their multiple functions in Black life and to the expansive rhetorical nature of Black music. The spirituals are one of the most important traditions in the African diaspora that survived the institution of enslavement. As a genre of songs that mixes elements of African and Western musical traditions with the turmoil, anguish, and pain of enslavement, the spirituals are much more than symbolic gestures of religious devotion. They are texts cocreated by performer and audience, full of improvisation, and malleable enough for use in numerous situations. These traits define the spirituals as a cultural praxis that unifies its practitioners around central components of their belief systems, including the most pressing existential question: Is my living in vain?[3]

Although traditional conceptions of rhetoric usually revolve around public oratory (e.g., Sojourner Truth) and confine rhetoric to alphabetic discourse (that is, speaking and writing), Tubman's use of the spirituals was rhetorically strategic and emblematic of how spirituals were vital to the enslaved in terms of mediating certain spaces and activities. Moreover, the spirituals helped the enslaved to cast themselves as worthy of God's presence and protection. When Tubman sang the spirituals on the shores of the Combahee River, she solidified an ethos as someone especially close to God and capable of delivering the enslaved out of bondage, like Moses. Tubman understood that if she used a certain style with particular inflections and embellishments, her audience would have a text with which they could engage (audience members shouting "Glory!" and "Hallelujah!") and identify. Her audience was persuaded by her authenticity, and singer and respondents became united in the truth of their common experiences.

Tubman's use of the spirituals demonstrates how music permeates the Black experience in America. Rethinking Black history through sound challenges the normative ways in which this history has been constructed. For example, this approach to Tubman frames her facility with the spirituals as a rhetorical tool, which was just as important as her verbal prowess and the pistol she carried. Imagining and appreciating her singing requires us to think through our ears and consciously acknowledge a fundamental truth: the rhetorical function of sound—or the interface of rhetoric and music—is as important as any other area of inquiry with respect to African American history and culture. Undeniably, there would have been no Harlem Renaissance, Civil Rights movement, or Black Arts movement as we know these phenomena without Black music. Such music always has been inextricably linked to the "spiritual strivings"[4] of Black folks. The spirituals, along with related genres such as blues and jazz, are also discursive fields where swinging, improvisation, call-and-response, blue notes, the groove, and other musical idioms are a form of literacy. I am contemplating much more than the impact of lyrics, though that impact is not insignificant. I am simply more concerned at this juncture with the ability of nonverbal music to articulate the feelings, emotions, and states of mind that have shaped African American cultural and political development. This is not to suggest, however, that this book confines the value of Black music to its politico-economic relevance or its impact on something beyond itself.[5] Aesthetics are always important. But my interest here is specifically on how Black music functions as rhetoric, to amplify its centrality to African American expressive culture and to draw attention to the operation of sonic Black subjects in the multicultural American public sphere.

Thelonious Monk said that if one really understands the meaning of bebop, one understands freedom.[6] Following Monk, understanding more about the nature of Black music broadens our grasp of its significance to Black life and culture. *On Rhetoric and Black Music* is like a bebop solo, one that plays through the changes of disciplinary discourses in rhetorical studies, African American history, and music while serving as a response to the call of leading scholarship on African American sociolinguistics and rhetorical traditions.[7] These include the landmark texts featured in the African American Life Series at Wayne State University Press, under which this book is also published, such as Keith Gilyard's *Voices of the Self: A Study of Language Competence* (1991), Kermit Campbell's *"Gettin' Our Groove On,": Rhetoric, Language, and Literacy for the Hip Hop Generation* (2005), Vershawn Young's *Your Average Nigga: Performing Race, Literacy, and Masculinity* (2007), Vorris L. Nunley's *Keepin' It Hushed: The Barbershop and African American Hush Harbor Rhetoric* (2011), and, arguably one of the most important texts written on African American vernacular English, Geneva Smitherman's *Talkin and Testifyin: The Language of Black America* (1977).

This book grapples with two central questions: One, how does African American music function as rhetoric? Two, what happens if Black music is posited as not merely reflective but central to the discourse of African Americans and Americans in general? Although there is no single way that African American music functions as rhetoric, *On Rhetoric and Black Music* examines *some* of the ways it does through a detailed rhetorical analysis of some of America's most iconic musicians and by suggesting that we all should take a moment to listen to them as public intellectuals invested in crafting rhetorical projects through their music. Toward this end, this book amplifies and contextualizes the relationship between musical innovation and rhetorical strategy.

Although the idea of shared experience helps to explain how the spirituals could and did function as a mode of communication for Tubman and her audience, that idea alone does not explain the internal mechanisms by which music functions as a communicative act. To explain such dynamics, one must consider parameters for describing how music communicates particular meanings and examine how those meanings may have an impact at the level of public discourse.

Inquiry into the relationship between music and communication stretches back to antiquity. Plato, for example, considered music to be a language, one particularly suited to conveying emotions. However, for this very reason he was suspicious of its ability to influence beliefs and behavior.[8] Similarly, Aristotle reasoned that music possessed "some influence over the character and the soul," and he believed furthermore that melodies could be ethical, active, passionate, or inspiring, depending on the genre and context.[9] The relationship between music and rhetoric became a topic of explicit debate during the Enlightenment era, and discussions of music and lyrics abound in many of the music treatises of the seventeenth and eighteenth centuries.[10] Composer and musician were tasked with moving people in a way similar to a well-delivered speech, which explains the origins of music terminology that describes musical ideas such as theme, phrase, and sentence. Composers like Joseph Haydn were commonly referred to as orators and praised for their musical accomplishments and rhetorical abilities.[11] However, disagreements about the nature of music's communicative power broke down into the two broad philosophical camps of naturalism and idealism.

Naturalism, the philosophical foundation for mimesis that prevailed prior to 1800, was the view that all things within the universe could be investigated or reduced to empirical, material processes. From this perspective, works of art were like instruments that functioned like the passions to induce a "corresponding emotional reaction in the mind and spirit of the listener."[12] Idealism was the product of Romantic thinkers who elevated the status of music by alleging that it was "precisely because of [music's] ability to function outside the strictures of language" that music had the "ability to transcend that which could be expressed in words." Contrary to naturalism, idealism framed the power of art as a product of its ability to reflect a higher ideal or truth and the audience's ability to perceive that truth.[13] While naturalism restricted music to the realm of emotional cause and effect, idealism suggested music could function epistemically, and listeners were expected to actively engage the music and their imaginations in the pursuit of a deeper meaning.[14] Thus the debate revolved around a question of effects versus essence. Does music perform its work by moving the passions through a language of emotions (effects) or by reflecting higher ideals via intellectual inquiry (essence)?

Although much ink has been spilled by Western musicians, musicologists, and philosophers wrestling within this binary, the African diaspora has never been overly fixated on, or bothered by, music's communicative plasticity.[15] This dynamic is a product of a broader feature of language use within the diaspora. Western deconstructionist debates over the instability of language and the capricious nature of signs have never had much purchase in Black lived experiences because the idea that language is subjective and constitutive has been largely taken for granted. The historical development of African American rhetoric makes use of both classical Western and African rhetorical traditions and instead treats the instability of language as a creative and competitive arena.[16]

Within African diasporic traditions exists a more explicit recognition of music's communicative agency. Although some societies in ancient Africa made extensive use of written documents, the "vocal-expressive modality" reigned supreme in communication culture. This "sum total of oral tradition," which included "vocality, drumming, storytelling, praise singing, and naming" survived the Middle Passage and is a distinctive feature of African American communication.[17] Additionally, all art is considered functional, meaning that all texts, sonic or otherwise, possess a meaning within the artist's and audience's world view.[18] This idea most strikingly contrasts with the notion of Western absolute music, or music celebrated for its supposed detachment from any programmatic or cultural context. This theoretical framework is held together by the concept of *nommo*, a term used to describe the power and force of the word to shape reality. Although *nommo* is usually discussed in relation to African diasporic language practices, it also conceptualizes the "productive capacity" of sound and the hybridity of speech and music.[19] The meaning-making process of *nommo* emphasizes collective activity, as there is no strict separation between artist and audience. The participatory function of audience during a communicative act (e.g., the shouts of "amen" during a sermon in a Black church) is another important distinction of African diasporic rhetorical traditions. Communication within the Western tradition, which privileged the autonomy and primacy of the speaker, relied on a conception of audience and the role of listening as passive and lacking in agency.

However, both African and Western conceptions of sound are reflected in the modern field of sonic studies (or sound studies), which is the study of the production and consumption of sound, the sociocultural milieu in which sound is embedded, and sound's impact on human behavior. In other words, sonic studies *is* a rhetorical approach to sound and has three emphases. First, it is spatial; it is attentive to sound's ability to impact the construction and experience of spaces (the case of Muzak in shopping malls, for instance). Second, it is epistemological in terms of exploring sound's ability to construct ways of knowing and to mediate memories and experiences (blues music as a way of coping with adversity). Third, it is identity-oriented in its preoccupation with the role of sound in constructing and deconstructing personal and cultural identity (the beat in hip-hop). *On Rhetoric and Black Music* expands the traditional work of sonic studies by explicitly focusing on Black sound, to focus on the intersection of sound, history, culture, and politics of the African diaspora.

Sonic studies incorporates empirical demonstrations of relationships among music and linguistic communication. The abilities to process language and to process music occupy the same region of the brain, and both functions are tied to a learned sound system. Aniruddh Patel uses the term "native sonic milieu" to discuss how one's native sound system "imprints on our minds" through a "mental framework of sound categories."[20] This explains why music derived from another culture can sound foreign. As is the case with verbal language, we hear with an accent, or the sum total of previous experiences and exposures. The hybridity of the spirituals, its mixture of European and African characteristics, was possible because Africans heard Christian hymns with their native sonic milieu intact.

Research also has shown that the perception of melody and harmony is not a static process. The human brain converts pitch and timbre into various relationships.[21] Some are prioritized over others, which accounts for the ability to memorize certain melodies more readily than others and for the proclivity to hear coherence between certain melodies and harmonies as opposed to other combinations.[22] The importance of timbre, or the quality of sound, cannot be overstated. The timbres that are used for the performance of the spirituals signify important cultural characteristics, and they serve as one of the principal vehicles for the intense emotions expressed in various songs. The shouts, cries, and guttural moans shape the timbre and texture of the spirituals. These ornamentations supply the spirituals with their temporal and spectral profile, their amplitude and distribution of frequencies.

Rhythm, too, is an important aspect of communication, and the native sonic milieu of the African diaspora features an implicit knowledge of common rhythmic characteristics that allow for "expressive timing in music," including the "musical allusion to physical movement."[23] Expressive timing capitalizes on the relationships between beat, meter, accents (structure), physical motion (dancing, swinging), and emotion (as in the pairing of slower tempos with darker emotions). When the rescued slaves at Combahee River responded to Tubman's singing by shouting "Glory!" they displayed their knowledge of expressive timing through their responses, an iteration of the call-and-response pattern.[24]

The empirically demonstrated connections between music and linguistic communication address what biomedical scientist Michael Arbib refers to as the "language-music continuum." At one end of the continuum is "pure" language, which contains a grammatical system (phonology, syntax, lexicon, discourse rules) that enables the communication of unlimited propositions.[25] A number of language-music mixtures (songs such as the spirituals) exist along the continuum. At the other end is instrumental music, with the ability to communicate emotions at a much deeper level than language alone. If we construct the language-music continuum expressly with regard to the language and music that has sprung from Black culture, we can determine more clearly the culture's "sonic and auditory distinctive features."[26] These features, a particular constellation of rhizomatous roots of sounds that unite Black musicological production and communicative practices, comprise what I term the *sonic lexicon of Black music*. This concept conjoins the foundational ideas about African American language, or African American vernacular English (AAVE), with the history and practice of Black music. Thanks to the scholarly contributions of those such as William Labov, J. L. Dillard, Lorenzo Turner, Robert L. Williams, John R. Rickford, and

Geneva Smitherman, which served to dispel many of the inaccuracies and misunderstandings concerning the language practices of Black communities, AAVE is not "lazy, ungrammatical speech." Much to the contrary, AAVE is a complex, rule-governed verbal system that began as a creole of African and European language mixtures. These mixtures were the products of African language structures overlayed with English words under the historical conditions of slavery and racial oppression. Due to the critical role that language serves as a cornerstone of racial and ethnic identity, AAVE thrives today as a rich tapestry of communication styles that remains tethered to those foundational African language structures and rhetorical traditions. The sonic lexicon of Black music incorporates those foundational structures as the sonic blueprint that undergirds both language and musical practices. Although Black music is an ever-expanding, multigenre enterprise, the sonic lexicon of Black music is a heuristic for the range of musical, stylistic, and thematic qualities, or roots, that unite around a distinctive lineage embedded in the Black experience in America. Further, the sonic lexicon of Black music thrives, as does AAVE, not through race per se but through rigorous and long-term cultural immersion in its traditions. This fact accounts for practitioners of AAVE and Black music who do not identify themselves as Black or African American.

While delineating the complex minutiae of any particular genre of Black music would immediately exceed the limitations of any single book, *On Rhetoric and Black Music* instead posits Black music as a storehouse of sonic commonplaces and common resonances. Following Kenneth Burke's notion in *A Rhetoric of Motives* that "you persuade a man only insofar as you can talk his language by speech, gesture, tonality, order, image, attitude, idea, *identifying* your way with his," *commonplaces* are viewed as the shared "common ground" of cultural beliefs, practices, and idioms that may serve as potent resources for constructing persuasive arguments.[27] *Resonance* is a term that refers to the alignment of sonic frequency patterns that oscillate (or vibrate) and amplify one another. I find commonplaces and resonance as useful for hearing the relationship between Black music and its audiences—in-synch, reciprocal patterns of sound waves that signify moments of musical meaning-making, "sonic thinking,"[28] and "sensorial solidarity."[29] If it succeeds, this book will fill a crucial gap between the fields of African American rhetorical studies,

African American literature, sonic studies, and musicology by amplifying the unique relationship between the rhetorical function of music and Black political consciousness.

W. E. B. Du Bois, one of African America's greatest intellectuals, certainly understood the discursive value of Black music, as indicated by *The Souls of Black Folk* (1903), a classic of American literature. The epistemological value of the bars of music that Du Bois situates at the beginning of every chapter performs the work of identifying African Americans with a particular musical heritage, and they potentially influence interpretation (see figure 1). Du Bois's approach is thus ethnomusicological, meaning that he identifies the music with the essence of African American experiences. Toward the end of the foreword he states, "Before each chapter, as now printed, stands a bar of the Sorrow Songs,—some echo of haunting melody from the only American music which welled up from Black souls in the dark past."[30] He goes on to comment that "the world listened only half credulously until the Fisk Jubilee Singers sang the slave songs so deeply into the world's heart that it can never wholly forget them again," and he remarks furthermore that "the Negro folk-song—the rhythmic cry of the slave—stands today not simply as the sole American music, but as the most beautiful expression of human experience born this side the seas."[31] He discerned a musical resource to be mined, harnessed, refined, and publicized as product for mass consumption.

Du Bois gestures repeatedly to the "endoxa" of Black music. According to Aristotle, *endoxa* are the commonly held beliefs that serve as the beginning of rhetoric.[32] Part of the *endoxa* of Black music, as Tubman knew, is the belief held by African Americans in the purpose, power, and significance to their lives of the Sorrow Songs. Although *endoxa* are contextual and are not beyond refutation, they serve as the foundation for broader claims.

While theorizing the Black experience in America, Du Bois invokes music for the strategic purpose of articulating what words alone fail to convey. A reading of just the written word that fails to seriously engage the musical notations is relatively impoverished. *Souls* is clearly a sonic text in addition to its value as a historical, sociological, political, storytelling, and autobiographical document. Although the music is only printed on the page, these musical epigraphs invite readers to imagine the sound of Black life.

THE SOULS OF BLACK FOLK

I

OF OUR SPIRITUAL STRIVINGS

O water, voice of my heart, crying in the sand,
  All night long crying with a mournful cry,
As I lie and listen, and cannot understand
    The voice of my heart in my side or the voice of the sea,
  O water, crying for rest, is it I, is it I?
    All night long the water is crying to me.

Unresting water, there shall never be rest
  Till the last moon droop and the last tide fail,
And the fire of the end begin to burn in the west;
    And the heart shall be weary and wonder and cry like the sea,
  All life long crying without avail,
    As the water all night long is crying to me.
                                ARTHUR SYMONS.

BETWEEN me and the other world there is ever an unasked question: unasked by some through feelings of delicacy; by others through the difficulty of rightly framing it. All, nevertheless, flutter round it. They approach me in a half-hesitant sort of way, eye me curiously or compassionately, and then, instead of saying directly, How does it feel to be a problem? they say, I know an excellent

Figure 1. This passage of music appears at the beginning of chapter 1, "Of Our Spiritual Strivings," in Du Bois's text. The melody is that of "Nobody Knows the Trouble I've Seen." In this chapter Du Bois introduces his understanding of double consciousness and discusses its painful impact on the Black experience.

How is this feasible without a recording or live performance of these musical passages? Can the experience of this music really be translated to the text? Du Bois does not need to reproduce completely such musical experience to exploit the significance of the spirituals' *musical syntax*, which is the relationship between the music's elements (such as timbre, pitch, and rhythm).[33] The musical notation invokes the memory of the spirituals and extends the musical syntax of the Sorrow Songs to other areas of the text. Describing, in the last chapter, the relationship between the musical notations and the discursive text, Du Bois states that "before each thought that I have written in this book I have set a phrase, a haunting echo of these weird old songs in which the soul of the Black slave spoke to men."[34] He explains that the songs, as well as the passages of poetry, relate directly to the material in each chapter. Moreover, he asserts that "these songs are the articulate messages of the slave to the world . . . the music of an unhappy people, of the children of disappointment; they tell of death and suffering and unvoiced longing toward a truer world, of misty wanderings and hidden ways."[35] For Du Bois, it is the echoes, sonic symbols, which he associates with the South and with the enduring beauty of Black life despite oppression.

Reading *Souls* as "total art," Anne Carroll speaks to the intertextuality between Du Bois's text and theories concerning the unity of the arts by opera composer Richard Wagner. A total work of art engages the multiple senses of an audience member with the goal of causing them to participate in the experience of reaching a higher truth or being transported to a new reality. While Wagner used these theories to support a problematic project of nationalism and folk heroism, Du Bois applied this idea toward the fight against racism and inequality. Given the time that Du Bois spent in Germany during Wagner's growing popularity in the world of opera and his reference to one of Wagner's operas in the section of *Souls* titled "On the Coming of John," Carroll's argument is worth considering.[36] In terms of the structural organization of *Souls*, Carroll points to the placement of the musical passages as similar to the use of *leitmotifs*, a term that describes a melodic idea developed through repetition, thereby unifying large-scale compositions.[37] We need not assume that Du Bois was consciously employing leitmotifs nor need we justify his project through its connection to Wagner's ideas, but it is clear that he indeed produced a total work of art and simultaneously drew on the rhetorical function of Black music.

Of course, reading *Souls* and deciphering the musical epigraphs is not enough to capture the full import of the spirituals, but that is beside the point. Music does the rhetorical work of galvanizing the argument of the text as a whole. The text proposes sonic possibilities and invites readers to become involved in Du Bois's creative practice and analysis.[38]

This outcome is linked to "representative thinking,"[39] a term Hannah Arendt coined to articulate the skill necessary for individuals to see different perspectives on particular issues. Building coalitions, a lifelong activity of Du Bois, requires genuine empathy, understanding, and cooperation through such work of representative thinking. Music helps to create and support representative thinking by traversing gulfs of experience and supplying substantive content in spaces where verbal discourse may lack effectiveness or accuracy. Moreover, music is rhetorical to the extent that rhetoric, as Gerard Hauser informs us, is "more than suasive discourse but also a method for thinking about communication, especially its heuristic concerns for invention."[40] Music shapes what can be said—and to whom—by expressing emotions, ideas, and courses of action, some of which are transformative.

Black music in particular has facilitated these processes by generating frames of reference that shape discourses of race and ethnicity. For example, to extend the analysis beyond the South and the Sorrow Songs, this book includes discussion of Scott Joplin's compositions of ragtime piano music. Joplin's incorporation of difficult melodic passages and syncopated rhythms defied the labeling of African American artistry as simple or unworthy of serious critical engagement at a time when the institution of minstrelsy sought to degrade every aspect of African American expressive culture. Anyone who applauded the genius of Joplin's achievement was also applauding Black humanity, the attempt by some public figures to sever ragtime from its Black origins notwithstanding. In a media landscape that has historically stereotyped, ignored, or exploited African Americans, Black music has been an indispensable counterargument to historical stereotyping, ignorance, and exploitation. It has communicated signs and symbols that have worked in tandem with cultural forces, social conditions, and social actors.

The rhetoric of Black music is not merely the catalog of musical artifacts and performances. It involves all of the discourse, including this book, directly attributable to the catalog. Take, for instance, the first episode of national and international acclaim for Black music, the tour of the same Fisk Jubilee Singers so beloved by Du Bois.

In 1871, to prevent the impending closure of Fisk University, the university's music director and treasurer, George L. White, sent a nine-member choir, led by twenty-year-old singer and organist Ella Sheppard, to travel and raise funds for the school. White recognized the novelty of the spirituals for white audiences and bet on the choir's ability to present authentic spirituals as a step above minstrel acts. Additionally, he played a major role in arranging the songs in ways that would be more palatable to white audiences by modifying certain stylistic elements and instructing the group to avoid harsh tones.[41] He stripped the songs of some of the timbre, texture, and pitches that clashed with conventional Western vocal performance standards. Additionally, he removed certain accents and the expressive timing that made the spirituals participatory texts in favor of some of the traditional Western standards of classical vocal performance.

In the year following the choir's debut, a hymnal book from the Jubilee Singers was released with an enigmatic preface that captured the way White and others sought to apologize for the distinctive characteristics of the spirituals. The preface began by addressing music critics and warning them that they will not know how to approach the music. The author of the preface, Theodore Seward, also referred to the group as the "Jubilee Band." Given that the group billed itself as the "Jubilee Singers" in the year prior, this subtle change appears to be a refusal to defend the group as a choir. It was an admission that the group's deviation from Western style was somehow erroneous; calling them a band carried connotations of less formal and less professional standards. Seward then stated that their songs came "from no music cultivation whatever, but are the simple, ecstatic utterances of wholly untutored minds."[42] Despite this devaluation, Seward admitted that the rhythmic style of the spirituals is complicated, "strikingly original," and "extremely satisfactory."[43] About half of the songs in the hymnal book utilized the same scale, one that omitted the fourth and seventh degrees, which Seward characterized as easy for the "uncultivated mind." He also described this scale (the pentatonic) as a "simpler alphabet" than the ordinary diatonic scale. Seward closed the preface by acknowledging the criticism that the group sounded "too good" and "too refined" for those who had been to the South and heard the singing in the camp meetings. Seward responded by arguing that the group was just matching the degree of culture in the congregation and that the Singers represented "the highest average of culture among the colored people," and that "the quickness with which they have received impressions and adopted improvements from the cultivated music they have heard, only affords an additional illustration of the high capabilities of the race."[44]

The construction of the Jubilee Singers and their sound as the highest average of culture among the colored people was important because it spoke to how the group was packaged for white consumption and the contexts in which their sound could be considered appropriate for high culture. Despite the watering down of their sound, they were still capable of having a considerable impact on their audiences, and their pleas for support and funding were met with a considerable number of donations.

The responses to the Jubilee Singers recorded in the press reveal some of the discourse surrounding the group in Black and White public spheres. In fact, some audiences were more drawn to the idea of real authentic "negro spirituals" than to the group's attempts to modify their style. However, the Jubilee Singers owed part of their success to their versatility and mastery of both classical music and the spirituals. During the beginning of their tour, the Singers had a variety of genres on their program, including some opera and sentimental pieces. However, racist attitudes about their capabilities led some to consider their attempts at classical music to be the work of "well-trained monkeys."[45]

Despite the challenges they faced, the Jubilee Singers understood their purpose of saving Fisk and representing the Black community. In 1880, Sheppard wrote a letter to the *People's Advocate*, a Black newspaper in Washington, D.C., in which she described the group's rebuff by a white minister in Louisville before a series of concerts. The minister warned that he would "not have any 'clap-trap singing' in his church."[46] Nonetheless, the concerts drew praise from audiences and the press. The minister would later bring his family and speak on the group's behalf, lauding their cause and accomplishments. This led Sheppard to remark, "wherever we go, we are converting friends to our cause, and enlightening the country regarding the Negro's capabilities."[47] Her use of the word "converting" is interesting because, unlike Tubman, the Singers were using the spirituals as a tool to communicate their acceptableness to white society. Their talents were hard to deny, and their sound was something unique within America's musical landscape. In this instance, ethos was derived from their mastery of vocal performance and their polished presentation.

The power of such conversions was not lost on other important African American figures, who, along with Du Bois, understood the value of the Singers to the causes of freedom and equality. For example, iconic orator and abolitionist Frederick Douglass provided the group a song entitled "Run to Jesus" to add to their repertoire.[48] Due to the international acclaim of the Jubilee Singers, the world became aware of the value of Black cultural production. In addition to challenging the negative stereotypes of African Americans circulating in American media from minstrel shows, the Singers played a significant role in disrupting the marginalization of Black artistic achievement and, consequently, narratives of Black inferiority.

Just as slave narratives pointedly demonstrate to readers the humanity of their authors in an intellectual context in which mastery of alphabetic print is equated with the ability to reason, the mastery of music by Black subjects illustrates the genius usually only ascribed to white, male composers and performers of Western classical music. I take up these concerns specifically in my later discussion of Mary Lou Williams. As a Black woman, Williams's musical abilities complicated and, at times, defied normal categorization within the coterie of jazz musicians that came of age during the era of big band jazz. Some downplayed her performance ability. On the other hand, those who did concede her performance talent attributed that talent to "playing like a man," thus reinforcing the construction of jazz as a genre of music for male instrumentalists.[49] Moreover, Williams's infusion of Black spirituality into her music situates her artistry within the tradition demonstrated by Tubman, as Williams uses the musical dimension and auditory apparatus of Black sounds to inspire intellectual and spiritual freedom.

Amiri Baraka wrote, in *Blues People*, that if the music of African Americans was "subjected to a socio-anthropological as well as musical scrutiny, something about the essential nature of the Negro's existence in this country ought to be revealed, as well as something about the essential nature of the country, i.e., society as a whole."[50] Similarly, Alexander Weheliye has suggested that scholarly investigations of Black music help us to better understand "sonic Afro-modernity."[51] I take their insights to mean that a rhetorical investigation of Black music is indeed a worthy scholarly enterprise.

The following chapters expound on the rhetoric of Black music through extended analyses of musicians, their work, and the Black public sphere. *On Rhetoric and Black Music* is about locating and amplifying evidence of the rhetorical function of Black music in myriad modes of communication, including oratory, the press, fiction, and poetry by a wide variety of rhetors and audiences. In each case, I pay close attention to the artists' compositional practices and styles of performance in connection to the public discourse animated by their music. I readily admit that any selection of artists for such an analysis leaves out others with equally compelling oeuvres. Besides my personal enthusiasm for these artists, they were also chosen based on the availability of archival materials, the amount of coverage they received by the national and international press, and their influence, both musically and rhetorically, within their respective genres. The next chapter discusses the compositions of Scott Joplin, particularly "Maple Leaf Rag" (1899) and his opera *Treemonisha* (1910) in conjunction with James Weldon Johnson's novel *The Autobiography of an Ex-Colored Man* (1912). I establish that both Joplin and Johnson saw Black music as a principal tool for articulating the humanity of African Americans and distancing Black music from the legacy of minstrelsy. The lives of Joplin, Johnson, and the fictional narrator overlap in interesting ways as all three individuals navigate the challenges facing Black performers during the dawn of American popular music.

In the second chapter, I discuss the work of Duke Ellington, specifically his "Black and Tan Fantasy" (1927), *Jump for Joy* (1941), and *Black, Brown and Beige* (1943). These compositions are notable for their clear expression of themes that engage identity, Africa, and history, and they portray Ellington's efforts to recreate the sonic archive lost to African Americans through slavery. Although Ellington is known as one of the most influential musicians in the genre of jazz, he was also critically important to evolving ideas of Black identity and Afrocentrism. Through music, Ellington was able to connect themes of racial uplift and modernism to his exploration of new tonal registers in ways that defied the marginalization of Black music.

In the third chapter, I explore the legacy of Mary Lou Williams through the lens of the African American jeremiad. I argue that Williams's experimental and spiritual compositions, including *Mary Lou Williams Presents Black Christ of the Andes* (1964), defied the norms surrounding female musicians and the secular confinement of jazz. After experiencing a life-changing religious conversion, Williams dedicated her life to helping others and teaching the value of the sonic lexicon of Black music to younger generations. Williams's claim to "play like a man" (as she embraced the description of her) exemplifies the ways in which the field of jazz, especially bebop, was constructed as male.

The fourth chapter discusses the rise of John Coltrane. During the 1960s, Coltrane's music, especially *A Love Supreme* (1965), became a symbol of the aesthetic qualities of Black Nationalism. Coltrane remains one of the most referenced jazz musicians in African American poetry and prose, and the rhetorical impact of his music suggests ways of understanding the genre of free jazz as constitutive, much like Ellington's work, of rhetorics of Afrocentrism.

The final chapter features the rhetorical mastery of Mahalia Jackson. I argue that, in addition to her status as an icon of gospel music, Jackson should be considered one of Black America's preeminent rhetoricians. I explore Jackson's music and career through six different dimensions of rhetorical practices, which include Jackson's navigation of the Black church, international audiences, gender, political activism, and ethos construction. I pay particular attention to the complexities of Jackson's rhetorical maneuvers between white and Black audiences while explaining how she used her distinctive style of performance in accordance with a rhetorical project invested in both the spiritual salvation and social liberation of her audiences.

1
Ragtime, Race, and Rhetoric

For African American ragtime musicians, musical form served also as a rhetorical form that animated a wide discussion about Black artistry and the intellectual ability of African Americans. Ragtime has come to be defined as a style of popular piano music that flourished from the mid-1890s to 1918 and featured "ragged" or syncopated rhythm. During the height of its popularity, almost anything innovative within the realm of instrumental, vocal, or dance music was called ragtime.[1] Such fluidity indicates that the term was used as a buzzword that signaled what was then considered to be new, popular, and in style. Therefore, one of the next great chapters in Black musical development following the spirituals and folk songs became part of the cutting edge of America's developing landscape of popular music at the turn of the century. The eventual mass appeal of ragtime with white youth ruptured simplistic negations of Black cultural production.[2] Yet, African-American artists, such as Scott Joplin and James Weldon Johnson, sought more. They used ragtime and its attendant discourses to debunk claims about the inferiority of Black cultural production.[3] This is particularly evident in Joplin's most important compositions, namely, "Maple Leaf Rag" (1899) and *Treemonisha* (1910), and in Johnson's groundbreaking novel, *The Autobiography of an Ex-Colored Man* (1912). They employ ragtime as rhetorical invention and exemplify the sonic as an available means of persuasion in the face of limited cultural power and authority. I turn to these artists not out of an attempt to replicate great-man narratives but for their representation of the many contributions by African American men and women active within the culture industry.

Joplin, an African American composer and pianist from Texarkana, Texas, became known as the "king of ragtime" for his piano compositions that captured audiences with their rhythmic and harmonic complexity, some of which were too difficult for most performers. Through music, Joplin contributed to the discourse of racial uplift that lauded education and respectability politics as tools to fight racial oppression. The sophistication of his music demanded that Black musical production be taken seriously and shifted the discourse around ragtime to include its potential for both entertainment and high culture.

Historical accounts of the development of ragtime explain its overlap with coon songs (the genre of music that accompanied minstrelsy) as coincidental.[4] However, if ragtime is characterized as a larger cultural response to such music, the importance of Joplin and Johnson's contributions are heightened. Minstrel shows were attempts to portray the culture, songs, and dances of African Americans in ways that were deliberately derogatory and exaggerated for comedic effect. These performances included variety acts, stump speeches, songs, dances, and comedic skits. Minstrelsy was an important part of the musical and theatrical development of American popular culture and one of the first vehicles of mass media to directly address the topics of class, politics, ethics, and enslavement through music and dance.[5] Further, anxiety about America's lack of an authentic culture drove the popularity of American minstrelsy as a medium for racializing culture itself. Minstrelsy supported the manufacturing of whiteness through the (dis)identification with racialized others.[6] In response to the growing competition from African Americans for jobs, land, and resources, minstrelsy "offered a way to play with collective fears of a degraded and threatening male 'other' while at the same time maintaining some symbolic control over them."[7] The minstrel show, and Black music in particular, thus became the space where many of America's anxieties about race, class, sex, and politics were explored. Moreover, minstrel characters were often mistaken for realistic African Americans.[8] Therefore, the authenticity of African American culture on the national stage was compromised as its production was coopted by a growing institution of racist propaganda.

Given that Scott Joplin was a minstrel performer during his formative years—beginning his musical career as a member of the Texarkana Minstrels in 1891—he understood these racial dynamics well. For many Black artists such as Joplin, minstrelsy was the only route to performing on stage. Minstrel groups made up of African Americans began to appear as early as 1855 and, despite the requirement of racial self-degradation, minstrelsy provided Black entertainers with a viable venue to perfect their crafts.

The most successful minstrel groups were those that stressed their authenticity as "real Negro" performers or former slaves with ties to southern plantations.[9] Groups such as Callender's Minstrels, The Simon Pure Negro Company, and the Georgia Slave Troupe Minstrels emphasized their ethnic legitimacy in order to compete with white minstrelsy groups.[10] Joplin and other Black artists found themselves in the precarious position of having to choose between complicity in minstrelsy's project of racial denigration or remaining excluded from America's most profitable and dynamic musical market.[11] Joplin would respond to this dilemma by creating a third option: elevating Black music on its own terms as high art with his widely popular compositions. Although Joplin published over ninety compositions throughout his lifetime, two pieces stand out for their rhetorical significance. The first is "Maple Leaf Rag," Joplin's most important song and one of the most well-known tunes of the ragtime era. The second is *Treemonisha*, a 230-page opera set near his hometown of Texarkana. *Treemonisha* is Joplin's magnum opus as well as a portrait of his political and social ideology.

Prior to the publication of "Maple Leaf Rag," there were few musical differences between minstrelsy coon songs and the genre that would become known as ragtime. The term "rag" functioned as both noun and verb. Songs such as Ernest Hogan's "All Coons Look Alike to Me" (1896), Joseph Howard and Ida Emerson's "Hello! Ma Baby" (1899), and Theodore Metz's "There'll Be a Hot Time in the Old Town To-night" (1896) included gestures or explicit references to "Negro rag."[12] The idea of "rag" or "ragging" had to do with a particular approach to rhythmic syncopation, which is the use of a variety of unexpected rhythms to cause differing strong and weak beats. Syncopation lends music a quality of being both on and off the beat for pleasurable effect. The most general ragtime rhythms featured syncopation in the melodic line set against duple or march-like bass lines. European classical music contained a rich reservoir of harmonic complexity and a modicum of rhythmic sophistication as well; however, the idea that rhythm could also be fluid and multifaceted (e.g., loose or ragged) rather than rigid and predictable (as in a march or waltz) represented a new horizon in American popular music.

The relationship between syncopation and race forms part of the foundation of America's orientation to music of the African diaspora.[13] For a period of time, African music was perceived as a dangerous threat in America. The African drum was classified as a weapon by South Carolina's Slave Code of 1740, otherwise known as the Negro Act. This effort was a response to the Stono Rebellion, a slave revolt that occurred near the Stono River on September 9, 1739. Around twenty slaves gathered weapons and firearms and marched south with signs that read "Liberty" while singing and beating drums. The drumming was a tool to recruit slaves in the surrounding area, and their numbers grew to around ninety before they were stopped by a group of white militiamen. The slaves were found in a field singing and dancing to the beat of their drums, uniting through a cultural practice that spanned regional and tribal origins. Along with banning the possession of drums, section thirty-six of the code prohibited "horns, or other loud instruments, which may call together or give sign or notice to one another of their wicked designs and purposes."[14] This precedent, the stigmatization of music created by the enslaved, became a part of the cultural foundation for a dichotomy between the high culture of Western classical music, with its emphasis on melodic and harmonic experimentation, and the low culture of popular music, with its emphasis on dancing and pleasure, which was mapped onto America's racial dichotomy. Ragtime would continue this legacy because its syncopation quickly became racially coded as Black.[15]

The Phenomenon of "Maple Leaf Rag"

"Maple Leaf Rag," though not the first ragtime publication by an African American artist, changed the paradigm of the genre by raising artistic standards.[16] Joplin was even aware of this fact before its publication, stating to one of his music students that "Maple Leaf Rag" would make him "tops among ragtime composers."[17] The first important difference is that "Maple Leaf Rag" featured syncopations that occurred mid-measure, across bar lines, and with octaves added for emphasis. The bass line, which in most songs would feature alternations between octaves and chords, features a line that abandons that pattern for a more fluid and complex mixture of chords and syncopation. Additionally, Joplin uses a higher degree of harmonic development, including precise voice leading and well-placed dissonance and resolution. Instead of beginning with the expected move of establishing the tonic of A-flat, Joplin introduces a bit of chromaticism with an inner voice moving from A-flat to A and then to B-flat in order to move to the dominant chord of E-flat. A few measures later, a shift occurs from the dominant E-flat to a flatted sixth chord, or F-flat. This melodic maneuver is similar to the flatted sixth scale-degree in a minor blues scale, a key part of that eponymous genre and one of the dominant sources of its affective power. These details comprise sonic Blackness, as such distinctions were freighted with symbolic meaning for listeners conditioned by racialized listening practices.

The structure of the first section of "Maple Leaf Rag," referred to as section A, differs from other songs by featuring a first half that is thematically unrelated to the second half of the song (ABCC) as opposed to the more common ABAA or ABAC.[18] The next three sections also present interesting harmonic and rhythmic innovations, including more chromatic lines, counterpoint, melodic motifs transposed to different harmonies, and Joplin's signature musical motif of a descending chromatic line of fourth intervals.[19] These compositional choices broke with convention in daring and significant ways and infused the song with a kind of energy and fluidity that was unique for its time. These innovations demonstrated the intellectual and creative prowess of African Americans and represented a symbolic challenge to discourses of racial inferiority. The absence of any vocal accompaniment is also quite significant, considering that most ragtime songs, as with American popular music in general, featured vocal accompaniment. Instead, "Maple Leaf Rag" was a technically challenging instrumental. Before its publication, there were concerns that the piece would be too difficult for most pianists to play, thus harming its potential sales.[20] However, those concerns were assuaged by the work's growing popularity. The success of "Maple Leaf Rag" would be evidenced by its unusual increase in sales years after its publication, reaching a half-million total copies by 1909.[21] Furthermore, the song carried uncanny staying power among the genre's most popular entries. In fact, "Maple Leaf Rag" would be recorded at least six times during the 1920s, two decades after its initial debut.[22]

Joplin's signature composition launched his profile as a profitable composer. His negotiation for royalties on the sales of his music helped to set a precedent for Black musicians who were often forced to relinquish all ownership and publishing rights in favor of one-time payments from publishers. Joplin's publishing contract with John Stark, a white music and instrument dealer in Sedalia, Missouri, included a one-cent-per-copy royalty, which significantly elevated Joplin's economic status. Joplin's example reflected the ways in which professional and cultural values were deeply connected, allowing Black performers to "advance facets of their political agendas alongside their profits."[23]

"Maple Leaf Rag" became part of a contentious public debate, no doubt marked by the specter of race, over the genre of ragtime and its role in society. Professional associations of classical musicians and dancers, such as the National Music Teachers Association and the National League of Musicians, passed resolutions against ragtime as early as 1886 in an effort to link ragtime to notions of a "crisis in taste, education, and skill."[24] However, such crude maneuvers to blunt or deny the growing cultural popularity and significance of ragtime would prove futile. Examining some of the diverse interpretations of the music by actual listeners, as opposed to focusing solely on academic circles and musicians' unions, presents a clearer picture of public discourse. Take, for example, an editorial featuring an unnamed doctor condemning ragtime in the *Evening News* of San Jose, California, in 1900:

> Why, in my day a young girl would trip daintily to the piano and sing "Lorena," or "Daisy Dean," or "Gentle Annie," or "Belle Mahone," or some other sentimental or ladylike ballad but now—well, I went out to call on some nieces of mine the other evening, and I asked one of them to sing. She had a short skirt on and boy's shoes, and she bounced across the room like what we used to call a "tomboy." My niece flung herself at the piano and began to bang out a "rag-time" accompaniment. A minute later she was bawling something through her stiffly contracted throat about "Nigger, give me back that night key." It's enough to make our grandmothers turn over in their graves—the thought of a young gentlewoman doing her best to imitate a field hand. It's destructive to voice and manners, the "coon" song is, and if I were the powers that be I'd put an end to it.[25]

The doctor's response depicts what Shai Burstyn refers to as "period ears" (and I would add "race ears"), which are the aesthetic responses of past listeners situated in a given place and time.[26] Such aesthetic responses are derived from the interaction of musical cognition and cultural influences. In this doctor's testimony, "coon song" and "ragtime" appear to be used interchangeably, along with the characterization of the music as that of field hands. Also present was the connotation of gender transgression and sexual perversion as endemic to the music itself. These sorts of remarks often accompanied ragtime's emerging popularity with younger fans as ragtime clashed with the "horizon of expectations" of those possessing the doctor's sentiments.[27] Further, public outcry would attach emphasis to the racial subtext of the music as justification for its condemnation. Ultimately, these instances indicate the potential impact of music and space on public and private experience. Through ragtime, Black music began to enter white living rooms and parlors, influencing auditors' relationships to Black expressive culture as an antecedent to physical integration. According to theorist Jean-Luc Nancy, sound is "tendentially methexic," meaning that listening does not occur separate from physical interaction with sound itself.[28] Put differently, "the auditory self is an embodied self that responds and (re)sounds."[29] What I appreciate most about this idea is that it conceptualizes the intimacy of listening as one of the defining differences from the visual realm. Because of this bodily involvement, the consumption of ragtime could not occur without also consuming its plethora of meanings, in this case the consumption of Blackness, a process in line with Mendi Obadike's concept of acousmatic Blackness, or the presence of Blackness without a Black body via the unification of socially conditioned listening practices and racially coded assumptions.[30]

Another dismissive response to ragtime involved a concerted effort to downplay its innovative characteristics. For example, Frank Hayes, a popular pianist during 1905, complained to the press about fans who assumed that he would play ragtime during his concerts: "I should consider it no distinction to be a rag-time piano player. I am not an admirer of rag-time and never was. There is nothing wonderful about it. I played the so-called rag-time before it was known by that name. It is no more or less than syncopation. That is as old as the hills; or, at any rate, as old as the piano. You may say that rag-time is accentuated, or elaborated syncopation.... But rag-time has not sufficient merit to be permanent."[31] Hayes's claim that syncopation was "as old as the hills" feigned ignorance about the particular use of syncopation in ragtime music while attempting to reduce ragtime's musical traits to a single characteristic. This theme would be echoed in corresponding academic discourses as well, with some critics highlighting the unique nature of "Negro music" while crediting various distinctive characteristics to other cultures.[32] In 1902, Thomas Preston Brooke, a Chicago Marine Band director credited with being the first nationally recognized musical authority to speak positively about ragtime, stated that ragtime was never "discovered" or "invented" but always present "like the light of the sun." He went on to state:

> It has been demonstrated beyond all semblance of a doubt that there is nothing so popular with the great masses of the people as rag-time, and, for my part, I am of the opinion that anything that everybody likes must have some merit. The American people are far too intelligent and too conservative to be carried away by any senseless fad. They have been listening to every kind and every grade of music since the foundation of the republic, and the fact that they express a decided preference for rag-time is not caused by any lack of knowledge of classic music. It is simply because there is something about it that awakens and thrills the sense of rhythm in every living creature.[33]

Brooke's comments demonstrate the ways Black achievement put pressure on America's paradoxical relationship with Black expressive culture and its creators. To recognize the success of ragtime without some sort of erasure or censure of Black contribution was tantamount to recognizing the achievement of Black musicians and, by extension, the Black community itself. Therefore, from this line of argument, the music was a product of all Americans and already existed within the Western canon. However, Brooke cannot neglect mentioning that there is just "something about it." That "something" was the distinctive sonic and auditory features of Black music that would prove difficult to ignore.

The reception of ragtime in African American communities was even more complicated. In 1899, the year "Maple Leaf Rag" was released, prominent African American scholar William Sanders Scarborough discussed the status of Black art in ways that echoed the most common critiques of Black entertainment. Speaking at the third annual Hampton

Conference, his address, "The Negro in Fiction as Portrayer and Portrayed," responded to the work of Charles Chesnutt and Paul Laurence Dunbar, calling for the necessity of the "novelist who will portray the Negro not in the commonplace way that some have done, but one who will elevate him to a high level of fascination and interest."[34] Adjoining his literary analysis to a broader social critique, Scarborough remarked, "We are tired of vaudeville, of minstrelsy, and of the Negro's pre-eminence in those lines. We want something higher, something more inspiring than that. We turn to the Negro for it."[35] Scarborough continued his critique by warning that the sway of the "almighty dollar" would cause many to "pander to low tastes and cater to public sentiment," like Esau ready to sell his birthright for a mess of pottage.[36] We find more nuance in the reported discussion that followed Scarborough's lecture:

> There was a rather general feeling that the Negro was thought incapable of anything better than "rag-time" music, and the so-called "coon songs" and it was also said that entertainments which included cake walks, and plenty of "rag-time" songs would draw larger audiences than those of a more "respectable" character. Several speakers referred to the coon songs and rag time music as natural expressions of a certain stage of civilization. "When real," said one, "they have a certain quality that appeals to the human race without distinction of color. We do not need to be ashamed of them: they are evanescent and will pass. From 'rag-time' we shall grow into something higher; we must pass from the known to the unknown."[37]

For many conference attendees, and a large swath of the African American community, ragtime was conceptualized as contrary to their notions of respectability and racial uplift. This was not necessarily because of the music in and of itself, but because of the music's relationship to coon songs and other forms of racial denigration. On this view, ragtime was a part of the forces working against a multifaceted effort to push back against negative portrayals of African Americans in all areas of the public sphere.

What would separate Joplin from composers such as the prominent William Marion Cook is that the latter wrote compositions that combined

European classical music with the influence of the spirituals.[38] Composers and musicians working within the classical tradition drew critical acclaim for their technical prowess, not unlike that of the Jubilee Singers. As the attendees of the Hampton Conference noted, such distinctions could be used to validate the aptitude of African Americans within a larger counterargument for freedom and equality. Eurocentrism notwithstanding, the musical profession presented "as many opportunities for solving the Negro problem as farming or some similar pursuit."[39]

However, Joplin's work would demonstrate that African Americans need not turn to classical music to develop a product of similar quality and caliber. Ragtime itself could be complex enough to support similar levels of virtuosity and communicate to the world Black identity and Black genius. In this manner, Joplin is a crucial rhetorical figure. His choices to market the nonclassical quality of his compositions and to eschew themes associated with minstrelsy would prove to be an important part of his growing public profile. Additionally, receiving acclaim from white critics and band directors would add credibility to his productions, one of the most important endorsements coming from Alfred Ernst, conductor of the St. Louis Choral Symphony. Ernst's role as a leader of an important American symphony and his status as a German solidified his authority in European music and culture. A meeting between Joplin and Ernst was deemed so important that it was covered elaborately in the St. Louis *Globe-Democrat* of February 28, 1901, with a large photograph of Joplin. Ernst stated to the press that he believed he had discovered in Joplin "an extraordinary genius as a composer of ragtime music."[40] Ernst went on to mention that he intended to take Joplin's compositions with him back to Germany to share with disciples of Wagner, Liszt, Mendelssohn, and other European masters.[41] After mentioning a few of Joplin's compositions, including "Maple Leaf Rag," Ernst remarked:

> With proper cultivation, I believe, his talent will develop into positive genius. Being of African blood himself, Joplin has a keener insight into that peculiar branch of melody than white composers. His ear is particularly acute. The work Joplin has done in ragtime is so original, so distinctly individual, and so melodious withal, that I am led to believe he can do something fine in composition of a higher class when he shall have been instructed in theory and

harmony. Joplin's work, as yet, has a certain crudeness, due to his lack of musical education, but it shows that the soul of the composer is there and needs but to be set free by knowledge of technique. He is an unusually intelligent young man and fairly well educated.[42]

The significance of Ernst's celebration of Joplin as a composer and not a minstrel cannot be overstated. Despite Ernst's Eurocentric and racialized view of education and culture, such positive remarks accorded to an African American were rare. Furthermore, these pronouncements from someone in his cultural and professional position would help catapult Joplin to national fame and respect as a composer while elevating the cultural status of ragtime.

Additional responses to ragtime defended the genre under the pretense of its similarity to classical music. In one of the most explicit examples of identification with ragtime, the women studying at the Enna Conservatory of Music in Des Moines, Iowa, divided themselves into ragtime and antiragtime sects. The latter argued that the music wasn't "proper" and that it was "trashy," while those in favor argued that the music was indeed "classical" and that "anyone who [could] not play it refuses because they can't."[43] In this case, the technical demands of ragtime left detractors vulnerable to the claim that they lacked the skills to play it, equating technical difficulty with quality and merit. Secondarily, there was an attempt to legitimize the music by identifying it as a subgenre of classical music, which was the approach that critics such as Ernst utilized. To validate ragtime for mass consumption, its status as Black music was minimized or outright denied.[44]

In 1903, an article was published in Joplin's city of residence, Sedalia, Missouri, crowning Joplin the "king of ragtime." He was celebrated as a local hero who had gained a national reputation for his compositions. However, the article described Joplin's accomplishments as occurring *in spite of* his "ebony hue and retired disposition," circumscribing Joplin's accomplishments as an exception for African Americans. Aside from the article's problematic accolades, it provided early evidence of Joplin's larger purposes: "Joplin's ambition is to shine in other spheres. He affirms that it is only a pastime for him to compose syncopated music and he longs for more arduous work. To this end he is assiduously toiling upon an opera, nearly a score of the numbers of which he has already composed and which he hopes to give an early production in this city."[45] Joplin would make good on his promise with the publication of *Treemonisha*, an opera that stands as his most audacious and socially conscious work. Despite his earlier successful publications, Joplin had difficulty securing a publishing contract for the opera.[46] This led to his decision to publish the opera on his own at great financial cost to himself.

Treemonisha's Vision

The plot of *Treemonisha* begins in the year 1866 as the recently freed Black inhabitants find themselves "in dense ignorance with no one to guide them" because "the white folks had moved away shortly after the Negroes were set free."[47] The opera presents the story of Treemonisha, who, upon her eighteenth birthday, takes on a leadership role in her community by espousing the value of education and attacking the presence of superstition and conjurors within the community. To block her efforts at reform, the conjurors kidnap her and attempt to throw her into a wasps' nest. As the community comes to accept Treemonisha's leadership, she pleads for the forgiveness of her attackers as a gesture toward unity among disparate segments of the Black community. The opera alludes to Joplin's view of the African American community following emancipation. On this view, education is the only solution to the ignorance and superstition that plagues Black America. Joplin's principal musical motif "represents the happiness of the people when they feel free from the conjurors and their spells of superstition."[48]

During the first act of the opera, Remus defends Treemonisha's role as teacher in the neighborhood by declaring that Treemonisha "is the only educated person of our race" in the area and that "she'll break the spell of superstition in the neighborhood."[49] Along with ragtime, Joplin includes spirituals and folk songs, and he associates Black music with intellectual awakening. Joplin also uses African American vernacular English to draw distinctions between the educated and the uneducated:

> **Zodzetrick**:
> You 'cuse me wrong
> For injury I'se not done,
> An' it won't be long

'Fore I'll make you from me run.
I has dese bags o' luck, 'tis true,
So take care, gal, I'll send bad luck to you.

Remus:
Shut up old man, enough you've said;
You can't fool Treemonisha—she has a level head.
She is the only educated person of our race,
For many long miles far away from this place.
She'll break the spell of superstition in the neighborhood,
And all you foolish conjurors will have to be good.
To read and write she has taught me,
And I am very grateful,
I have more sense now, you can see,
And to her I'm very thankful.
You'd better quit your foolish ways
And all this useless strife,
You'd better change your ways today
And live a better life.

Zodzetrick:
I don't care what you say,
I will never change my way.

(Starts to leave.)

I'm goin' now, but I'll be back soon,
Long 'fore another new moon.
D'y'all hear?[50]

Joplin's idea of education is tied to a particular performance of respectability. Given that he was educated in a similar manner (his parents worked for a white family who agreed to tutor him), the opera expresses his broader understanding of education as the solution to the empowerment and self-determination of Black America. This idea was supported by a large number of important figures in the African American community, including Booker T. Washington, one of the most authoritative leaders in Black America. Joplin previously celebrated Washington with his piece "A Guest of Honor" (1903), which was written to commemorate Washington's visit to the White House.[51] It is likely that such a tribute was, at least in part, a product of admiration and allegiance to Washington's rhetorical project of racial uplift through industrial education. The same mindset was also expressed in W. E. B. Du Bois's notion of a Talented Tenth, the mechanism by which the "best" of the race would guide the masses "out of contamination and death of the worst."[52]

The opera presents many instances of African American rhetorical traditions, such as a scene featuring the call-and-response between the community and the local pastor, Parson Alltalk, which provides a subtle critique of hypocrisy in the Black church. African American folklore is also alluded to, with clear connections between Treemonisha's potential demise in the wasps' nest and Brer Rabbit's use of the briar patch. At the same time, the opera's form and structure show the influence of Wagnerian operatic conventions.[53]

Treemonisha also demonstrates the importance of Joplin's experiences within the vibrant, politically conscious African American rural communities of Texarkana and Sedalia, specifically the Queen City Band of Sedalia, a cornerstone of the community and one of its primary sources of entertainment, and the Colored Vaudeville Benevolent Association (CVBA). The CVBA was founded by musicians and entertainers with the intention of elevating the status of vaudeville entertainment, including the securing of more equitable pay and treatment for African American performers. Joplin served on the association's arrangements committee and performed at fundraising events. He even dedicated one of his compositions, "Paragon Rag," to the CVBA. Joplin eventually would rise to a position on the association's executive committee and play a critical, though brief, role in the association's daily operations until its relocation to Harlem in 1912.[54]

From a musical standpoint, *Treemonisha* was Joplin's most dynamic composition in terms of complexity and narrative depth. However, the piece was not without its weaknesses, relying too much on a long preface (which was supposed to be read by the audience prior to the performance) and recitatives to communicate the plot instead of action by the characters.[55] However, these weaknesses do not fully account for Joplin's difficulty in publishing the opera or staging its performance. It is most likely that a combination of these issues, along with the racial content of the opera, was too off-putting for most publishers. The opera (eventually self-published) did, however, receive a detailed review in the *American Musician and Art Journal* in June of 1911 that claimed the "remarkable point about this work is its evident desire to serve the negro race by exposing two of the great evils which have held his people in its grasp, as well as to point them to higher and nobler ideals." The review would further characterize Joplin's opera as a "mission" to produce a "thoroughly American opera." But having been composed by "one of the Ethiopian race," it would "hardly be accepted as a typical American opera for obvious reasons."[56] Although *Treemonisha* would not see success until a revival of Joplin's oeuvre during the 1960s and 1970s, it did not diminish Joplin's reputation as a composer, and not because it remained under the radar. Because of Joplin's promotional efforts and small performances of sections of the opera, the wider community was aware of his accomplishments.[57] On the contrary, it proved, along with other successful operas such as William Marion Cook's *Clorindy* (1898), that any artistic endeavor was possible within the purview of Black music, even the high culture of the operatic tradition.

Ethnomusicologist Bruno Nettl suggests that the way musicians "think musically" depends on the ways they think of their world in general.[58] As such, Joplin, with a clear sense of his rhetorical objectives, was able to recast ragtime as intellectually and technically sophisticated on its own terms outside of the classical tradition. He understood the power of music as an aid in displacing racist stereotypes and defending Black cultural authenticity.

Listening to *The Autobiography of an Ex-Colored Man*

Along with Joplin, James Weldon Johnson used music to solidify the authenticity of African American culture and heritage. Johnson's *The Autobiography of an Ex-Colored Man* is a fictional biography of an anonymous narrator who, due to his light skin complexion, believes he is white, that is, until an embarrassing episode of racial segregation at school shatters the narrator's image of himself. He later approaches his mother to ask, "Mother, mother, tell me, am I a nigger?"[59] It is a psychic blow comparable to the experience described by Du Bois in *The Souls of Black Folk* involving his rejection by a fellow classmate.[60] With part of his identity destabilized, Johnson's narrator begins to try to understand and accept his Blackness. He becomes enamored with African American music and culture, especially ragtime, and decides to undertake the cause of preserving the slave spirituals in "an unselfish desire to voice all the joys and sorrows, the hopes and ambitions, of the American Negro, in classic musical form."[61]

The narrator is introduced to Black music through his mother's singing. He explains how he "used to stand by her side and often interrupt and annoy her by chiming in with strange harmonies."[62] He links the music to a sense of maternal love and ancestry through his admission of his "fondness for the Black keys."[63] Music comes to signify the relationship between the narrator's mother and her mysterious, mystical Southern past, a world that he spends a considerable amount of time attempting to capture later in his life.[64]

Despite his resolution to unite the white and Black worlds of music, as well as the white and Black aspects of his identity, he regretfully gives up his quest after witnessing a lynching and realizing anew the racial horror to which Black lives in America could be subjected. Instead, he decides to pass for white. He marries a white woman, has children, goes into real estate, and assimilates into the white world, later symbolized by his abstention from playing ragtime in favor of practicing the works of Chopin. The narrative concludes with one of the most memorable passages in African American literature: "when I sometimes open a little box in which I still keep my fast yellowing manuscripts, the only tangible remnants of a vanished dream, a dead ambition, a sacrificed talent, I cannot repress the thought, that, after all, I have chosen the lesser part, that I have sold my birthright for a mess of pottage."[65] The narrator echoes Scarborough's exact words from the Hampton Conference. Both men were critical of those who would accept rewards to betray their Blackness, whether through culpability in the dissemination of racist stereotypes, as in Scarborough's warning, or through the adoption and performance of whiteness, as in the narrator's self-admonishing case. However, the narrator's anguish demonstrates—at least in the context of the novel—that such rewards pale in comparison to the sacrifice of denying one's own truth and abandoning the struggle against racial oppression.

The narrator had acknowledged "Go Down, Moses" to be a prime example of the spirituals in their purest and most powerful form. He remarked: "I doubt that there is a stronger theme in the whole musical literature of the world. And so many of these songs contain more than mere melody; there is sounded in them that elusive undertone, the note in music which is not heard with the ears. I sat often with the tears rolling down my cheeks and my heart melted within me."[66] Statements such as these reveal a lot about his occasional self-contradictory remarks about Black culture that, at times, utilize the connotations of "primitive" and "natural" in ways loaded with racial essentialism. Such comments are representations of the narrator's struggle to untether himself from the hegemony of racist discourse.[67] Nevertheless, Black music presented a subversive incongruence with racist stereotypes that were predicated, the narrator understood, on pseudo-scientific observations of moral, biological, and intellectual inferiority. Thus, the novel utilizes the sonic both to ground its narrator's internal racial angst and for its commentary on America's racial dynamics.

The narrator's failure to achieve the goal of transcribing the spirituals for fame and financial gain represents an unexpected sense of responsibility to the people the music represents. The beauty he hears in the music is the experience of Blackness translated to the sonic, and his attempt to marry the spirituals to European classical music ultimately fails due to his lack of courage to face the repercussions of Black life.[68] The narrator understands that the amount of time and work required to transcribe the spirituals correctly would also involve becoming a part of the Black community and endangering his ability to escape its constraints or avoid its suffering. If Black music is embedded in the daily experience of Black life, as Johnson's narrator comes to realize, it is also mediating that experience. The rhetorical work of music is extended by its ability to disjoin or unify disparate identities, reorienting one's sense of interiority.[69] This novel challenges readers with the sound of race by presenting the interaction of the visible, the racial, and the audible. On one level, this text presents the movement of music between Black and white worlds, and, on another, the movement of the narrator himself as he racially "passes" between both worlds. Johnson's text reflects the dueling representations of Black music within the public sphere where traits or markers of African American music are tied both to the authenticity of the Black experience and stereotypical tropes, which complicates the process of coming to a stable Black identity. Arguments supporting the "inherent" qualities of Black music and "racial essence" are weighed against an understanding of race as socially constructed.[70] Because the narrator's light skin does not make him appear phenotypically African American, he attempts to fashion his identity from allegiance to African-American cultural products. Thus Black music facilitates his confrontation with the cognitive dissonance inherent in America's binary, racial paradox as a constitutive signifier of authentic Black identity.

Johnson, in addition to his notoriety as an author, diplomat, and leader of the National Association for the Advancement of Colored People (NAACP), was also embedded in the music industry of Tin Pan Alley. Through his songwriting partnership with his brother, J. Rosamond Johnson, and Bob Cole, a prominent musician and performer, Johnson was privy to the intersection of entertainment and racial dynamics confronting African American musicians and composers.

In his autobiography, *Along This Way* (1933), he explicitly described his songwriting trio's attempt, in response to coon songs, to bring greater artistry to Negro music, thus moving beyond crude and racist songs concerned primarily with "jamborees of various sorts and the play of razors, with the gastronomical delights of chicken, pork chops and watermelon, and with the experiences of red-hot 'mamas' and their never too faithful 'papas'."[71]

Johnson and his partners met the challenge of maneuvering their music through the racial dynamic of Tin Pan Alley and Broadway by marketing their music as a more sophisticated version of ragtime, in ways similar to Joplin except for two important differences. Johnson and his partners packaged their music for mass consumption in two ways: by selling the performance rights to white vocalists and by changing the covers of their sheet music from the imagery of minstrelsy to pictures of whites (see figures 2 through 5). The presence of elegantly dressed and posed white urbanites provided a comfortable buffer to, and visual substitute for, the audible Blackness of the songs. Johnson and his collaborators were therefore the forerunners of a particular music industry strategy that entailed the recruitment, grooming, and management of

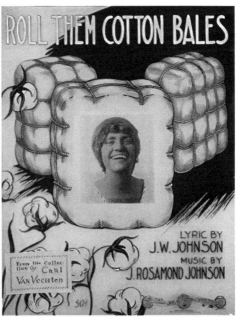

Figures 2–5. The cover pages for the Cole and Johnson Brothers songwriting trio varied between displays of minstrelsy, as with "Gimme De Leavin's" and "Roll Them Cotton Bales," and images of whites, as with "Every Woman's Eyes" and "The Spirit of the Banjo." The artwork for sheet music was usually handled by publishing companies with input from the composers.

white artists by Black musicians and producers for the purposes of performing Black music for white audiences.[72]

Further explaining the strategies that his team used to sell their music, Johnson recalled:

> We had a theory that great popularity in the case of any song was based upon a definite and sufficient reason; that it was not merely accidental. A song might be popular because it was silly; but silliness sufficient to give a song popularity would have to be the result of a certain cleverness.... In those days the royalties of a writer depended largely upon the young fellow who would buy a copy of the song and take it along with him when he went to call on his girl, so that she would play it while the two of them gave vocal vent to the sentiments.... It needed little analysis to see that a song written in exclusive praise of blue eyes was cut off at once from about three fourths of the possible chances for universal success; that it could make but faint appeal to the heart or pocketbook of a young man going to call on a girl with brown eyes or Black eyes or gray eyes. So we worked on the chorus of our song until, without making it a catalogue, it was inclusive enough to enable any girl who sang it or to whom it was sung to fancy herself the maiden with the dreamy eyes.[73]

The team's theory for "universal success" and reference to "blue eyes" indicate that the "cleverness" they deployed incorporated their ability to assess the artistic, racial, and rhetorical dimensions of their musical enterprise. Although the Johnson brothers and Cole never denied their racial identity, neither did they explicitly state it. In a demonstrative, and somewhat humorous, episode, Edward Bok, the editor of *The Ladies' Home Journal*, announced that the magazine would publish a song that was submitted by "a young Negro composer in Georgia." In response, a woman sent a letter protesting the inclusion of works by Black composers in the publication. This reader claimed that "no Negro had the musical skill or the artistic taste to interpret even his own race, much less the ability to do anything worthy of going into the pages of *The Ladies' Home Journal*" and finished her critique with the command to "give us some more of those little Negro classics by Cole and Johnson Brothers."[74]

Johnson would continue his discourse on Black cultural production in his 1922 *Anthology of Negro Poetry* by declaring ragtime one of only four distinct American artistic products, along with the Uncle Remus stories, the spirituals, and the cakewalk.[75] Setting aside Johnson's overstatement that "no persons, however hostile, can listen to Negroes singing this wonderful music without having their hostility melted down," his claim about the music's ability to shape the American social landscape is noteworthy.[76] Although Black cultural production could never usurp oppression on its own without other political, social, and economic action, it could certainly articulate the lived experience of Black life and help others identify with Black America, perhaps lessening anti-Black racism in the process.

In what could be described as a sardonic admission of ragtime's national influence, America's first political satire magazine, *Puck* (1912), charged that it was the "principal ailment of the American nation . . . which has crept into everything social, political, and intellectual."[77] Similarly, in an expression of his bewilderment at the idea that the national anthem might as well be "A Hot Time in the Old Town To-night" instead of "The Star-Spangled Banner," music critic J. Lawrence Erb, writing in *The Etude* (1899), asked:

> Why is this condition? Surely there is enough music that is popular and yet good; just as surely there is an abundance of music that is good and yet popular. It is not that the supply is not adequate to the demand. Is it not a direct result of the conditions that obtain in our American life of to-day in all its manifestations? We work at such high pressure that there is not energy left to devote to the higher things of the intellect and the heart.[78]

Erb's reference to "There'll Be a Hot Time in the Old Town To-night" is significant because, in what was arguably the most important linkage of ragtime and the American nation-state, the song became widely popular within the American military and was sung by the American victors in Spanish Santiago to signal the end of the Spanish-American War, in addition to cropping up during the Boxer Rebellion and becoming the theme song for Teddy Roosevelt's Rough Riders.[79]

Natalie Curtis, the pioneer ethnomusicologist celebrated for her transcriptions of music from Native American tribes as well as her collection of African American music at the Hampton Institute, provided one of the first explicit articulations of ragtime as central to the American landscape. In her 1913 article, "The Negro's Contribution to the Music of America," she boldly proclaimed: "Your children dance, our people sing, even our soldiers march to 'rag-time', which is fast becoming a national 'Pied Piper' to whose rhythm the whole country moves. This bizarre and fascinating music with its hide-and-seek of accent has not only swept over the United States, but it has also captured Europe, where it is rightly known as 'American Music', and is taken quite seriously as typical of this country."[80] Curtis concluded that a force for better understanding between whites and Blacks has been unleashed by the acceptance of Black musical achievements.[81] Her relatively progressive embrace of African American music as part of the fabric of America, a minority opinion to be sure, was received as a buzzworthy and provocative proposition.[82]

Also provocative were the identity maneuvers of white musicians, who were negotiating perceptions of their authenticity and their relationship to the Black community. Although there were many who used the arena of minstrelsy to deride and mock Black music and aesthetics, those with noble desires to perform the music were nevertheless confronted with a racial dynamic in which it was more socially acceptable to wear blackface and perform minstrelsy than to perform Black music in ways respectful of its styles, traditions, and creators.

For example, consider the strange and curious case of Ben Harney, who perhaps understood and benefited from the widespread rhetorical force of Black music—its mainstreaming, if you will—more than any white American of his day. In one of the earliest press notices he received, on August 26, 1896, the *Daily Inter Ocean* noted, "Ben Harney gave a delightfully entertaining performance on the piano. Mr. Harney is a young Kentuckian, and his imitation of a negro's musical methods are truly characteristic."[83] The description of Harney's performance as imitation stands in stark contrast to his later claims to be the originator of ragtime.[84] Although the historical record clearly contradicts that assertion, Harney was the first white performer to publish a ragtime song and in many ways validated Johnson's critique of white men "taking down" Negro tunes.[85] Harney's publications and performances of minstrelsy—accompanied by his uncommon all–African American ensemble—capitalized on America's burgeoning sheet music industry and its ability to function as a gateway to national recognition.

For a brief period, there were conflicting reports concerning Harney's ethnicity.[86] Rather than to dismiss such confusion as a product of erroneous journalism, I draw attention to the racial ambiguity because Harney navigated the music industry in ways that would enable the errors. Performing in blackface with an African American ensemble (which also performed in blackface) could certainly have confused his audience members. Ironically, once Harney's ethnic identity was clearly established toward the latter part of his career, he was better positioned to reap financial rewards from ragtime and even claim ownership of the genre. Although some white tastemakers viewed ragtime as problematic, their opinion often changed when they thought the inventors were white. The question of imitation became moot when whites could claim to be originators. Instead of being viewed as a minstrel and mimic of Black music, Harney would come to be celebrated as an innovator of ragtime and be seen as instrumental to its promulgation in America. In fact, upon his death, *Time* (1938) magazine referred to him as "ragtime's father" and credited Harney with launching "a nation-wide school of ragtime composers" while listing Scott Joplin as a "prominent follower."[87] An article by Broadway star Fred Stone in the *New York Times* titled "The Origin of Ragtime" (1924) also assigned credit for the music's development to Harney.[88] So despite the seminal role of Joplin, the Johnson Brothers, Cole, and other African American artists in creating the genre of ragtime and innovating within it, as well as their efforts to separate it from the sphere of minstrelsy, white artists, in a pattern that repeated itself throughout the century, received a disproportionate share of the credit and financial rewards.

Whatever the historical trajectory, when auditors heard ragtime, they heard the fissures within America's construction of race, opening new avenues to a Black modernist subjectivity. As artists navigated social and political constraints, their artistry impacted aesthetic values while laying the groundwork for what Eric Watts describes as the "aesthetic regimes" invested in the production of the New Negro during the Harlem Renaissance.[89] In his extensive historical treatment of Black musicians within the development of Manhattan's music industry, David Gilbert observed that African American musicians "strategized about how to become professional entertainers as much as they dreamed of symbolizing a vanguard of African-American citizenship."[90] Joplin, the Johnson brothers, and Cole were important figures in these deliberations, along with James Bland, Sam Lucas, Joe Jordon, Gussie L. Davis, Ernest Hogan, and many others.[91]

For Joplin, Johnson's protagonist, and Harney, ragtime functioned as a musical rendezvous, or "contact zone," for identities, bodies, and ideologies.[92] It engendered both symbolic and physical subversions of racial boundaries by pitting the desire for Black cultural production against racial segregation. Therefore, it is no coincidence that some of the first instances of desegregated clubs and musical theaters featured such music.[93]

For an understanding of the American rhetorical landscape, it is instructive to notice how and why Ben Harney was dubbed the father of ragtime. But it is essential to a true account of the rhetorical force of African American music to comprehend that he was *not* the father. Although ragtime has no "natal occasion," it was a product of Black communal collaboration and experimentation that became a critical and powerful rhetoric of humanity and social justice.[94] That it also has been central to overall American identity and expression, sometimes in vexing ways, only indicates, as Toni Morrison suggested in *Playing in the Dark*, the persistent, often troubling, and, above all, rhetorical "Africanist presence" in American life.[95]

2
Duke Converses with the World

Throughout his career of more than fifty years, during which he produced more than two thousand compositions, Edward Kennedy "Duke" Ellington used his music to articulate Black identity and history while becoming a symbol of modernism and racial progress. This chapter outlines the rhetoric of Ellington by examining three of his most important works. First, Ellington's "Black and Tan Fantasy" (1927) marked his ascendance to national notoriety. This song was performed during Ellington's residence at the famous Cotton Club in Harlem, New York, and its success positioned Ellington as the foremost innovator of a new array of sonic material popularly referred to as "jungle music." Second, the racial pride of *Jump for Joy* (1941), an all-Black musical revue that Ellington argued "would take Uncle Tom out of the theater," took aim at the stereotypical images of African Americans exploited by Hollywood and Broadway.[1] Third, *Black, Brown and Beige* (1943), a long-form orchestral composition that Ellington premiered in Carnegie Hall, became what he called "a tone parallel to the history of the Negro in America."[2] Through these three works, Ellington helped to define jazz and Black identity for several generations.

As the popularity of ragtime gave way to the rising genre of jazz, racist criticism predictably kept pace.[3] Texts such as Rollo H. Myers's *Music in the Modern World* (1943) characterized jazz as "debased" and "hysterical" noise that was penetrating every corner of the globe.[4] Despite the popularity of jazz in Europe and its welcome by authoritative voices in classical music, early criticism of jazz often emphasized its so-called links to crime, sexual perversion, and primitivism.[5] Ellington's music worked to dissociate African American culture from these connections by producing alternative narratives of history and identity through sound.

The two musical characteristics through which Ellington's contributions became manifest are swing and dissonance. Swing, the dominant rhythmic idiom of the big-band era, is signifying on time itself, going against the flow of a stable pulse.[6] Therefore, as the rhythmic identity of jazz, swing is a literal suggestion of resistance.[7] In Western musical traditions, dissonance is constructed as the lack of harmony and tonal resolution. Further, dissonance is a moment of transition often associated with conflict, while its counterpart, harmony, signifies peace, conclusion, and stability. Dissonance is also associated with darker colors and emotions, confusion, and the presence of evil. However, Ellington framed dissonance as a way of life for a people he described as "something apart, yet an integral part."[8] Dissonance became both a musical preference and a statement about the political status of the Black community as a "nation within a nation."[9]

Ellington, of course, was an important member of the cadre of intellectuals exploring Black history and identity under the auspices of what became known as the Harlem Renaissance, and his music contributed just as much to that exploration as Langston Hughes, Countee Cullen, and Aaron Douglas. Ellington even went so far as to characterize his work as "conversation music."[10] Although he may have been describing the call-and-response qualities of his style of arranging, it is an apt description for his music in terms of content, context, and rhetorical effect, as his music did indeed animate public discourse.

The Rise of "Black and Tan Fantasy"

The source material for "Black and Tan Fantasy" arose from trumpeter Bubber Miley's experience of a spiritual his mother would sing titled "Hosanna." Ellington and Miley worked together to arrange the sounds of the spiritual into what became one of Ellington's most popular early compositions. With the aid of a plunger mute technique that can imitate the human voice, Miley creates a sorrowful, growling sound with his trumpet.[11] The dark and foreboding feel of the song also is created with the use of a slow march-like tempo, low saxophone textures, and melodic lines reminiscent of Stephen Adam's "Holy City," a Western traditional song. The song begins in B-flat minor (which is a significant transformation of the source text's use of major keys) with a twelve-bar introduction of the central theme before modulating to B-flat major for both a sixteen-bar saxophone solo and Miley's extended blues solo on trumpet. Miley's phrasing imitates all of the tropes of vocal performance, including moans, growls, and mumbles. Ellington then follows Miley's solo with a stride piano solo that features a characteristically rhythmic left-hand accompaniment. The song concludes with a statement of Frédéric Chopin's "Funeral March."[12] Folding Chopin's march and the Western classic "Holy City" into the dark blues texture of the orchestra was a unique juxtaposition displaying the range and dexterity of the spirituals and the blues idiom. These musical gestures opened a wider range of emotional colors and signaled a distinct break from the music of Ellington's peers. In one account of "Black and Tan Fantasy," the song was used as the context for a contest between Miley and fellow trumpeter Johnny Dunn. Ellington had the stage set up to resemble an old church. As the orchestra began to play, Miley began playing off-stage, "cutting loose with his jungle-iron, choking and wailing like a lost soul."[13] This particular fusion of sacred and profane showed that jazz was a vehicle capable of exploring the wide realm of emotions and experiences of Black life.

Ellington's melodic and harmonic innovation could not be easily categorized into the "hot" and "sweet" categories that had become monikers for jazz performed by Black and white musicians, respectively. "Hot" jazz was said to have originated with Black musicians who, in lieu of traditional techniques, imitated Black vocal performance. They utilized tone modification devices (plungers and mutes) along with the liberal use of glissandos, vibrato, growling, and other tonal effects. Using traditional instruments to make such human sounds involved acts of virtuosity that were often dismissed or devalued by (generally white) critics. "Hot" jazz also emphasized improvisation with an emphasis on spontaneity over adherence to a rigid form. Additionally, the role of syncopation and strong rhythmic qualities were paramount.

"Sweet" jazz, which arose from the performance of jazz by whites, became known as a more "disciplined" instrumental performance that was seen as more professional, intellectual, and substantive. The term was used to describe the music of figures like Paul Whiteman, a popular leader of an all-white band who referred to his music as "symphonic jazz." Songs like "Black and Tan Fantasy" disrupted this dichotomy because the harmonic and melodic content displayed a much more robust musical statement that could not be easily dismissed as lacking in substance. Although other bands could perform transcriptions of the song, the style in which Ellington's orchestra performed the music was almost inimitable.[14]

The success of "Black and Tan Fantasy" solidified Ellington's profile as a prominent public figure.[15] In addition to record sales, the broadcast of Ellington's concerts over the radio spread Black culture and music to new swaths of the American public in a medium that, like printed music, concealed the bodies of the performers and heightened the need for labels to distinguish between Black and white ensembles. To ensure that the radio was never "blind," ubiquitous racialized discourse, such as the "hot" and "sweet" dichotomy, became a critical tool for demarcating Black culture in the public sphere. Managing white audiences' expectations of "exotic" Black entertainment was a significant rhetorical constraint for Black artists seeking to expand the medium of jazz to reflect the many-sided authentic experiences of Black life.[16] Ellington's considerable success with radio was due, in part, to his ability to control his image and sound to entice white audiences while appearing nonthreatening, a task which was complicated by the need to remain authentic to African American audiences as well.[17] "Black and Tan Fantasy" was sophisticated enough to perform this double role. While some listeners heard wild "jungle music," others heard the sounds signifying on the sonic material of the spirituals as a recalibration of its resources for a new genre of music.

Once Ellington's popularity became too great to ignore, white critics began to credit him (albeit grudgingly) as an entertaining performer of "Negro music." For example, the editors of the *Greensboro News and Record* stated, "If we were asked to name the ten best American composers, living or dead, we would put Duke Ellington on the list, not because of the intricacies of his compositions, but because he has expressed the soul of his people better than any other man."[18] Underneath the condescension and backhanded compliments was a growing realization that Ellington's music was so impactful that it could not be dismissed. In a second instance, Lawrence Tibbett, a celebrated American opera singer, defended Ellington during an NBC radio broadcast by arguing that "serious" musicians attended Ellington's performances in Paris and that his music was loved by all. He went further to declare Ellington's compositions, including "Mood Indigo" and "Black and Tan Fantasy," central parts of the American school of music.[19]

Even Ellington's white competitors were not beyond paying homage to his growing influence. Rudy Vallée, one of the most popular white bandleaders in America, argued that Ellington had "done more than anyone else to shape the tendencies of present day dance music."[20] Ellington's profile was further elevated when famous classical composers such as Percy Grainger, one of the most eminent wind ensemble composers in classical music, refused to participate in the collective cold shoulder of musical elites. Grainger compared Ellington's music to the "melodic mastery of British composer Frederick Delius."[21] Classical music critic R. D. Darrell reasoned that "the most brilliant flights of Rimsky's or Strauss's orchestral fancy are equaled, if not surpassed by many passages in Ellington's records."[22] In his commentary on "Black and Tan Fantasy," Darrell described his initial reaction to the song as amused and dismissive before experiencing a profound change:

> With the majority I did not recognize it when it first came to my ears in the form of the "hottest, funniest record you ever heard." . . . But as I continued to play the record for the amusement of my friends I laughed less heartily and with less zest. In my ears the whinnies and wa-was began to resolve into new tone colors, distorted and tortured, but agonizingly expressive. . . . Beneath all its oddity and perverseness there was a twisted beauty that grew on me more and more and could not be shaken off.[23]

Once Darrell listened beyond the rhetorical construction of jungle music, he began to hear the actual innovation and creativity that contributed to the song's success. Foreign critics were even willing to label Ellington's music as the most original art form to emanate from America besides Mickey Mouse.[24]

This creativity extended to the film *Black and Tan* (1929). Directed by Dudley Murphy[25] and starring Fredi Washington[26] as Duke Ellington's wife, the plot features Washington as a successful dancer and entertainer while Ellington (who plays himself) and his orchestra suffer financial difficulties. To assist Ellington, Washington offers the orchestra the opportunity to perform with her at a club. Washington is then diagnosed with a heart problem that threatens her dancing career, but she remains determined to perform despite the risk to her health. During the performance with Ellington and his orchestra, Washington stumbles. To hide her condition, she falsely assures Ellington that she is healthy enough to continue with the performance, which ultimately leads to her death. As her last request, she whispers, "Duke, play me the 'Black and Tan Fantasy.'" Toward the end of the song, the camera takes on the viewpoint of Washington. Ellington is then shown playing in front of her while the picture becomes blurry and eventually fades out. Despite the tragic ending for the film's heroine, *Black and Tan* was advertised as a showcase of the Cotton Club Orchestra and "jungle syncopation." Terms such as "jungle" and "primitive" were loaded with negative racial stereotypes, but one of the important impulses of the Harlem Renaissance era was a willingness to challenge the stigmatization of all things Africa. Additionally, there was a great deal of commercial cachet in the use of such terms for white audiences attracted to what they perceived as "exotic" entertainment. This, in part, accounts for Ellington's ambivalence concerning the use of these terms to describe his music. The film offered audiences the "primitivist" spectacle worthy of the Cotton Club's reputation, including scantily clad dancers and a glimpse into the "primitive piety" of Black worship.[27] But more important, *Black and Tan* was one of the first films to portray the emergence of Black artists during the Harlem Renaissance. Just as the song "Black and Tan Fantasy" expanded the range of styles and sounds for Ellington's orchestra, *Black and Tan* expanded the dimensions of Black performance on screen beyond the racist imagery of minstrelsy.

The totality of Ellington's performance of "Black and Tan Fantasy," including its translation to film and its various iterations on subsequent recordings and radio broadcasts, became a critical part of a paradigm shift concerning representations of Black culture in the public sphere. Throughout Ellington's career, he often bristled at the description of his music as just "jazz" because, at that time, that label could render one's music trivial entertainment. Ellington wanted to be taken seriously as a composer, and he often articulated a much more robust rhetorical intention with his music: "Our aim as a dance orchestra is not so much to reproduce 'hot' or 'sweet' 'jazz' music as to describe emotions, moods, and activities which have a wide range, leading from the very gay to the somber. Every one of my songs is taken from the life of Harlem. . . . [I look] to the everyday life and customs of the Negro to supply my inspiration."[28] Thus "Black and Tan Fantasy" was part of an effort to better communicate the interiority of Black life, including its diversity of emotions and moods, which went beyond the capacity of "hot," "jazz," or any of the other racialized genre descriptors.

Consider the written transcription of "Black and Tan Fantasy" and its apparent simplicity (see figure 6). What cannot be transcribed into standard musical notation is the performative aspects of this melody. The texture and sound quality of the notes are what provide the song with its distinctive characteristics and resonance. Therefore, the "jungle syncopation" reference is an attempt to name its "sonic and auditory distinctive features."[29] In accordance with ethnomusicologist Gerhard Kubik's claim that jazz harmony and textures are in fact derived from African matrices, musicians like Ellington created blues tonalities by converting the tonal-harmonic resources provided by Western instruments and music.[30] This claim subtly repudiates the common narrative that the rhythm of jazz originates in Africa and the harmony exclusively from the West.

Ellington's exploration of harmony and texture in "Black and Tan Fantasy" was indeed a genuine inquiry into diasporic sonic material. However, despite Ellington's noble intentions, the distinctive sound that he and his orchestra worked to cultivate became increasingly attached to descriptors like "jungle music" and other primitive motifs. Ellington eventually became one of the musicians (in addition to his predecessors

Figure 6. Duke Ellington, "Black and Tan Fantasy" (1927). This excerpt presents the first seven measures of the score's reduction for piano.

Joe King Oliver and Red Allen Sr.) primarily associated with the term, and he was often referred to as the "king of jungle rhythm."[31]

Commentary about the popularity of "Black and Tan Fantasy" in the Black press (which also struggled with resisting anti-Black hegemonic discourses) was equally ambivalent on "jungle" discourse and often included terms such as *eerie*, *weird*, and *mournful* in connection with "the mystery, enchantments, and undertone of the jungle."[32] Describing Ellington's music as a mixture of strange rhythms and tempos, the *Pittsburgh Courier* noted that his ballads became "plaintive jungle beats" that were "cradled in queer and unrecognizable harmonies."[33] Such publications framed the jungle discourse as an aural extension of the exotic/primitive stereotype described by critic Sterling Brown in his 1933 essay "Negro Characters as Seen by White Authors." Brown made direct and explicit connections between racial stereotypes and the influx of whites seeking entertainment in Harlem.[34] According to Brown, these stereotypes arose from America's revolt against Puritanism and from Sigmund Freud's theories about sex. In his view, white authors exploited Black life and culture for what they saw as the "Negro's savage inheritance of hot jungle nights."[35] Brown further characterized these authors as rushing to Harlem for a taste of color, hoping to experience "Negro, *au naturel*."[36] This cultural dynamic, combined with the employment of Ellington's orchestra at the infamous Cotton Club (a club that featured Black entertainment for white audiences) and the recurrent radio broadcasts of his shows nationwide, produced a complicated rhetorical landscape for Ellington's larger ambitions of elevating Black music and culture.

The conceptual relationship among hot jazz, jungle music, and Africa presented both obstacles and advantages for Ellington. He began expressing a desire to compose music that spoke to the African diaspora. In some respects, the "jungle music" fetish provided cover for honest exploration of African-inspired motifs in his music.[37] For example, in the *Christian Science Monitor* on December 13, 1930, Ellington stated: "I am just getting a chance to work out some of my own ideas of Negro music. I stick to that. We as a race have a good deal to pay our way with in a white world. The tragedy is that so few records have been kept of the Negro music of the past. It has to be pieced together so slowly. But it pleases me to have a chance to work at it."[38] Ellington framed Black music as the cultural and aesthetic currency that could be used to represent authentically the presence of African Americans. This idea would become a lasting motivation for his subsequent large-scale works, including *Jump for Joy* and *Black, Brown and Beige*. Additionally, Ellington was speaking to the loss of historical records concerning the African diaspora, both verbal and sonic, which contain the intangibles of culture, religion, and aesthetics. Ellington positioned his music as an articulation of this lost sonic material. In a subsequent interview, Ellington elaborated on his rhetorical aims of composing Black life:

> I am not playing jazz. I am trying to play the natural feelings of a people. I believe that music, popular music of the day, is the real reflector of the nation's feelings. Some of the music which has been written will always be beautiful and immortal. Beethoven, Wagner and Bach are geniuses; no one can rob their work of the merit that is due it, but these men have not portrayed the people who are about us today, and the interpretation of these people is our future music.[39]

Ellington was neither a cynical opportunist nor an ardent Africanist; rather, he understood Black music through a diasporic lens.[40] Therefore, Ellington's tacit acceptance of the "jungle music" label masked a serious attempt to locate and build upon a tradition that, according to Ellington, required rediscovery for its potential impact on the future of music.[41] For Ellington, such music could lead to a stronger sense of collective identity and history. This idea is not dissimilar from Racquel Gates's exploration of "ratchet" (a form of Black cultural transgression) television and her claim that, freed from the burdens of respectability politics, such spaces can offer the room for rich and complex experimentation as well as subversive challenges to hegemonic discourses.[42] It's safe to say that we can view that which was categorized as "jungle music" as the "ratchet" music of its time from the perspective of cultural elites.

While music critics were just beginning to discover and theorize African music during the late 1920s, the desire to create a genealogy for jazz was important not only to academic elites but also to Ellington and other jazz musicians. For example, on January 10, 1931, an article appeared in the *Baltimore Afro-American* that profiled a group of experts from the Institute of Paris and their trip to Africa to seek out a scientific answer to the origins of the syncopated rhythms most often associated with people of African descent. Their findings were to be presented in a series of programs that would discuss lullabies from Madagascar and folk songs from Senegal, as well as religious chants from the Congo.[43] The article then shifted its focus to America by claiming that there were those, such as Ellington, who refused to look further for the true origin of jazz than African American history. However, the article went on to credit Ellington with not only playing quality jazz but also a "new type of modern music."[44] Ellington, for his part, was quoted by the newspaper remarking that jazz was not the "outgrowth of free jungle life" but of the oppression of the slaver.[45] In this instance, Ellington decoded the subtle limitations that were being applied to Black music rhetorically, and he was responsive to attempts at erasure concerning the role of the Black experience in America within the development of jazz. He also sought to distance jazz from the negative connotations of "jungle music" when it was used to signify superficiality or insignificance. However, Ellington's efforts ran the risk of completely dissociating jazz from Africa.

Alain Locke, editor of the 1925 anthology *The New Negro*, described the complexities of the discourse that surrounded Africa as a mixture of "compensating interests" enabled by the work of those like Ellington:

> Fortunately, there are constructive channels opening out into which the balked social feelings of the American Negro can flow freely. Without them there would be much more pressure and danger than there is. These compensating interests are racial but in a new and enlarged way. One is the consciousness of acting as the advance guard of the African peoples in their contact with Twentieth Century civilization; the other, the sense of a mission of rehabilitating the race in world esteem from that loss of prestige for which the fate and conditions of slavery have so largely been responsible.[46]

From Locke's perspective, works such as "Black and Tan Fantasy" were the "channels" through which previously forbidden social feelings could be expressed.

Poets such as Langston Hughes and Countee Cullen wrote extensively about the complex relationship they shared with the concept of

Africa. For example, Hughes's poem "Afro-American Fragment" presents the role of Africa as a site for constructing African American identity:

> So long,
> So far away
> Is Africa.
> Not even memories alive
> Save those that history books create,
> Save those that songs
> Beat back into the blood—
> Beat out of blood with words sad-sung
> In strange un-Negro tongue—
> So long,
> So far away
> Is Africa . . .[47]

Hughes positions music as an archive of what remnants of Africa survive in African American culture. In his 1926 essay "The Negro Artist and the Racial Mountain," Hughes connected his work directly to jazz: "Most of my own poems are racial in theme and treatment, derived from the life I know. In many of them I try to grasp and hold some of the meanings and rhythms of jazz."[48] The connection Hughes makes between his poetry, jazz, and the inheritance of Africa was shared by Ellington and many other artists concerned with exploring African American identity.

Countee Cullen, also a popular writer and contemporary of Hughes's, dealt with the concept of Africa in his poem "Heritage":

> What is Africa to me:
> Copper sun or scarlet sea,
> Jungle star or jungle track,
> Strong bronzed men, or regal Black
> Women from whose loins I sprang
> When the birds of Eden sang?
> *One three centuries removed*
> *From the scenes his fathers loved,*
> *Spicy grove, cinnamon tree,*
> *What is Africa to me?*[49]

Cullen's "Heritage" is full of the jungle discourse used (rather longingly) to describe Ellington's music. However, Cullen's incisive question is key to his search for a conception of Africa that is more authentic and upends racist discourses.

Visual artists were also exploring these ideas. The work of Aaron Douglas, one of the most prolific painters of the Harlem Renaissance, depicts the jungle with dark, faceless figures. However, the impressions Douglas creates are not those of mockery or exoticism. For example, Douglas's *Into Bondage* presents a haunting portrait of the abduction of Africans and their impending enslavement. The painting depicts the jungle with shadowy shapes of men who have brightly colored chains on their wrists, reminiscent of a chain gang. The brightest spot of the painting shows two ships at sea. The painting functions rhetorically as an ironic commentary on the "darkness" of the jungle and the "light" of the approaching slave ships. The area that is shaded in darkness actually signifies safety while the light highlights modernity's dark side: the acceleration of violent conquest and economic exploitation of human beings. The ideological reversal that Douglas's painting performs visually, Ellington's "Black and Tan Fantasy" performs sonically, turning the jungle music sound into modern innovation. Thus, along with his contemporaries Hughes, Cullen, and Douglas, Ellington was a coarchitect of a diasporic frame of reference.[50] Edwin Black defines "frame of reference" as the body of convictions, attitudes, and values that form around a particular idea. Ellington's music suggests that Black music was not just a vehicle for a diasporic frame of reference, but also a space for theorizing its contents.

A sense of the image that Ellington cultivated in the minds of his fans speaks to the rhetorical success of his endeavors, both from the vantage point of record sales and the perceived meaning and impact of his music. In a widely publicized national competition for the top band in America by the *Pittsburgh Courier* in 1931, fans of the Ellington orchestra were given the opportunity to describe why Ellington deserved the highest honors. Throughout the more than fifty thousand votes cast in Ellington's favor, their statements illustrate the salience of the meanings attached to Ellington's music. For example, while explaining his support for Ellington, one respondent, Alexander Wilkins, echoed Ellington's self-description when he argued that, "Duke Ellington is not playing jazz, but is playing the natural feelings of the people."[51] Due to Ellington's success, he began to be seen not only as a celebrated musician but as a leader of the race.

As Ellington's success continued, he grew even more ambitious concerning the rhetorical dimensions of his music. Ellington went so far as to characterize himself as "crying out in the wilderness to be heard," with a desire to create "true negro music."[52] On February 12, 1941, Ellington presented a sermon at a local church in Los Angeles in conjunction with the community's Lincoln Day festivities. In the sermon, titled "We, Too, Sing 'America'," he proclaimed that "the Negro is the creative voice of America" and "the personification of the ideal begun by the Pilgrims almost 350 years ago."[53] Ellington acknowledged the privilege of free speech in light of the silence imposed by Europe's dictators.[54] He then stated that it was "our voice that sang 'America' when America grew too lazy, satisfied and confident to sing . . . before the dark threats and fire-lined clouds of destruction frightened it into a thin panicky quaver."[55] Ellington translated his statements into action with his production of *Jump for Joy: A Sun-Tanned Revu-sical* during the following summer. He convinced producer Joseph Pasternak and actor John Garfield, as well as a number of other writers associated with the Hollywood Theatre Alliance, to finance the production, one that contributed to progressive and Popular Front sensibilities.[56]

The Jubilation of *Jump for Joy*

Ellington's goal with *Jump for Joy* was to address the issue of race in America through a "form of theatrical propaganda."[57] The cast for the show, staged at the Mayan Theater in Los Angeles, was strictly forbidden from using blackface and from employing negative caricatures. The production was also a response to works such as George Gershwin's *Porgy and Bess*, an opera written specifically for African American performers, which Ellington viewed as an example of white composers borrowing from African American composers without due credit.[58] The revue featured actress Dorothy Dandridge and the collaboration of arranger Billy Strayhorn, poet Langston Hughes, and numerous up-and-coming Black entertainers, such as comedian Wonderful Smith and singer Big Joe Turner.[59]

Jump for Joy was not structured around a plot per se. Instead, it featured a series of sketches that could be altered or changed between nightly shows with the assistance of over fifteen writers, not dissimilar from the improvisational practices that governed Ellington's concert performances. In addition to the title song, "Jump for Joy," Ellington produced other notable songs that became central to his repertoire, including "The Brownskin Gal in a Calico Gown," "I Got It Bad and That Ain't Good," and "Blue Flame." The central ideas of the production were resistance to racial oppression and cultural pride, and those sentiments were echoed in the titles of the various skits, such as "Cotton Lisle Is Out of Style," "*Green Pastures* Was Just a Technicolor Movie," "The Sun-Tanned Tenth of the Nation," and "Uncle Tom's Cabin Is a Drive-In Now," which were derived from the lyrics of "Jump for Joy." The show began with a monologue from Ellington:

> Now, every Broadway colored show,
> According to tradition,
> Must be a carbon copy
> Of the previous edition,
> With the truth discreetly muted,
> And the accent on the brasses.
> The punch that should be present
> In a colored show, alas, is
> Disinfected with magnolia
> And dripping with molasses.
> In other words,
> We're shown to you
> Through Stephen Foster's glasses.[60]

The show then continued with vocal performances and dance routines. Actor Paul White sang "I've Got a Passport from Georgia," which included the lyrics "Farewell, Charlie, so long Joe / Good-bye, Jim, and I do mean Crow." Ellington's superb orchestration, in addition to the groundbreaking performances, presented the highest degree of African American talent combined with a bold critique of racism that eventually caught the ire of the Ku Klux Klan. The Klan demanded that White's song be cut from the show and left a picture of a coffin under the stage door.[61] Along with a series of other death threats, one cast member was beaten while leaving the theater. However, such actions only emboldened the cast.

The music added to the potency of the social critique of the skits, especially "Jump for Joy," which is an up-tempo swing chart that featured an elegant call-and-response riff between a muted trumpet and the orchestra, following a contrasting saxophone line led by the baritone sax. Ivy Anderson, Ellington's celebrated full-time vocalist, provided lyrics to the verse and chorus sections previously played by the orchestra. Imitating train sounds was an important staple of Ellington's orchestra and a critical component to the genres of blues and swing. "Jump for Joy" presents this technique in an effort to pull its listeners away from the Jim Crow South and toward the exuberant promises of a better future (see figure 7). Fittingly, every performance of the revue concluded with Strayhorn's "Take the 'A' Train," a more explicit exhortation toward upward mobility and the pursuit of a better life. In addition to the performances, the revue also introduced the nation to zoot suits, linking the flamboyant attire to the revue's spirit of protest. According to Ellington, "every setting, every note of music, every lyric, meant something. All the sketches had a message for the world."[62]

Figure 7. This example excerpts the first six measures of the saxophone parts from the score of "Jump for Joy." The series of eighth notes creates the "chugga-chugga" sound associated with trains, a symbol of modernity and mobility.

One important element of the show was the strategic reversal in point of view. Instead of Black entertainers performing for whites and catering to a white point of view, the show presented Black entertainment from the Black point of view, decentering what was considered the traditional American audience.[63] Due to his time spent at the Cotton Club, Ellington was quite aware of the rhetorical difficulty of his undertaking. The social critique had to be handled with sophistication and care if the production were going to be successful, and Ellington worked closely with his team of writers to ensure that he could say "everything [he] wanted to say without saying it."[64]

The revue opened to capacity crowds of whites and Blacks so enthused that they refused to leave after the shows, leading to jam sessions that went on for hours on end.[65] As news about the production spread across the nation, thousands of requests for souvenirs and programs poured in from fans excited about the show's positive message.[66] Ironically, the production initially received mixed reviews from the Black press, with Almena Davis, editor of the *Los Angeles Tribune*, remarking that the show represented the death of Uncle Tom and "a new mood in theater" that reflected "the happy satire of colored life" while questioning the show's use of white writers and producers.[67] Additionally, some reviewers, such as George T. Simon in *Metronome*, were critical of the show's organization and execution. Simon took issue with the notion that the orchestra—which performed in the pit and off stage—could be the feature of the show.[68]

The production ran for 122 performances in Los Angeles before succumbing to lagging ticket sales in September, ending the total span of its run at eleven weeks. However, hopes for taking the show to Broadway or on a national tour were quickly dashed as the message of antiracism and cultural pride proved to be more politically charged than what other venues were willing to tolerate. But despite *Jump for Joy*'s short-lived run, it left a lasting impact, particularly with African American audiences. Writing two years after the show's conclusion, Alyce Key of the *Los Angeles Tribune* remarked that the significance of the production spoke directly to "a people sick to death of being burlesqued and caricatured on the American stage."[69] The "ghost of *Jump for Joy*" would now rise to "protect the standard for Negro shows."[70]

The frustration of his hopes to take *Jump for Joy* to Broadway was a major disappointment for Ellington in light of his overall satisfaction with the show's execution. He remarked, "All the sketches had a message for the world. The tragedy was that the world was not ready for *Jump for Joy*."[71] Decades later, when asked by a protester in San Francisco what his contribution to the Civil Rights movement would be, Ellington stated, "I did my piece more than 20 years ago when I wrote *Jump for Joy*."[72]

A *Black, Brown and Beige* State of Mind

The origin of *Black, Brown and Beige* began with a smaller work entitled *Boola*, which was one of Ellington's unfinished operas. In preparation for the composition, Ellington, according to his statements to the press, had collected up to eight hundred books on African American history.[73] Ellington explained the title of *Black, Brown and Beige* as a reference to "the [Black] state of mind, not the color of the skin," an effort to connect a collective self-image to the social ascension of the Black community.[74] However, his son, Mercer Ellington, suggested that the title was also a subtle gesture toward the legacy of colorism in the Black community.[75] In either case, Ellington's rhetorical aims were in line with the social consciousness present in his previous work.

The debut of *Black, Brown and Beige* at Carnegie Hall followed what became known as "Ellington Week" (January 17–23, 1943), as Black musicians decided to honor the twenty-year anniversary of Ellington's first appearance in New York.[76] Carnegie Hall represented the pinnacle of American artistic excellence as well as a significant color line. Ellington's success in securing his first performance in the venue broke a significant barrier and was a testament to his efforts to advance the popularity and authenticity of jazz.[77] His time spent touring nationally and internationally, in addition to performing on national radio broadcasts, had increased his stature to the extent that few members of the classical music community could deny his significance as a composer and arranger. In addition, the performance was organized as a benefit for the Russian War Relief effort.

The first movement of the piece, "Black," begins with the musical relationship between African American work songs and spirituals. Thunderous timpani open a dramatic sequence featuring a booming, majestic brass line that presents one of the central musical themes, before settling into a swinging, robust groove. Ellington's arrangement provides the textures of swing, blues, and spirituals with a grandiose and pictorial narrative. The piece then shifts to "Come Sunday," a sermon in song led by alto saxophonist Johnny Hodges. Ellington described this section as "intended to depict the movement inside and outside the church, as seen by workers who stood outside, watched, listened, but were not admitted."[78] The conclusion of the movement features what Ellington called "the promise." Ellington reasoned that an unfinished ending was "in accordance with reality," as there remained so much work to be done in terms of the struggle for equality.[79] The quick transitions between textures and tones sounded disjointed to some listeners, but Ellington explained this context as reflective of Black temperament, which "passed quickly from the extremes of joy to gloom and back again," as well as a gesture to the dramatic changes that had occurred in the rhythm of Black life in America.[80]

The second movement, "Brown," focuses on the contributions of African Americans to American culture and history, particularly those made by soldiers. The first section, titled "West Indian Dance," features a Latin-style feel as a dedication to the rescue efforts of free Haitians in the Viscount François de Fontanges Legion (a Black unit of the French Army), who provided critical aid to American soldiers at the siege of Savannah during the Revolutionary War. The second section takes on the Civil War and is titled "Emancipation Celebration." This section presents the mixture of joyfulness and bewilderment confronting the recently emancipated. The joy is attributed to those who were freed in their youth, and bewilderment suggests the uncertain conditions of older adults who found themselves free but also stripped of security and stability. The third section, "The Blues," addresses the Spanish-American War and presents a celebration for returning soldiers in conjunction with the broader emergence of Black life in urban centers. "The Blues" is the work's sole vocal feature, which was performed by Betty Roché. The dark timbre of Roché's voice is a more than suitable match for the mournful and pensive texture that concludes the movement.

The third and final movement, "Beige," features Harlem as a symbolic site representing the many centers of Black life across the nation. "Beige" is structured as a waltz depicting a sophisticated panorama of Black life in all of its struggles for expression, education, and equality. The first section, "Sugar Hill Penthouse," gestures toward the upward mobility of Harlem before concluding with a nod to World War II. Sugar Hill became a popular neighborhood for wealthy African Americans, and its residents included prominent public figures such as W. E. B. Du Bois, Cab Calloway, and Adam Clayton Powell Jr., among others. Ellington described the conclusion of this section as representing the loyalty of African Americans to a society that misunderstands them: "So, just as always before, the Black, Brown, and Beige were soon right in there for the Red, White, and Blue."[81] In many respects, *Black, Brown and Beige* became a sonic transcription of the sermon he delivered in 1941:

> We stirred in our shackles and our unrest awakened Justice in the hearts of a courageous few, and we recreated in America the desire for true democracy, freedom for all, the brotherhood of man, principles on which the country had been founded. We were freed, and, as before, we fought America's wars, provided her labor, gave her music, kept alive her flickering conscience, prodded her on toward the yet unachieved goal, democracy—until we became more than a part of America! . . . We are more than a few isolated instances of courage, valor, achievement. We're the injection, the shot in the arm that has kept America and its forgotten principles alive in the fat and corrupt years intervening between our divine conception and our near tragic present.[82]

Following the concert, Ellington was presented with a plaque with a conductor's baton attached and received a standing ovation from the musicians and entertainers, both on stage and in the crowd, who were there to celebrate Ellington's accomplishments and leadership. The plaque was inscribed with thirty-two signatures from diverse political and artistic figures, such as William Grant Still, Edward Johnson of the Metropolitan Opera, Earl Hines, Marian Anderson, Paul Robeson, Aaron Copland, Paul Whiteman, Benny Goodman, Cab Calloway, and Artie Shaw.[83]

Black, Brown and Beige ignited an intense public debate concerning the relationship between jazz and classical music. Paul Bowles of the *New York Herald-Tribune* was highly critical of the piece, describing it as "formless and meaningless" and a patchwork of bright ideas that failed to coalesce into an integrated large-scale work.[84] Bowles dismissed

Ellington's ideological commitments to the importance of African American history and culture, referring to them as a "gaudy potpourri of tutti dance passages and solo virtuoso work."[85] He then challenged Ellington's allegiance to the genre of jazz by claiming, "If there is no regular beat there can be no syncopation . . . no jazz."[86] Although Bowles clearly misinterpreted the relationship between jazz and syncopation, he was right in noticing the rhythmic fluidity of *Black, Brown and Beige*. However, this fluidity was not the result of careless mistakes or poor preparation. Ellington positioned rhythm as an improvisational category, along with melodies and individual solos, which reflected the larger improvisational character of the sonic lexicon of Black music. The rhythm, as with other dynamics of the work, was also reflective of the improvisational quality of the Black experience in America.

Mike Levin of *DownBeat* magazine came to Ellington's defense, claiming that anyone who sought to pass judgment after listening to the piece only once could not possibly be relied on. Levin attributed the flaws in the performance to limited rehearsals and a lack of familiarity with the score. However, he described Ellington's work as a "tremendous step forward for music."[87] Despite his praise of Ellington's musical accomplishments, Levin dismissed the programmatic material and, like many other critics, was noticeably silent about the work's rhetorical engagement with African American history and the cultural contribution of Black music.

Some critics questioned the very idea of the project. John Hammond of *Jazz* magazine accused Ellington of abandoning jazz and its most basic virtues (traditional twelve/thirty-two bar blues structures). Hammond concluded his critique with the plea, "I hope that someday [Ellington] will be able to find himself once again and continue his contributions to the folk."[88] It is an ironic request given the scant attention paid either to Ellington's opening monologue or to the role of music in African American history. Leonard Feather, responding in *Jazz* magazine, rejected Hammond's criticism: "I think it is a dirty rotten, lowdown nogood shame that somebody like John Hammond, who had done so much to eliminate race prejudice in music, should be so completely befuddled by personal prejudices himself."[89] Feather claimed that Hammond's comments were motivated by jealousy and envy over the orchestra's success, and he agreed with Mike Levin's claim that one hearing of *Black, Brown and Beige* was not enough to offer an objective criticism. However, he also emphasized the importance of the work's emotional and historical content by recounting some musicians' experiences with the work, such as cornetist Rex Stewart's recollection of coming to tears upon hearing Johnny Hodges perform "Come Sunday" for the first time. Regarding the question of Ellington's "betrayal" of the dance-band tradition for the cultural status of European classical music, Feather repudiated the false dichotomy: "Who the hell wants to dance in Carnegie Hall? And what does Hammond know about music for dancing, since he doesn't even dance? Duke's music has gone a little beyond the stage where it has to tickle the toes."[90]

Some of the responses in the Black press were also critical. Writing in the *New York Amsterdam News*, J. A. Blades charged Ellington with betraying not only jazz but also the race. Instead of striving to push jazz further in the world, Blades argued that Ellington had given up the racial struggle and was seeking to "escape his racial responsibilities."[91] In perhaps the most damning critique that could be leveled against another's claim to Blackness, Blades declared that Ellington had "sold his birthright for a mess of pottage."[92] Thus, according to Blades, Ellington had followed the same path as the narrator from James Weldon Johnson's *The Autobiography of an Ex-Colored Man*, who, at one point, sought to profit from translating the spirituals and eventually fled from life as a Black man in order to pass as white. Blades contrasted *Black, Brown and Beige* with Ellington's previous work, stating, "Gone is the racial purity of his 'Black and Tan Fantasy', and in its place is the weak and colorless grey of his latest work."[93] According to Blades, Ellington had long sought the "white light" and now the "fires of his desires [were] beginning to smolder in his most serious compositions."[94]

For those with Blades's point of view, Ellington's experimentation with symphonic forms was an implicit endorsement of the white cultural hegemony to which jazz had been functionally and rhetorically opposed. Yet there was at least one critical response that did engage the rhetorical context of the performance in its totality, including its dedication of proceeds to the Russian War Relief effort. Writing for the *Chicago Defender*, Langston Hughes recalled the beauty of the audience's diversity and the power of music to bring various races together. He reflected, "I couldn't help thinking about the more backward and barbarous regions of our country where people are prevented from sitting together in concert halls by law."[95] Hughes remarked that he was reminded of the influence of Black music on America, and he described American music as flavored with the "honey of the Negro soul."[96] Hughes mentioned that he held back tears as he thought about the connections between Black music and the Red Army and how the Russians were "driving the Nazis—who hate colored and white people sitting together listening to music—back with their ideology of hate and murder toward Berlin."[97] In addition to his expression of appreciation for those "fighting on the coldest front in the world," Hughes drew explicit lines to the rhetorical aspects of Ellington's oeuvre. Hughes stated that Ellington reached "down into the hearts of millions of all colors all over the world" to affirm for all people the right to life, joy, and happiness.[98] Aside from his political sentiments and his personal relationship with Ellington, Hughes was keen on the extent to which Black music signifies cultural and ethnic heritage.

The dedication of the performance to the Russian War Relief effort aligned with the sentiments of a large number of the Black intelligentsia, such as Hughes, Adam Clayton Powell Jr., Paul Robeson, and Louise Thompson Patterson, who at that time saw Russia as an ally in the cause of racial equality.[99] Although Ellington's views on communism would change drastically after World War II, he followed the majority of Harlem in its support of Communist Benjamin J. Davis's campaign for New York City Council later that year.[100] However, it is doubtful that Ellington's collaboration with Communists went beyond music. His activities only earned a superficial interest from the Federal Bureau of Investigation, who eventually concluded that his activities did not go beyond being a Black, liberal artist.[101] His collaboration with the Hollywood Theatre Alliance on *Jump for Joy* would be the only explicit participation with a semipolitical entity on a project of similar scale. Despite Ellington's common refrain that he was not interested in partisan politics, *Black, Brown and Beige* became the quintessential statement of his deep patriotism and his commitment to the struggle for civil rights.

Aside from Blades's attempted racial policing of Ellington's work, he was right to attempt to place *Black, Brown and Beige* in context with Ellington's prior work. However, the piece is certainly not an abandonment of the sonic virtues that lent to Ellington's earlier successes. On the contrary, *Black, Brown and Beige* is a sustained meditation on the entire corpus of sonic material that had helped to shape African American history. Although Ellington's efforts may have failed with some of the critics, it certainly impressed many white audience members. Dan Burley of the New York *Amsterdam Star-News* heard someone comment during the performance, "the Negro was put ahead twenty years culturally as a result of this affair." Another white audience member responded, "negroes don't suffer when they are publicly represented by such obvious class, poise, dignity and assurance as Duke Ellington presented here tonight."[102] Peter Suskind of the Norfolk *Journal and Guide* made a similar argument with his claim that "Ellington destroyed for himself and a whole race of people the last vestige of doubt which might have existed among many whites that the contribution of the Negro to music is universal."[103] Suskind indicated that it was the sense of dignity inspired by the performance that caused even those without musical training to sense the gravity of the occasion. Ellington's appearance at Carnegie Hall meant that his genius and prowess as a composer could no longer be denied and that jazz was in fact a vast intellectual enterprise on par with Western classical music. Despite most critics' pointing to the work's failure to comply with certain symphonic traditions of theme and development, few considered the rhetorical strategy of playing such a work in Carnegie Hall. After years of being labeled the "king of jungle music," Ellington had proved that African American expressive culture was worthy of the highest echelons of American cultural prestige.

Black, Brown and Beige opened a new avenue for Ellington; he began to make regular appearances on the concert stage. For each performance, Ellington attempted to perform music with a significant social message. He returned to Carnegie Hall on December 11, 1943, to premier *New World a-Comin'*, which was written in dedication to Roi Ottley's book of the same name. Inspired by the author's prediction of improved conditions for African Americans after World War II, Ellington said that he "visualized this new world as a place in the distant future where there would be no war, no greed, no categorization, no nonbelievers, where love was unconditional, and no pronoun was good enough for God."[104]

On November 23, 1946, Ellington presented *The Deep South Suite*, which featured the nostalgia and beauty of Black life in the South in four parts. The first movement, "Magnolias Just Dripping with Molasses," was what Ellington called a reproduction of the "Dixie Chamber of Commerce dream picture." The second movement was titled "Hearsay" as a reference to the misassumptions about life in the South. The third movement, "There Was Nobody Looking" presents one aspect of the complicated racial dynamic of the South as an illustration of a governing theory: as long as no one was looking, interaction was okay. This theory, according to Ellington, suggested that people of diverse backgrounds could indeed live and thrive together in the South—as long as they were not under the watchful eye of the guardians of America's racial caste system.[105] The final section of the suite, "Happy-Go-Lucky Local," presents another celebration of the mythic symbol of the train in African American culture. This piece presents a narrative of a Black fireman on a small train who travels through towns and villages in the South. The conductor uses the train whistle to communicate with members of his community by turning the whistle into an instrument to play the blues, spirituals, and boogie-woogie rhythms. The following year, on December 26, 1947, Ellington introduced *The Liberian Suite* as a commission by the Liberian government to celebrate the country's centennial anniversary as an independent republic.[106] Eventually, *My People*, a recapitulation of some of Ellington's earlier themes concerning Black history, would follow in 1963.

Ellington never referred to himself as a rhetorician or an intellectual leader, but considering his plethora of interviews and statements to the press, it is clear that he saw his music as a contribution to public discourse. In fact, Ellington saw his music as a way to respond directly to work of writers such as Hughes and Richard Wright. Hughes and Ellington worked closely together on *Jump for Joy* and, as mentioned earlier, Ellington was prone to bragging about his consumption of African American literature and history. However, if there is any doubt about how seriously Ellington took engaging other Black, public intellectuals with his music, one should consider that a year before his performance of *Black, Brown and Beige* he wrote to Wright to inquire about collaborating on a project. Ellington stated that he was "an ardent admirer" and that he wanted to meet in order to express his appreciation of Wright and "offer something that would fit with [Wright's] work."[107] Wright's groundbreaking novel *Native Son* had been published only two years prior, in 1940, and he was becoming a leading intellectual in the Black community.

Although this letter marks the only correspondence received from Ellington in Wright's archived papers, it portrays a composer in dialogue with his artistic and intellectual peers.

The social and political context of Ellington's music reflects the cultural changes occurring from the influx of African American migrants to urban centers. Increased social freedom and improved economic status created the opportunity for rhetorical invention with new mediums, such as jazz, to formulate a basis of solidarity and emotional bonds in new conceptions of Black identity. Ellington's articulation of these new identities and histories would encourage the next generation of jazz musicians to explore, with greater depth, the themes of Africa, identity, and history. Exactly twenty years after Ellington's "Black and Tan Fantasy," Dizzy Gillespie and George Russell's *Afro-Cuban Drum Suite* (1947), otherwise known as "Cubano Be" and "Cubano Bop," would launch a new paradigm in jazz featuring authentic Afro-Cuban and African music. Gillespie would later premier this work alongside Cuban composer and percussionist Chano Pozo. Just as Ellington sought to engage the discourses of his community, Gillespie was influenced by Kingsley O. Mbadiwe, founder of the African Academy of Arts and Research, as well as the writings of Melville J. Herskovits and Rudi Blesh. Following Ellington's innovations in rhythm and dissonance, the first movement of "Cubano Be" begins with a rhythm played on the conga that sets the stage for Russell's "Lydian Chromatic Concept," which builds in intensity and dissonance through the use of the B-flat auxiliary diminished scale and accented off-beats.[108] To add to the rhetorical dynamics of the performance, Chano Pozo performed in traditional African garb, displaying his background as a member of the Abakuá, a male secret society in Cuba that upheld African traditions. Ellington's music contributed to the increase in racial pride during the 1930s and 1940s while providing a rhetorical framework for artists, such as Gillespie—and later John Coltrane—who could begin a new chapter of exploration involving Afrocentrism and Black Nationalism.

3
The Rhetoric of Mary Lou Williams

On February 28, 1978, Mary Lou Williams, pianist extraordinaire, walked onto the small stage of Les Mouches, a cabaret and restaurant in New York. As the crowd cheered her entrance, she appeared calm and regal while she took her place at the piano. Before she began her performance, she grabbed a nearby microphone and told the crowd, "What I would like to do for you tonight is the origin of jazz. Often *I'm* [emphasis mine] called the history of jazz because I played through all the histories." Williams then acknowledged the contentions around the use of the word jazz by some musicians, but then countered by emphasizing that what was important was that it was a label for art, in fact, the only "true" art in the world because it "came out of the suffering of the early black slaves." And with that, she returned to the piano and began methodically supporting this thesis by working through each era of jazz. She began with "Old Time Spiritual" (from *Mary Lou's Mass*, 1975) and then flowed, seemingly effortlessly, through ragtime, the blues, boogie-woogie, and then on to a variety of canonical jazz tunes such as "On Green Dolphin Street," "I Can't Get Started," "My Blue Heaven," "Medi II," "Over the Rainbow," "St. Louis Blues," and "Surrey with the Fringe on Top."

Williams's concert that evening was a masterclass of jazz style and technique, the culmination of decades of performances. Although the audience was thoroughly entertained, this was more than just a routine performance for Williams, and her opening speech was more than traditional introductory greetings. This concert was part of a larger call to action, an attempt to raise awareness about Black history, and an important component of an evolving rhetorical project. This chapter examines the contours of Williams's artistry as part of a larger tradition of Black women's rhetorical practices. Williams's legacy of composition, experimentalism, spiritual exploration, and subversion of limiting gender constructs echoes throughout the careers of Black women artists of the twenty-first century.

Williams's influence is an understated force in the development of modern jazz. Her daring and inventive approach to composition—combined with her mentorship of, and collaboration with, younger, influential musicians (e.g., Thelonious Monk, Miles Davis, Bud Powell, and Charlie Parker)—places her technically at the center of the evolution of jazz, though her influence has been underplayed by critics and scholars relative to the attention devoted to her male counterparts. Williams defied the status quo and disrupted simplistic narratives surrounding the role of women in a racially demarcated and male-gendered jazz industry.[1] Though Williams's peers, such as Duke Ellington and Count Basie, were able to solidify their places as masters of a particular style of jazz, Williams was never elevated to such a pedestal.[2] Further, in each stylistic period of jazz, such as swing or bebop, the music accompanied a particular style of Black masculinity that held great appeal for both Black and white audiences. While masculine tropes such as "cool cat" dominated jazz discourses, there were parallel tropes created for women, which included "hip chicks" and "kittens on the keys." These designations only reinforced gender stereotypes, further complicating the marginalized space in which women in jazz already found themselves.[3]

In this chapter, I explore Williams's life and music with an ear toward the rhetorical dimensions of her spirituality, her efforts to care for others, and her desire to spread the knowledge of jazz history to America's youth. She saw Black music, particularly jazz, as an articulation of the deep sense of love and piety that is central to the Black prophetic tradition, a tradition African American religion scholars have contextualized as the struggle against spiritual, physical, and social oppression combined with an unyielding faith in humanity's potential grasp of social freedom.[4] Thus far I have discussed music as a critical part of the public sphere, where musicians and composers actively participate in important issues and debates. However, the sociopolitical barriers that have historically impeded the participation of women in the public sphere (disparate domestic responsibilities, unequal compensation, hostile work environments, and so on) have also circumscribed the activity of women composers and musicians.

This chapter is divided into two parts. First, I take a broad view of Williams's life and music, viewing her work as exemplary of the dynamic and creative contributions of Black women to the public sphere through music. My specific aim is to construct a narrative about Williams that includes important biographical details while emphasizing the rhetorical value of her contributions. Further, her personal experiences, such as her religious conversion and her status as a woman in a male-dominated field, resonate deeply with her audiences and weigh heavily in the overall reception of her music.

In the second portion of this chapter, I examine how Williams, through a lifetime of performing and teaching Black musical traditions, composed a rhetorical project that mirrors both the tenants of Black pragmatism and what David Howard-Pitney has called the "African-American jeremiad." Black pragmatism, a form of pragmatism that incorporates the Black experience in America, helps contextualize facets of Williams's life while illuminating her agency and acts of resistance to a gendered status quo. The African American jeremiad is a rhetorical and literary mode of social critique based on the biblical prophet Jeremiah's warnings to the Hebrew people about the necessity of repentance to avoid God's judgment. As an offshoot from the American, Puritan tradition, Black America adopted this rhetorical form for the purposes of protest beginning with early abolitionist critiques of white America for the "sin of slavery." Like the celebrated icons included in Howard-Pitney's analysis (Frederick Douglas, Booker T. Washington, Ida B. Wells, W. E. B. Du Bois, Mary McLeod Bethune, Martin Luther King Jr., and Malcolm X), Williams expressed an enthusiastic commitment to liberation as well as a strong conviction about the potential perils that could await Black communities if they strayed too far from the "right" path. The recognition of a jeremiadic structure in Williams's rhetoric helps to explain its dominant themes surrounding the protection of jazz for future generations and her admonitory approach to other emerging genres of Black music.

The Evolution of Mary Lou Williams

The early life of Mary Lou Williams (born Mary Elfrieda Scruggs in 1910) took place in Pittsburgh, Pennsylvania, and was immersed in strong ties to family and community. Her mother, Virginia Riser, was a church pianist and organist. Williams's autobiographical accounts state that as a toddler she often sat beside her mother as she played. One day, Williams played a song note for note to the astonishment of her mother, who subsequently prevented her daughter from receiving any formal training in order to preserve her innate musical knowledge and acute ear.[5] Williams began her music career as a child with her stepfather, Fletcher Burley, who took her to parties and clubs to perform for tips. Later she began accepting invitations to play with established big bands and other professional groups. Her family was always supportive of her musical development, often allowing her to travel outside of town with local bands. Such support challenged the common opinion that the involvement of women in public entertainment should be discouraged.[6]

Williams made her first entrance onto the national stage with her admission into Andy Kirk's Twelve Clouds of Joy, a territory band located in Oklahoma that played high society dance halls across the nation. It was in this band that Williams became a nationally recognized composer and arranger. Before Williams was formally allowed into the group, she was only permitted to perform as a substitute pianist and drive the bus used to haul instruments to various performances. According to Williams, her former husband, John Williams, had to engage in "shrewd" tactics to expose others to her talent, such as finding creative ways to get her on stage with the band. Williams was only allowed to perform when audiences grew impatient with the ensemble's prior pianist—essentially rescuing the band from poor performances.[7] However, her talents became undeniable as her visibility with the band increased. Williams pointed to gendered double standards as the explanation for the continued resistance to her acceptance into the band and stated that, during that era, women vocalists were acceptable but most men did not want women to participate as instrumentalists. However, it was the rare presence of a woman who could "play so heavy like a man" that increased the band's notoriety.[8]

As the band's popularity grew, so did curiosity about Williams and her role in the band. Although Kirk once denied Williams full membership, he served as an early musical mentor, providing Williams with assistance in arranging music for the group. However, Williams's skill and experimentation would eventually become the defining essence of the band's sound, much to the chagrin of members who disapproved of the presence of a woman in the band.[9] Although Williams received encouragement from some men in the world of jazz, her reception in the music industry overall was not always welcoming. Williams once described her appearance in a music rehearsal hall as completely unsettling for the bandleaders:

> He said, "What's that girl doing, sitting at the piano?" Nobody would say anything. He said, "Well, get her off the stage so we can play." Nobody would say anything. So I didn't move so he said, "Let's start the rehearsal." So I started playing and both of them had a fit. They didn't know that John [Williams] had a woman with them. . . . So he said, "We can't take her. We can't let the manager see her because she's a Black woman and we've got to put pants on her."[10]

Williams's appearance always had to be negotiated. While it was customary for women to dress as men in some bands, she was often encouraged to dress "as a woman" or to perform gender in particular ways for greater visual appeal. Despite constant comparisons between her and other women musicians considered more feminine, Williams openly embraced the "playing like a man" label.[11]

In 1929 the band received a request to record a few songs in Chicago, and the group decided to leave without Williams, an egregious professional snub. However, the organizer of the recording session, Jack Kapp (later founder of Decca Records) refused to record anything without her, reasoning that the band did not sound the same. Once she arrived in Chicago, Kapp recorded her without her consent or the existence of a recording contract through a deceptive request to hear her "audition." This exploitative recording session produced two songs titled "Night Life" and "Drag 'Em," which became Williams's first recordings.

A remarkably modern jazz composition for its time, "Night Life" (see figure 8) is an impressive display of Williams's dexterity and creativity as a composer and improviser. The song begins with an elaborate four-bar introduction before launching into a thirty-two-bar AABA form that features a complex mixture of ragtime-style walking bass lines, stride piano rhythms, and various pauses and tremolos that create a striking lucidity with rhythm.[12]

74 Chapter 3

Figure 8. Excerpt from "Night Life," by Mary Lou Williams. As played by Mary Lou Williams on April 24, 1930.

Combined with flashes of uncommon chords and thematic development with the melodic lines, the piece is shockingly original for its time. "Drag 'Em" is a medium-tempo blues by which Williams shows off the capabilities of her right hand through a series of smooth, soulful melodic lines that are supported by the strong rhythmic prowess for which she became known. In both tunes, one finds clear evidence of Williams's immersion in ragtime and stride piano traditions practiced by Earl Hines, Jelly Roll Morton, Art Tatum, Fats Waller, and Eubie Blake, as well as women pianists Lovie Austin and Lil Hardin Armstrong. Moreover, Williams's musical ideas were a forerunner to the harmonic experimentation that was later popularized by Thelonious Monk, a musician she mentored.[13]

Unfortunately, Williams did not receive proper compensation for her work, and the larger context of the Chicago recording session was mired in tragedy. According to biographer Linda Dahl, Williams experienced two rapes just prior to the recording session. The first assault occurred at a party in Kansas City the evening before she received the telegram requesting her presence in Chicago. The second assault was made during her train ride to Chicago by one of the train's porters. The attacks left Williams in so much pain that she had trouble sitting, and she would later discover that her uterus was permanently damaged.[14] Despite being in immense pain, Williams disembarked from the train and went straight to the recording studio. She had paid, and continued to pay, an enormous price to establish a stronger national profile. Her compositions were no less than acts of survival. Williams refused to have her (musical) voice silenced by her fellow band members or the attacks. In the documentary *Mary Lou Williams: The Lady Who Swings the Band* (2015), critic Farah Jasmine Griffin suggests that Williams saw her creative practice with music to be more than a translation or transcription of the traumas she experienced. It was also a triumph over them.[15] The jubilance of "Night Life" certainly provides credence to Griffin's assertion. Williams's efforts to be heard correlate with Deborah Atwater's summation of the prevailing theme of African American women's rhetoric as a "driving need to establish personhood, dignity, and respect . . . in a society that was often hostile and degrading."[16] Atwater locates ethos as the central rhetorical obstacle for African American women, except her conception of its application both includes and goes beyond the term's common use to refer to a person's perceived character or morals. Instead, Atwater is concerned with a definition of ethos that includes the way discourse can transform space and time into dwelling places where "people can deliberate about and 'know together' (con-scientia) some matter of interest."[17] Therefore, to grapple with the specific rhetorical challenges of Williams, as well as other Black women in jazz, means viewing their enormous efforts to be heard as more than attempts to elevate their personal careers, but as, instead, efforts to transform the spaces and places of jazz into spaces of freedom, dignity, and personhood.

Williams traveled with the band for several years before growing weary of the bleak financial situations and the hectic (and often dangerous) traveling conditions for Black professional musicians during the 1930s and '40s.[18] After Williams's departure from the Twelve Clouds of Joy orchestra, she relocated to New York and became a popular writer and arranger for other artists such as Duke Ellington and Benny Goodman. One of the most explicitly political phases of Williams's career occurred during her time in the 1940s performing at the Café Society (both uptown and downtown venues) in New York, a local hub for progressive causes. Unlike the Cotton Club in Harlem, which featured segregated seating for audiences, the Café Society catered to integrated audiences. Williams performed for benefits and rallies for a range of politicians, including President Franklin Delano Roosevelt and African American Communist Benjamin Davis's successful run for the city council in 1943.[19] Although Williams was never a formal member of any political organization, she remained preoccupied with the material conditions of the African American community. Moreover, this period of her life represented the beginning of her community activism and spiritual devotion that led to later musical statements.[20] This period also represented a new level of exposure and prestige for Williams. No longer attached to Andy Kirk and the Twelve Clouds of Joy orchestra, Williams would be featured as the main act, performing three shows per night for thousands of New York's most influential politicians, artists, and other professionals. However, despite breaking barriers within the world of jazz, Williams continued to encounter unscrupulous business partners and aspersions cast on her character in the press. For example, notices were often accompanied by veiled (and occasionally explicit) critiques of her performance of gender:

> Mary Lou Williams, the temperamental pianist whose genius is forever going un-recognized because of her personality, has a trio now and is headed for a date at The Composer. A former Andy Kirk keyboard girl, Mary Lou is one of the few really real artists with records to prove it. If her smiles were but sincere, or better still, if she would only give out a whole smile instead of a smirk, she'd win over her audiences so much faster.[21]

Similar accounts in the press presented Williams as contrary to other women who were seen as more commercially viable novelties. Such critiques attempted to stigmatize women who, from the critics' viewpoint, were not conforming to gender expectations.[22] Further, Williams was often compared to her friend Hazel Scott, a pianist who was viewed as more feminine than Williams, through implicit references, in a manner similar to a *Time* magazine article that combined a recognition of Williams's undeniable talent with backhanded commentary about her appearance:

> If you shut your eyes you would bet she was a man. But last week's audiences at Manhattan's Downtown Café Society had their eyes open. They heard a sinewy young Negro woman play the solid, unpretentious, flesh-&-bone kind of jazz piano that is expected from such vigorous Negro masters as James P. Johnson. Serene, reticent, doe-eyed Mary Lou Williams was not selling a pretty face,

or a low décolletage, or tricky swinging of Bach or Chopin. She was playing blues, stomps, and boogie-woogie in the native Afro-American way—an art in which, at 33, she is already a veteran.[23]

Following critic Susan McClary's assertion that music functions as a public forum for the negotiation and contestation of various models of gender organization, Williams's music and its attendant discourses point to the sexual politics of jazz and its structural organization around the male gaze.[24] Indeed, claims that Williams played "like a man" reflect the assignment of gender to invisible sonic material socially constructed around essentialist notions of femininity and masculinity. Black women musicians and composers like Williams were challenged by a hostility that was pervasive in many areas of the world of jazz, as evidenced by the discussion of women in a 1938 issue of *DownBeat* magazine, the genre's foremost publication, in which an anonymous critic wrote, "Outside of a few sepia females, the woman musician never was born capable of sending anyone further than the nearest exit. As a whole [women are] emotionally unstable [and] could never be consistent performers on musical instruments."[25]

Such casual cruelty and misogyny were also, at times, directly leveled at Williams and could escalate to physical assaults. Williams once recalled being "slapped off the piano stool"[26] and described violence, or the threat of violence, as part of the culture of jazz at the height of its popularity in Kansas City. Once, while describing the nature of her early musical training in Kansas City bands, she remarked, "You come out with a black eye if you didn't do it right. Shake you up in a minute. There was a band leader in Kansas City, he'd go to rehearsal with a paper, a big thick paper, and a gun under the paper. The first one that missed a note, he'd shoot at them. That was real tough."[27] Perhaps even more scarring was the barrage of verbal micro-aggressions. For example, Andy Kirk, one of the earliest supporters of her arrangements and compositions, went so far as to admit in an interview to referring to Williams as "the Pest":

> Andy smilingly looks back on those days. He used to call Mary Lou "Pest," but that was before he learned that she really could bang along on the ivories with the best of them. On one 1933 day, the Clouds of Joy had an important record date. The regular man

pianist tottered into the studio, stewed to the gills. Kirk turned to sax man and husband, Johnny Williams. "Quick, man," he snapped, "call up the 'Pest' and have her sit in for this date!" The Pest was called up and in and proved to be such a sensation that she's been in ever since."[28]

Despite being a child prodigy, Williams was constantly asked to prove herself and was often only accepted when her male colleagues considered her performances masculine enough. Although Williams often embraced the label of "playing like a man," it reflected an atmosphere that denied that womanhood, intellect, talent, and emotional stability could coincide. Even favorable or celebratory coverage of her work could not avoid commenting on her gender, often framing her as an exception. For example, a review of big band music written by John Hammond in *DownBeat* magazine stated, "Mary Lou Williams, in Andy Kirk's band, is not only the swingingest female alive, but can outplay all but three or four males in the business."[29] Similarly, more than a decade later, Barry Ulanov offered a glowing review of her work aside from its gendered connotations: "Mary has made it, made it three times or four or a dozen, made it for the twenties, made it for swing and made it for bop. So fully has she made it, that one can almost measure the success or failure of the music of her time by her music. So fully has she made it, that in discussing her work one almost forgets that she is a woman. Ah, but that's another story."[30] On the other hand, Williams's embrace of this label could be seen as an act of subversive signifying. Her mastery of music that was gendered "male" meant that there was nothing naturally male about it.[31] Such irony was not lost on many of her fans and fellow colleagues: "The past month's Deccas are shaded by a piano solo called 'Overhand', by Mary Lou Williams. She is none other than the colored pianist, mentioned last month, who holds down Andy Kirk's fourteen-piece band from Kansas City. Taking a bit of the best from Pine Top Smith, Meade Lux Lewis, and Earl Hines, she plays all the styles and the results are sensational. It sort of knocks the props out from under those who say a woman can't swing."[32]

Although such discourses continued to characterize Williams's performances, they did not detract from her musical aspirations to be taken as a serious artist, composer, and arranger. Despite suggestions from the owner of Café Society, Barney Josephson, that she should perform like Hazel Scott, he held a consistent interest in helping Williams expand her profile in New York. Josephson, in fact, helped Williams make the transition to radio personality by helping to launch *The Mary Lou Williams Piano Workshop* in 1943, which was broadcast weekly on WNEW. The show provided Williams with the opportunity to reach a wider category of jazz listeners, especially those without the opportunity to hear her perform in person, while providing a space to experiment with new sounds and ideas. One of those ideas became the *Zodiac Suite* (1943), which was inspired by Duke Ellington's *Black, Brown and Beige* (1943). Williams underwent an extensive phase of preparation for the composition process, which included the close study of composers in the classical tradition, such as Igor Stravinsky and Paul Hindemith. Williams also used her performances at Café Society to work out pieces of the larger work. That year, Williams had read a book about astrology and found some connections to her own spirituality, which was then closer to a budding, organic mysticism than the more polished structures of Catholicism she adopted later in her life.[33] Each movement of the suite was dedicated to a particular sign and musician that she believed embodied the sign's characteristics.

Williams penned a lengthy explanation of her rhetorical motives behind the suite for the reissue of the work in 1975. Williams suggested that she always thought that studying the stars helped one understand some of the influences on people's destinies.[34] Therefore, the *Zodiac Suite* represented a way of pointing her listeners toward a truer path. The work is an impressive display of Williams's modern jazz sensibilities and a forerunner to the sounds that would be explored by the following generation of musicians. More important, it suggested that Black women were also working within the vanguard of Black music cultures, placing the imprint of their genius on American culture. In addition to its production on radio, *The Zodiac Suite* was performed by an orchestra on December 31, 1945, and on June 6, 1946. Three movements of the piece were also performed at Carnegie Hall by the Carnegie Pops Orchestra, solidifying its status as the work of a prodigiously talented composer.[35] This performance was warmly received by music critics, with Barry Ulanov writing that Williams's unique fusion of classical and jazz was "the way music must go from here on" and that "classical music will stop short unless it is infused with the warmth and spontaneity of jazz."[36]

Despite the success Williams achieved during her time in New York, she found it difficult to secure long-term stability without reliable partners with whom to perform. Her ability to land lucrative contracts was challenged by shifting currents within the world of jazz that favored younger, male musicians. Biographer Tammy Kernodle aptly described Williams's career challenges as the result of being excluded from a "male jazz fraternity," that her talent and "honorary membership" could never fully pierce.[37] Such challenges were part of her decision to agree to a string of performances in Europe. However, her time there was fraught with unfair wage compensation and mental and emotional exhaustion from years of rigorous touring schedules and fractured personal relationships. After the death of one of Williams's close friends, pianist Garland Wilson, Williams eventually reached her breaking point in 1954 and decided to request release from her performing contract at Le Boeuf sur le Toit in Paris. Her desire to return to the United States accompanied an extended hiatus from jazz where Williams turned to prayer and spiritual devotion. It was during this time that Williams purportedly had a vision of Charlie Parker's death and returned to New York with a great deal of internal struggle about her future with jazz.

Although Williams had a complicated relationship with religious institutions, her spirituality became an important part of her identity as a response to the emotional turmoil she was experiencing. After her return to New York, Williams began attending various churches in pursuit of an institution that met her needs, eventually becoming a member of Adam Clayton Powell's Abyssinian Baptist Church in Harlem. However, she found intrachurch politics off-putting and tangential to her spiritual quest. Then, in perhaps her most explicit use of her music for evangelical purposes, Williams left Powell's church to work with tap dancer Baby Laurence and perform on street corners in Harlem. She played a spinet piano while Laurence danced, and they both preached the gospel while using music to connect with lost souls.[38]

Eventually, Williams began attending Our Lady of Lourdes, a Catholic church in New York, and she devoted herself to the mission of rescuing musicians suffering from substance abuse. Charlie Parker's death in 1955 was traumatizing for Williams, and she saw his death as emblematic of larger problems with the world of jazz. Largely neglecting her own physical welfare, she sold many of her possessions to turn her small apartment in Harlem into her own personal drug rehabilitation clinic.[39] She then opened a thrift store with the goal of financially supporting her endeavors. Williams employed what she termed "methods of my own" to care for the musicians, which included prayer, music performance, and composition.

Williams's focus on her spiritual journey received mixed reactions within the world of jazz. Altevia "Buttercup" Edwards, who was in a common law marriage to one of Williams's friends, pianist Bud Powell, described both the unique ways Williams navigated her role as an elder within the world of jazz as well as some of the impact of Williams's religious devotion on her circle of friends and supporters:

> And how many musicians learned on that little spinet [piano] she had in her apartment? Ate out of [her] pots? . . . And Bud would say profanity is unbecoming of a lady, and I would get so mad, so uptight, because I use to fathom myself being like Mary Lou. She always had command of the situation no matter how it got hot and heavy. I mean sometimes cats would get outside themselves, but she always used a soft tone of voice. She'd get them straight, and everybody would always listen to her. And I mean some rough characters baby. . . . There's all kinds of people in the musical world and she knew how to handle them all and still maintain her ladyship. You ask Lorraine [Gillespie], you ask anybody that knew Mary Lou and they will tell you the same thing. At one time we did. . . . some of us used to shy away from her because we thought she was becoming a religious fanatic, and we were afraid of what she was getting into. We didn't understand it ourselves. But she was searching for her own identity. She found it. Thank God she found it.[40]

In interviews recorded by Father O'Brien, the priest admits that Williams was so committed to the Catholic faith that she seriously considered becoming a nun on more than one occasion. She was so serious, in fact, that he had to convince her otherwise, each time, by reminding her that there was just as much drama within the church as there was without.

However, Father O'Brien's comments support viewing Williams as a sister or nun in all but name. Although Williams never sought nor was granted any official designation or recognition, details of Williams's life during this period indicate that she fully embraced the vows of poverty, chastity, and obedience. This includes the fact that upon her return to New York from Europe she was living on $300 quarterly royalty checks, which she used to care for a range of community and family members she housed in her small apartment. She sold everything in her wardrobe except one dress and one pair of shoes, using much of the proceeds for charity work. Williams also fasted constantly (for both spiritual reasons and from financial difficulties), consuming only water and apples for periods that could last up to nine days at a time.[41]

Beyond Williams's embodiment of the vows and her personal journey of faith, her religious devotion was also a response to the urgent needs of her community, a response that echoes within the rich tradition of Black activist nuns and sisters who understood their roles as concomitant with service to Black communities. Sisters such as Sister Mary Antona Ebo, the sole Black member of the inaugural delegation of Catholic sisters to join Black voting rights marches in Selma, Alabama, in 1965, and groups such as the National Black Sisters' Conference, a Black power federation of Catholic nuns formed in 1968, understood how their social service ministries challenged a host of racist stereotypes as living testaments to the virtue and moral authority of Black women.[42]

But before Black sisters began protesting for racial justice and equity in the 1960s, they were pioneering teachers of Black history who produced some of the nation's first Black leaders.[43] Williams, too, would go on to become deeply concerned about the education of America's youth, particularly around matters related to Black history and music.

Sacred Jazz

Over time, Williams's intense devotion to the goal of direct drug rehabilitation calmed, and she became open to the pleas of her spiritual advisers in the Catholic community to return to performing music professionally. She agreed on the condition that her music be spiritually motivated. Brother Mario Hancock, a Black friar in the Catholic church and a close friend to Williams, encouraged her to write a composition dedicated to St. Martin de Porres, an Afro-Peruvian of the seventeenth century elevated to sainthood in 1962. Although Williams had produced other works that alluded to religion, this piece stands as her first religious jazz composition. As a choir arrangement, "St. Martin de Porres" features complex harmonies and antiphonal sequences that stylistically pushed the boundaries of liturgical music. The piece was written with the intent of being performed in an actual Catholic mass and was first played in public on November 3, 1963, the anniversary of the saint's death and his feast day. Williams's arrangement of "St. Martin de Porres" for big band included dancers, soloists, and the full gamut of jazz styles that she mastered during her career. It was one of the first works of jazz to be written specifically for religious purposes; nevertheless it did not receive the critical attention of similar projects from artists such as Duke Ellington and John Coltrane. "St. Martin de Porres" was one of the first translations of the Negro spiritual to the context of the Catholic church, and it became the centerpiece of the album *Mary Lou Williams Presents Black Christ of the Andes* (1964), which signaled Williams's return to recording music. She saw "St. Martin de Porres" as an exemplary model of Christian devotion, humility, and conviction and regarded her piece as an effort to "heal troubled souls, especially those of African Americans."[44]

Along with the release of her music, Williams undertook an intense campaign to integrate jazz into the Catholic community and expand jazz education to youth, going so far as to have a pamphlet distributed at her performances that stated her specific beliefs about the characteristics of jazz and her creative process.[45] The pamphlet stated:

Origin
From suffering came the Negro spirituals, songs of joy, and songs of sorrow. The main origin of American jazz is the spiritual. Because of the deeply religious background of the American Negro, he was able to mix this strong influence with rhythms that reached deep enough into the inner self to give expression to outcries of sincere joy, which became known as jazz.

Creative Process of Improvisation
The creative process of improvisation cannot be easily explained. The moment a soloist's hands touch the instrument, ideas start to flow

from the mind, through the heart, and out the fingertips. Or, at least that is the way it should be. Therefore, if the mind stops, there are no ideas, just mechanical patterns. If the heart doesn't fulfill its role, there will be very little feeling, or none . . . at all.

The Spiritual Feeling: The Characteristic of Good Jazz
The spiritual feeling, the deep conversation, and the mental telepathy going on between bass, drums, and a number of soloists, are the permanent characteristics of good jazz. The conversation can be of any type, exciting, soulful, or even humorous debating.

YOUR ATTENTIVE PARTICIPATION, THROUGH LISTENING WITH YOUR EARS AND YOUR HEART, WILL ALLOW YOU TO ENJOY FULLY THIS EXCHANGE OF IDEAS TO SENSE THESE VARIOUS MOODS AND TO REAP THE FULL THERAPEUTIC REWARDS THAT GOOD MUSIC ALWAYS BRINGS TO A TIRED, DISTURBED SOUL AND ALL "WHO DIG THE SOUNDS."[46]

This pamphlet highlights three important components to Williams's theory of Black music. First, her emphasis on the "spiritual feeling of jazz" undoes the sacred/secular binary. In a later interview of Williams during her years spent teaching jazz at Duke University, she emphasized that "jazz is spiritual music. Nobody's going to believe it except for those who really know . . . feel it. It should be played everywhere because it has that terrific spiritual feeling. All of it is spiritual music."[47] This assertion adds context to Williams's rhetorical strategy: she viewed her music as performing a particular kind of spiritual work, a ministry, produced from the liberatory and restorative continuum of the Black sonic lexicon. Second, for Williams, jazz does not simply *symbolize* conversation or represent communication abstractly. Instead, jazz was quite literally a form of conversation for musicians and audiences properly oriented to its means of expression.[48] Finally, her mention of mental telepathy not only indicates her belief in the supernatural underneath the intense and intimate forms of communication between performers but also galvanizes the Black sonic lexicon as a durable communicative fabric.

Williams then went on to write her first full, jazz-influenced Catholic mass. The multimovement work, titled *Pittsburgh Mass* (1967), utilized blues and jazz styles for the Kyrie, Gloria, and Credo that featured lyrical content consisting of a mixture of biblical references and traditional prayers.[49] In addition to a writing a second mass in 1968 entitled *Mass for Lenten Season*, Williams worked fervently to have her music performed in the Vatican but was met with stiff resistance. In 1975, Williams produced her third mass, *Mary Lou's Mass*. This mass contained components of her earlier work and stands as Williams's most complete mass. The album begins with an entrance hymn for the congregation ("The Lord Says") and proceeds to the penitential rite ("Act of Contrition" and "Lord Have Mercy"). "Glory to God" signals the congregation's acceptance of pardon. The congregation is then led to pray and meditate on the proclamation of scriptural passages ("Medi," for meditation). The congregation next rises for the proclamation of the gospel ("In His Day" and "Lazarus"), expresses its belief ("Credo"), prepares for the Communion ("Our Father"), and sings a hymn accompanying the rite ("It Is Always Spring"). After a period of prayer, the postcommunion hymn is sung ("People in Trouble"), and the mass concludes with a final prayer and hymn ("One" and "Praise the Lord").[50] Although Williams was one of the first jazz musicians to compose works that fused jazz and sacred music of such length, most of the credit for this innovation would go to Duke Ellington, who, after declining to play Williams's work, saw much success with his own *Sacred Concerts*.[51]

Williams's compositions and performances should be understood, in part, as a product of her lifelong experiences with spirituality and the paranormal. Her numerous experiences of spiritual or paranormal events were guided by what would commonly be referred to as "an anointing" in the Black church tradition.[52] Her autobiographical accounts state that she was "born with a veil"[53] (or caul) and was privy to powerful spiritual experiences, such as seeing or hearing spirits, at a very young age. Williams would experience episodes so intense that those around her would be forced to tie her down for her own safety.[54] She stated that her family, particularly her mother, began to avoid taking her places as a child because her visions would frighten them: "One day we were walking in the field, and I saw a little white dog and the white dog grew into a cow. I said, 'Come on down, Mother' but she ran and left me, but she came back. Everybody was afraid to be around me because I was seeing so many weird things."[55] This element of Williams's lived experience was also a critical part of her music, evidenced not only by her explicitly religious music but also in her way of being as a performer and collaborator. Williams once remarked, "I think when anybody has anything like that, ESP, if you're an artist it should be put into your music, because at one time I could hear a musician playing and could hear the note he was going to make next. It was just that fast. It was just like seeing spiritual or telling someone's fortune, I knew exactly what he was going to do."[56] From this perspective, Williams should be included in discussions of Black women's contributions to, or manifestations of, Afrofuturism as part of a broader African diasporic tradition that engages with otherness, separation, and escape.[57] The theoretical construct of Afrofuturism presents the fusion of Black history and themes with futurism, fantasy, and science fiction. Afrofuturism and its attendant discourses may inform critical methods of exploration while functioning as forms of hermeneutics, epistemology, ontology, or spiritualism. In this case, Williams's music was a critical method of exploration and communication firmly tethered to an African diasporic experience "rooted in the past but not weighed down by it, contiguous yet continually transformed."[58] This push and pull between the natural and spiritual world, between images of the future and past, are central to Afrofuturism's practice of imagining other worlds and using the past to reshape or reimagine the future.

Jazz Jeremiad

However, Afrofuturism does not fully capture the prophetic nature of Williams's music and public discourse. Instead, Williams's musical, spiritual, and social concerns began to merge into a broader rhetorical project that emphasized the constitutive relationship between the health and well-being of Black communities and their musical production. Williams's rhetorical project mirrors the structural components of an African American jeremiad. The Puritan variation of the jeremiad became central to America's development of a "civil religion" or fabric of rituals, myths, and symbols that lies at the intersections of American society and its view of itself as a chosen people. The African American jeremiad embraces the survival of Black communities and, with missionary zeal, their eventual triumph over all obstacles and oppression. As a chosen people among a chosen people, Black America shares qualities with the children of Israel and their plight under Egyptian captivity; both groups are chosen by God to experience extreme hardships, and both groups were held in bondage and eventually freed as a testament to God's promise of provision.

The jeremiad contains three necessary components. First, there is the promise, which relies on the belief that the target audience is a chosen people with an important destiny that will later manifest itself. Second is the critique of current declension, or failure to remain steadfast on the right path. Finally, there is a "resolving prophecy" that if the audience will find the right path and turn from their wicked ways, they may reclaim the promise of salvation.[59]

While the extent to which Williams was conscious of the African American jeremiad and its history as such is unclear, Williams's proximity to Black church communities would have provided her with the requisite exposure. However, whether Williams's use of the jeremiadic form was intentional or not, its application to her rhetorical project is one way of identifying coherent narrative threads across her project's evolution. During the 1950s, Williams had a vision that "a strange foreign sound would enter into . . . jazz and would destroy the heritage, would destroy jazz completely."[60] Williams may have interpreted the evolution of Black music more than a decade later as a fulfillment of that prophecy. In either case, when Williams began to speak of jazz in a sermonic register, the components of the African American jeremiad became more pronounced. For example, in the early 1970s, Williams began distributing handbills throughout Harlem that exclaimed: "JAZZ is your heritage—born of the suffering of the early American Black people—the only true American art form—it is spiritual and healing to the Soul.—Listen with the ears of your heart and go home healed—keep jazz alive call your favorite TV-radio stations and record stores NOW."[61] Williams viewed Black music as a gift from God to a chosen people, a product of suffering with divine origins. This gift was quite literally world changing, spiritually powerful, and worthy of protection. Further, Williams's forceful critique of what she considered Black, communal declension in the form of backward musical developments was paired with her pleas to "keep jazz alive" and reconnect to a rich Black musical tradition. Williams was alarmed by the prospect that younger generations were not receiving jazz education and more so by the lack of education about Black history. She later clarified, "I had those handbills printed up because I want Black people to realize their own importance. American Blacks are the most inventive, creative, and original people in the world. But most of us don't fully realize that when God gave us jazz, he gave the greatest art in the world."[62]

In 1977, Williams had artist David Stone Martin illustrate some of her additional rhetorical aims regarding jazz (see figure 9). The drawing captures the essence of Williams's beliefs about the centrality of Black music to Black life. It also portrays three of Williams's main critiques of jazz and the general state of Black music during the 1970s. On the left side of the tree are three branches that lack leaves and are cut off, signifying musical dead ends. The first branch at the top is labeled "Commercial Rock." Williams saw much of the new wave of crossover experiments into R&B by jazz artists such as Herbie Hancock and Grover Washington as variations of commercial rock music, a decidedly different genre than the jazz she performed throughout her life. The middle branch is tagged "Black Magic," "Cults," and "Avant Guard" [sic]. This expresses a conservatism that seems puzzling given Williams's long career of musical innovation. Williams was the penultimate Jeremiah of jazz discourse and pedagogy (I would call Wynton Marsalis her successor), fiercely chastising those she thought were straying from the authentic traditions of Black music. She believed that such waywardness risked a spiritual destruction that would eventually harm Black communities. While it may be easy to dismiss Williams's jeremiad as the normal generational reaction to new forms of music ("Back in my day . . ."), Williams was legitimately concerned about the state of Black America and—given her grassroots efforts in drug rehabilitation—she was uniquely in tune with urban Black communities and an encroaching addiction epidemic and economic crisis. Moreover, Williams's rhetorical project sought to address what Cornel West would more than a decade later describe as the "nihilistic threat" to Black America, "not simply a matter of relative economic deprivation and political powerlessness" but involving "the profound sense of psychological depression, personal worthlessness, and social despair so widespread in Black America." West, in conjunction with a broad spectrum of Black literary authors and cultural critics, addressed the critical issues of "identity, meaning, and self-worth" as foundational to grappling with the Black experience in America.[63]

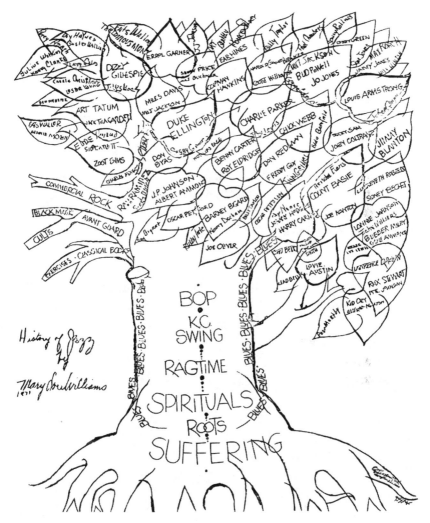

Figure 9. A drawing by Mary Lou Williams and David Stone Martin, 1977. This image was included with the liner notes of *Mary Lou Williams Presents Black Christ of the Andes*, Folkways, 1977.

Williams understood the state of Black musical production as a barometer of Black communal well-being and futurity, and her commitment to jazz education included orienting her students to a particular ontology of the Black experience where the learning, teaching, and performance of jazz was part of a larger praxis of Black expressive culture.

Williams took exception to the newer styles of jazz that she felt were performed without any connection to the traditions of Black music she held so dear. In light of that concern, toward the latter part of her career Williams came to see herself as a savior and protector of jazz for the next generation. On numerous occasions she explained that she played through all of the jazz eras, and that the blues feeling, since the spirituals, had always been a part of Black music. She announced, "What I'm trying to do is bring back good jazz to you with the healing in it and spiritual feeling."[64] Although Williams bristled at what became known as free jazz, a style dedicated to more harmonic and rhythmic experimentation than previous eras, she held the genre's central representatives, such as John Coltrane and Cecil Taylor, in high esteem and, in Taylor's case, performed with them. In 1978, Williams and Taylor, the pianist she celebrated with the title "My Giant of the Avant Garde," recorded a live concert that led to the album *Embraced*.[65] Taylor, known in the jazz community as one of the pioneers of free jazz, considered Williams one of his sources of inspiration. Therefore, the conclusion that Williams was against the genre of free jazz is contradicted by her own actions. Instead, Williams took issue with musicians using free jazz as a pretense to cover their lack of knowledge of jazz traditions, perhaps feigning artistic motivation to cover for what she considered subpar musical performances.

The third dead branch is labeled "Exercises" and "Classical Books." Williams always took pride in the fact that she was never formally trained.[66] Yet Taylor, whom Williams adored, was a classically trained product of the New England Conservatory of Music, and many of the musicians Williams collaborated with had some degree of formal musical training. Williams may have been reacting to the commodification of jazz pedagogy that occurred with its formal entrance into American collegiate music curriculums during the late 1960s and early 1970s. Williams may have perceived books and other materials that claimed to teach one how to perform jazz "like the experts" as cheap gimmicks that promised unrealistic, overnight success. Such material was completely incongruent with Williams's musical development, which included years of apprenticeship and applied learning through performance. D. Antoinette Handy asked Williams specifically about her warnings to students to avoid formal music education. The interview took place during Williams's tenure as a professor of jazz at Duke University in 1980. Noting the clear contradiction between her statements and her job, Williams clarified that she didn't mean *all* kinds of teaching. Handy asked, "I once heard you say to a group of students, 'Get away from some of the teaching'. You probably didn't mean it quite the way it sounded. I believe you meant 'Stay away from certain kinds of teaching'. Am I right?" Williams responded, "Yes, I think so."[67]

Additionally, Williams disagreed with displays of technique for technique's sake if there was no emotional sincerity in the music. This idea was a product of her internal struggle with the secular nature of jazz. By explicitly connecting jazz to the soul, it could not be the devil's music: it was a gift from God meant to heal the soul. In addition, Williams's perspective represented a way for her to continue to blend the secular and sacred in Black life generally and to reclaim the heritage of jazz as authentically Black. Her liner notes for *Embraced*, some of which took exception to the popular music of James Brown and Aretha Franklin, reiterated her rhetorical conceptualization of jazz as a healing force. She concluded: "Now I feel that one should play all forms of music—yet to inject another basic feeling into Jazz destroys the soulful feeling that is unique to Jazz. As I said, Coltrane never lost this feeling in his music. What is this great spiritual healing force in the music that is so important? Once again; The Blues. The Blues are actually the spiritual content and feeling in the music."[68] Williams, now immersed in the Catholic church, never gave up on the idea of integrating jazz into a musical world that was often portrayed as its antithesis. Williams was able to express her jeremiad not only through pamphlets but also through her artistry as a performer. Her performance lectures on the history of jazz, which reached their height during her time working with Father Peter O'Brien in the 1970s, animated her conviction and deep commitment to the soul-stirring power and promise of Black music.[69]

But Williams's jeremiadic phase should not be considered as separate from the early part of her career where she was breaking the glass ceiling in jazz. Her jeremiad was a culmination of a set of practices and beliefs that takes the form of a particular kind of pragmatism, Black pragmatism, which scholar Eddie Glaude described as "a longstanding tradition of African Americans explicitly taking up the philosophical tools of pragmatism to respond to African-American conditions of living."[70] As a form of pragmatism that "can sing the blues," it contains the traditional Deweyan construction of pragmatism—antifoundationalism, experimentalism, contextualism, and solidarity—while addressing the tradition's most egregious blind spot: racism and the lived experiences of Black life.

The four components of Black pragmatism figure strongly throughout Williams's life and performing career. For instance, antifoundationalism has to do with the rejection of sources of knowledge production considered beyond criticism. For Williams, this is most obviously evident in her many challenges to gender norms within the world of jazz. However, Williams's positions on the role of women in jazz were complex, shifting, and, at times, contradictory.[71] Although her work helped to transform assumptions about women jazz artists and, consequently, to increase the visibility of African American women in the public sphere, she never referred to herself as a feminist or characterized her creative practice along those lines.

Meritocracy can be inherently antifoundational, allowing individuals to disrupt social hierarchies based on race, class, and gender. Key to Williams's experience of the world of jazz was her advocacy for a meritocracy in Black music that reached its height during the jazz era where popularity and success was directly tied to one's musical abilities. For all the mistreatment and abuse that she endured throughout her career, Williams's undeniable talent opened doors normally closed to Black women, and she witnessed how jazz's embrace of democratic meritocracy led to many moments of both interracial and unisex musical success. For most of Williams's life, mastering an instrument ensured a modest, stable income, if not fame and fortune, for many artists, and this embrace of meritocracy aligned with projects of racial uplift that positioned Black excellence as a way to disprove or defeat notions of Black inferiority. This also may explain her distrust and rejection of more modern forms of Black music that deemphasized an artist's technical skill in favor of incorporating other dynamics of both American and Black popular culture (style, appearance, showmanship, and so on) as the gateway to commercial success and popularity.

The second element of pragmatism, experimentalism, is reflected most forcefully in Williams's dogged commitment, throughout her career, to musical experimentation, the defining quality that allowed her to thrive during multiple dramatic innovations in jazz music. This trait extends beyond her compositions and includes her personal life as well as her social and political commitments. Third, contextualism denotes an awareness of the historical conditions of beliefs, choices, and actions. Williams's insistence on teaching jazz as a matter of Black history was a critical pedagogical move during the rise of jazz in American academia, where it was often stripped of cultural context.[72] Moreover, Williams refused to bifurcate music and values, which fueled, for her personally, the necessity to reconcile the sacred and secular divide within her work. Composing her way out of this theological conflict was essential to enabling her to return to performing music following her period of retirement as an active musician and her conversion to Catholicism.

Finally, from her personal outreach to musicians battling drug addiction to her evangelism on the streets of Harlem, solidarity, the fourth characteristic of pragmatism, is a fitting description of her commitment to Black communities and the survival of its history, music, and people. Throughout the 1940s, Williams performed numerous times with all-women ensembles. Despite these instances of collaboration, Williams said she often found difficulty building relationships with other women. In some cases, this could be attributed to a dynamic in which the small minority of women were often pitted against each other, sometimes literally on stage, to compete for the title "the first lady of jazz," a title accorded to Williams for many years. She was uneasy competing against other women and stated that she would rather resign than to embarrass another woman in such a public spectacle.[73] Although Williams stated that she never had trouble being accepted as a musician by other women, her comments provide insight into the complicated landscape of her earlier years as a performer and her sense of fealty to other women. In any case, for Williams, being a jazz musician involved an ethics of care and a sense of duty to her community and future generations.

Williams's jeremiad is also a product of two motifs within the tradition of Black women's rhetorical practices: the ethos of religion and spirituality, and the "blues woman" aesthetic. Based on careful analysis of the rhetorical practices of African American women rhetoricians (among them Frances Ellen Watkins Harper, Maria W. Stewart, Sojourner Truth, and Anna Julia Cooper), scholar Shirley Wilson Logan describes a spiritual tradition steeped in histories of African priestesses, diviners, queens, and other prominent religious women in Africa and the African diaspora who used their status as spiritual women to cultivate ethos as a tool for social critique.[74] Williams's music contributes to this rhetorical tradition, especially *Mary Lou Williams Presents Black Christ of the Andes* (1964) and *Mary Lou's Mass* (1975). Her explicit mixture of jazz and sacred music is both a modern innovation and an emphasis on the music's older forms (spirituals).

Williams's compositions also reflect the motif of the "blues woman," which gestures toward the dynamic legacies of performers such as Gertrude "Ma" Rainey, Bessie Smith, and Billie Holiday. Blues women were often leaders and mentors in their communities who functioned as communal spokespersons capable of transcending social and religious differences through their exceptional literacy and authenticity in secular music. They were also agents of change regarding gender relations and sexual politics. Therefore, the rhetorical aspects of Williams's music belong to what Angela Davis posits as the "unacknowledged traditions of feminist consciousness in working-class Black communities."[75] Davis characterizes the blues as a unique space for feminism due to its ability to reconcile seemingly polar and at times antagonistic identities.[76] Blues women used musical performance to transform their artistry into self-reflective, poetic expressions.

For Williams, this tradition was evident in works such as "Roll 'Em" (1938), which she wrote for the Benny Goodman orchestra (see figure 10). It was a clear demonstration of her mastery of the blues idiom and an obvious product of the hard-swinging, riff-oriented styles that she mastered during her time in Kansas City. "Roll 'Em" became one of Goodman's biggest hits, and its popularity had much to do with Williams's ability to translate the boogie-woogie piano style to a large-scale jazz orchestra while maintaining intricate ensemble writing. The beginning of the piece features Williams's unique approach to call-and-response among musical lines which, though usually played by the rhythm section, she placed with the saxophones. The piece then opens up for Goodman's clarinet solo and a following trumpet solo that ushers the song toward its climactic shout chorus. "Roll 'Em" is representative of the work Williams performed for other band leaders and established her reputation as an authority in the blues and swing-style jazz.[77]

Williams saw the blues as one of the central components of jazz. Later in her life, she stated, "The Blues is really the healing force in all

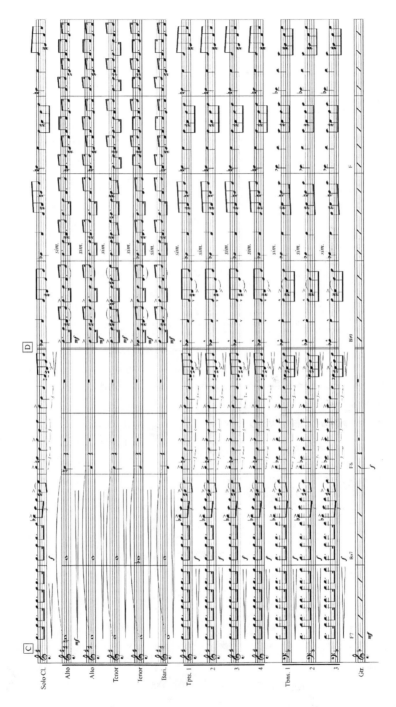

Figure 10. Excerpt of Mary Lou Williams's "Roll 'Em." Transcribed by Ted Buehrer. *Essentially Ellington: Jazz at Lincoln Center Library*, 2009.

forms of jazz—no matter how far out. You can play all of it—way out chords, fast technique and everything, and put this feeling and approach of the blues in it."[78] Williams's notion of healing is a sonic corollary to Tamika Carey's discussion of literacy and Black women's rhetorics of healing. Carey discusses the belief in the restorative powers of literacy as a product of a long, African tradition of healers and conjurers, a fusion of spiritual practitioners and social workers that labored within a variety of modalities to address the trials and tribulations of the human condition as well as the emotional and physical trauma of racial oppression.[79] Carey focuses on the legacy of Black women writers who utilized "language as a form of preventative and restorative agency," anticipating modern Black women's wellness initiatives. Carey also emphasizes the mastery of cultural memory and language as steps to self-reclamation, restoration, and actualization. This resonates with Williams's jeremiad, which also emphasizes cultural memory and the literacy of Black music (the sonic lexicon of Black music), and positions Black music as a conduit for healing—a spiritual and pedagogical practice crucial to the success and well-being of future generations of Black communities.

For women such as Ida B. Wells, discourses of women's rights were often concomitant with discourses of racial oppression.[80] Despite differences in class, geographical region, and religion, African American women were often the embodiment of their message, authenticating their arguments for equality, visibility, and respect by their very presence in a hostile public sphere.[81] Williams's work operates along similar lines; its power and importance extend from both its content and its creator. Although the impact of Williams's legacy can be readily traced through the scores of artists that cite her as an influence and the jazz festivals that are held in her honor each year, the personal testimony of musicians and fans provides insight into the scale and degree of Williams's impact on their lives.[82] These testimonies, some captured by Williams's manager, Father O'Brien, before and after Williams's death, provide nuanced accounts of Williams in a plethora of roles, from mentor to personal friend. For example, in O'Brien's interview with jazz violinist Joe Kennedy Jr., Kennedy described his lifelong admiration for Williams, the impact of her presence as a leading woman in the world of jazz, and the lengths Williams went through to support younger musicians through his account of Williams's personal involvement in producing his first album with the Four Strings, titled *Trends* (1949), for the Asch Records label.[83]

Although conditions have dramatically improved for Black women since Williams's tenure as a traveling musician and recording artist, what's been categorized as the urban musical landscape—Hip Hop, R&B, and Neo-Soul—has largely remained a male-dominated space. Black women have used their contributions to that scene to navigate a music industry shaped by the whims of corporate expectations and commercial viability. Such constraints often include the objectification of women, Eurocentric standards of beauty, the glorification of materialism, and the prioritization of profit over quality and authenticity. Nevertheless, Black women artists have managed to subvert these challenges with great artistic flair.

Ultimately, Williams's artistry made the case for Black women as serious composers of experimental and innovative music by using her spirituality as a site of creative practice, identity, and purpose. Her music participated in a rhetorical practice that transcended the limitations imposed by her gender and skin color and altered public discourse about the role of women in jazz. Though her moral character was repeatedly called into question, and her ability to speak from a position of authority in the world of jazz was, at times, undervalued, Williams's compositions allowed her to reshape the genre itself and, consequently, the possibilities of women in the public sphere, especially those working in modalities outside of the commercial and corporate interests of the music industry. She parlayed "playing like a man" into a significant career that has served as a model for other women musicians. While the commodification of Black music has always presented a threat to its vitality and authenticity, subsequent generations of Black artists have carried forward the creativity and commitment to excellence Williams so fervently championed. Williams's jeremiad captured her deep concern for the future of Black music and offered the hopeful prophecy that her precious treasure, what she described as "the product of the suffering of slaves," would continue to anchor Black communities through the turbulent storms of the twenty-first century.

4
A (Rhetorical) Love Supreme

In his celebratory remarks during a program at Pennsylvania State University honoring Dr. Martin Luther King Jr., leading African American scholar Cornel West stated that after four hundred years of struggle, "Black people have taught the world so much about how to love." While acknowledging the auspiciousness of his address on the same day as the 2017 presidential inauguration—a unique day to discuss American culture and politics—West proclaimed, "Instead of giving my speech, I could just play John Coltrane's *A Love Supreme* (1965) and sit down."[1] He saw a direct relationship among this album, the totality of Black experience, and the life and teachings of King. Both King and *Supreme* are part of a grand tradition of piety and resistance, one that encompasses, West noted, a Gramscian sense of critical self-inventory.

As I sat listening to West's comments, I couldn't help but be brought back to my first encounter with Coltrane's music while simmering, along with the audience, within a collective sense of anxiety and uncertainty on that day. Yet I instantly understood what West was describing. I encountered my first Coltrane album, *Giant Steps*, while searching through the jazz section in the media department of a public library during my senior year of high school. I was just beginning to take seriously the idea of pursuing music in college, and I had developed an almost insatiable desire to listen to jazz as much as I could. When I first heard the song "Giant Steps," I was completely spellbound. As a young, fledging saxophonist, my nascent comprehension of the virtuosity at work in that song was at once deeply intimidating and incredibly exciting. There was an electricity to Coltrane's tone that I didn't have language to describe. However, his music gave me the sense that jazz was so much more than great music. I recognized then that Coltrane was doing something incredibly subversive. Now, years later, West's celebration of Coltrane at such a *kairotic* (uttered during an opportune or "supreme" time) moment further underscored my view of Coltrane's iconicity and relevance to the story of America.

However, scholars disagree about how to read John Coltrane. On the one hand, he has been cast as a prominent figure in the Black Nationalist movement of the 1960s.[2] On the other, he has been described as an apolitical musician concerned primarily with spirituality, an image Coltrane himself readily promoted in his statements to the press.[3] These constructions of Coltrane are, of course, reductive, yet they point to an important cultural and aesthetic tension. Coltrane's music encompasses both of these personas through an active, rhetorical engagement with the issues of his time. Coltrane's oeuvre, including his iconic album *A Love Supreme*, represents a synthesis of competing discourses and sensibilities: that of moderate integrationists of the Civil Rights movement (with the closest musical extension being Motown and a new chapter in Black popular music), a countercultural and antimaterialist spiritualism, and Afrocentrism. In this chapter, I argue that such syntheses propelled Coltrane's status as a cultural symbol of Black innovation and aesthetics. I view Coltrane as a purveyor of epistemic sonic schema—a body of sonic material that produces knowledge both as an aural analog to Kenneth Burke's critical practice of "perspective by incongruity" and as the communication of the kind of doubled meanings associated with African American rhetorical traditions known as signifying. My contention that music can communicate knowledge relies on audiences' attempts to recognize and assign meaning to sonic, symbolic referents. Burke's notion of perspective by incongruity describes a critical method for rhetorical inquiry that involves juxtaposing incongruent concepts and terminology for the purposes of illuminating potentially unexamined meaning-making processes. In this context, I use it to refer to the juxtaposition of disparate sonic material that similarly reveals new meanings. Signifying, one of the foundational features of African American rhetorical traditions, involves the communication of myriad levels of meaning simultaneously. Notwithstanding music's constant invitation to subjective interpretation, Coltrane's music indexes the Black sonic lexicon with a degree of self-reflection that allowed listeners within the Black community to hear his music as critical commentary. Both concepts, perspective by incongruity and signification, help to explain how epistemic sonic schemas shape the rhetorical function of Coltrane's music as one of the key qualities of his musical experimentalism.

To explore the rhetorical dimensions of John Coltrane's music and its larger impact on American culture, it will be helpful to begin by reviewing Coltrane's musical development prior to *Supreme*. The practice of jazz improvisation was for Coltrane a career-defining skill and a critical part of his ethos. I will then read *Supreme* in the light of various thematic relationships among writers and thought leaders in the African American community in order to show how discussions of cultural pride, Black aesthetics, and social and political liberation were activated by Coltrane's music. The chapter ends by exploring the discourses surrounding the subgenre "free jazz" (also referred to as avant-garde jazz), which Coltrane often employed to powerful effect. This style of jazz challenged standard musical conventions and structures and became an important part of the rhetorical landscape of the 1960s.

Coltrane's Musical Evolution

Blue Train (1957), *Giant Steps* (1959), *My Favorite Things* (1961), and *Africa/Brass* (1961) each foreground a particular set of ideas that culminate in *Supreme*'s composition and performance. *Blue Train* was Coltrane's first record as a bandleader after his engagements with Miles Davis and Thelonious Monk from 1955 to 1957. He is joined by pianist Kenny Drew, drummer Philly Joe Jones, bassist Paul Chambers, trumpeter Lee Morgan, and trombonist Curtis Fuller. On this project, Coltrane began to manifest his unique approach to expanding and exploring melodic ideas and increased his mastery of the blues and ballads. Due to his growing ability to use one or two musical lines and develop them—seemingly without end—writer and jazz critic A. B. Spellman compared this period to the career of Johann Sebastian Bach.[4] To Spellman's point, Coltrane gained a reputation for his inventive approach to improvisation and for a sound often described as wailing, sharp, and resonant.[5] These characteristics gave his artistry a mysterious and probing sensibility that began to shape his public profile as a musician constantly searching for new sounds and forms of expression.

On the tracks "Blue Train" and "Locomotion," Coltrane presents energetic and hard-hitting solos that incorporate the evolving style of bebop jazz known as hard bop.[6] In one of the first published transcriptions and analyses of Coltrane's improvisation, pianist Zita Carno described "Blue Train" as a virtuosic blues solo with the unusual qualities of a constant buildup of energy combined with a deceptive simplicity where nothing is just what it seems.[7] This tune and its technical innovations began to concretize the identification of Coltrane with the larger tradition of the railroad train as an African American cultural and literary trope of progress, mobility, technology, and continuity. This trope involves a set of rhizomatic discursive practices stretching back and forth from the underground railroad to the blues men and women within African American folklore to the singing and dancing on the hit television show *Soul Train* and beyond: Coltrane comes to embody a distinctive sonic translation of this tradition.

On "I'm Old Fashioned" (originally written for the 1942 musical *You Were Never Lovelier*, starring Fred Astaire and Rita Hayworth), Coltrane uses a popular show tune to showcase his ability to take familiar work and transform its emotional contours without losing the melodic identification with the original version. On "Moment's Notice" and "Lazy Bird," Coltrane presents his talent for creating complex harmonic compositions, later referred to as Coltrane (chord) changes, which are harmonic chord progressions that feature the use of chord substitutions for the common II-V-I progression. This innovative change created the effect of polytonal improvisation, or dual tonal centers for a single song. Such musical innovations helped to engender the recognition of jazz as a source of Black genius, where breaking barriers artistically resonated with breaking barriers socially and politically.

On *Giant Steps*, Coltrane perfects a difficult technique of playing a series of notes and arpeggios at rapid speeds, famously referred to as "sheets of sound" by jazz critic Ira Gitler (see figure 11).[8] Although he had displayed flashes of this technique in his earlier work, *Giant Steps* is far more advanced in its theoretical complexity and difficulty. As a display of tremendous virtuosity, this album added yet another dimension to Coltrane's public reputation. In addition to being known for his soulful and emotional music, Coltrane further solidified his status as one of the jazz community's greatest musical minds, combining both innovation and highly skilled technical ability. In fact, the title song on the album has now been canonized in jazz pedagogies as a test of improvisational

A (Rhetorical) Love Supreme 103

Figure 11. This excerpt from "Giant Steps" begins in measure twenty-six and features the conclusion of the main chorus (head) and the beginning of Coltrane's improvised solo in measure thirty-two. Notice that the tempo is quite fast; a quarter note equals 290 beats per minute. Coltrane's rapid-fire deployment of ascending and descending arpeggios begins to take flight.

maturity and dexterity. However, Coltrane was after more than academic exercises. He cared about how his music was received and about reaching audiences authentically.[9] This concern was entangled with larger issues surrounding modern jazz and Black aesthetics. Black artists choosing to explore the highest realms of their talents outside of Western classical music often saw their credibility called into question. But the creation of innovative and experimental music had to be balanced against the demands of producing commercially acceptable jazz, and this balance became a central preoccupation for Coltrane and, in part, motivation for his subsequent album, *My Favorite Things*.

Borrowed from the Rodgers and Hammerstein musical *The Sound of Music*, the title song was also the first to feature Coltrane's soprano saxophone. Coltrane began to demonstrate what critic Houston Baker calls the mastery of form and the deformation of mastery. Baker uses this concept to describe the rhetorical strategies of either using mastery of form to conceal or disguise subversive or radical ideas in ways that "float like a trickster butterfly in order to sting like a bee" or using explicit displays of disruption that strike outsiders as a "deformity" or as "alien" to a set of expected norms.[10] This aptly describes Coltrane's deconstruction of the melodic and harmonic ideas that undergird the song. The original version features an AABC structure that presents two sections in E minor (raindrops on roses and whiskers on kittens), a section in E major (girls in white dresses with blue satin sashes), and then a final section that provides both a change in texture and the conclusion of the chordal sequence (when the dog bites, when the bee stings). However, Coltrane dispenses with section C until the end of the song and frames the majority of the piece as a modal composition that alternates between E minor and E major. Modal compositions, although present in European music, are most generically related to Asian, African, and Middle Eastern musical practices. Whereas Western music since 1600 has generally emphasized a tonal progression of chords constructed in a key, modal music is constructed on scales that are not derived from a key but from groupings of notes that do not align to form chords in the strict sense. Stylistically, modal music is more concerned with the horizontal plane of melody. Additionally, Coltrane's extension of these sections into pedal point vamps (a note sustained, usually by the bass guitar or double bass, through a series of harmonies) creates a linear or horizontal orientation to the improvisation. The improvisational challenge then evolves from playing through and around intricate chord changes to a focus on the development of motifs and other musical ideas in ways that build in intensity and euphoric effect, a decidedly different orientation from the original's brief waltz-like structure. Coltrane transforms the soprano saxophone, one of the most genteel instruments in the woodwind family, into an instrument capable of much darker and introspective colors. It is a display of processes of transformation and reinterpretation capable of turning mainstream, Eurocentric artwork and cultural ephemera into distinctly Black texts that represent Black experience. Such transformations have political overtones, as acts that claim space, via the sonic, for the Black experience in Western media and public discourse (see figure 12).

Of course, this kind of revision was not uncommon in jazz, and Coltrane was certainly influenced by Miles Davis, who was also known for his creative reinterpretations of popular tunes. However, Coltrane does not just depart from the conventions of the original version of "My Favorite Things." He also contributes a new sound and approach to jazz itself, further solidifying his reputation for experimentation and breaking boundaries. With the addition of pianist McCoy Tyner, drummer Elvin Jones, and bassist Jimmy Garrison, Coltrane was able to bring together individuals who supported his musical exploration and were critical to the execution of his ideas. Through the deformation of the

Figure 12. This excerpt of Coltrane's solo in "My Favorite Things" begins right after pianist McCoy Tyner's solo. Coltrane repeats the chorus (head) of the song before launching into one of the solo's climactic moments, with dramatic sixteenth-note lines ascending toward the higher limits of the soprano saxophone's register.

original "My Favorite Things," and the juxtaposition of such contrasting musical material, Coltrane's music communicated the depth of the sonic lexicon of Black music via epistemic sonic schema and the music's potential for usurping Western aesthetics, thereby forging a rhetorical relationship between avant-garde jazz and Black aesthetics writ large.

The album *Africa/Brass* signaled yet another important shift in Coltrane's artistry. Its release caused a stir in the jazz community, leading reviewers to celebrate its originality and daring experimentalism with claims that Coltrane was "rewriting the rules of jazz" and placing himself in the center of a new musical movement.[11] However, Coltrane's critical success was due, in part, to the strong narrative qualities of the album, which present a transformative journey from Africa to the posh jazz clubs of New York. Specifically, Coltrane's compositional maneuvers were also a rhetorical response to the waves of African nations gaining independence from foreign powers, a historical sea change that couldn't but impact conceptions and representations of Africa in America.[12]

As jazz became an important vehicle for the support of revolution and liberation from Western colonialism, Coltrane's music offered a sonic topos of Africa, juxtaposing Black sonic subjectivity with vibrant political awareness. For example, consider the featured song on the album, "Africa." This song begins with not one but two bass players. One plays the pedal point while the other performs a prolonged trill using the bow. Soon the piano and wind instruments enter with trilled notes as well, which creates the effect of swarming insects. As Coltrane begins playing the first theme, the wind section adds a layer of scattered slurs, growls, and swells that imitate the vocal utterance and animalistic sounds found in the jungle. After this theme the piece settles into a smoother groove led by drummer Elvin Jones and takes on the form of a modal vamp. Toward the middle of the piece is an extended drum solo with strong Afro-Cuban and African inflections that further improvisational development and the accumulation of energy. Taking the title of the album, *Africa/Brass*, as a literal juxtaposition, the epistemic sonic schema helps us name what is, for Coltrane, a methodical compositional process. This album thus offered a foretaste of a process that could be extended to support large-scale narrative structures, a feat Coltrane would attempt in a four-part suite entitled *A Love Supreme*.

The Cultural Impact of *A Love Supreme*

A Love Supreme presented the reflective and emotional blues of *Blue Train*, the complexity and dexterity of *Giant Steps*, the modal experimentation of *My Favorite Things*, and the Afrocentrism of *Africa/Brass*. *Supreme* was instantly heralded as a jazz classic, winning Coltrane two Grammys for jazz performance and composition. Evidence of the album's extraordinary cultural impact abounds and can be observed, quantitatively, through its consistent rankings on the iTunes list of the top one hundred bestselling jazz albums, as well as *Rolling Stone*'s list of the top five hundred albums of all time.

The album's release in 1965 coincided with a pivotal moment of the Civil Rights era. The first quarter of that year, which is when *Supreme* appeared, witnessed the assassination of Malcolm X and the landmark protest march from Selma to Montgomery. A devastating riot in the Watts neighborhood of Los Angeles would follow in August. The release of an album amid such tensions was nothing short of *kairotic*. Coltrane's liner notes for the album indicate the origins of his inspiration and his rhetorical strategy. They are worth quoting at length:

DEAR LISTENER: ALL PRAISE BE TO GOD TO WHOM ALL PRAISE IS DUE. Let us pursue Him in the righteous path. Yes it is true; "seek and ye shall find." Only through Him can we know the most wondrous bequeathal.

During the year 1957, I experienced, by the grace of God, a spiritual awakening, which was to lead me to a richer, fuller, more productive life. At that time, in gratitude, I humbly asked to be given the means and privilege to make others happy through music. I feel this has been granted through His grace. ALL PRAISE TO GOD.

As time and events moved on, a period of irresolution did prevail. I entered into a phase which was contradictory to the pledge and away from the esteemed path; but thankfully, now and again through the unerring and merciful hand of God, I do perceive and have been duly re-informed of His OMNIPOTENCE, and of our need for, and dependence on Him. At this time I would like to tell you that NO MATTER WHAT . . . IT IS WITH GOD. HE IS GRACIOUS AND MERCIFUL. HIS WAY IS IN LOVE, THROUGH WHICH WE ALL ARE. IT IS TRULY—A LOVE SUPREME—.

This album is a humble offering to Him. An attempt to say "THANK YOU GOD" through our work, even as we do in our hearts and with our tongues. May He help and strengthen all men in every good endeavor.[13]

Coltrane's liner notes, as well as the album itself, present an Augustinian conversion narrative that should be read alongside two other famous conversion narratives belonging to this historical moment: those of Malcolm X and Martin Luther King Jr. One important dimension of such a narrative is that there are in essence two conversions. Augustine describes two distinct points of conversion, with the first occurring with his intellectual acceptance and belief in the truth of Christianity. Yet according to Augustine, his conversion was not yet complete because although he had "ceased to doubt that there was an incorruptible substance, whence was all other substance," he was lacking a degree of certainty and steadfastness required for his beliefs to change his actions. Augustine then reasoned, "But for my temporal life, all was wavering, and my heart had to be purged from the old leaven."[14] The completion of Augustine's conversion occurred during a moment of great personal crisis wherein he experienced an encounter with the voice of God. After following God's commandment to read scripture, he states, "by a light as it were of serenity infused into my heart, all the darkness of doubt vanished away."[15] This pattern is immediately identifiable in Coltrane's narrative and comports with biographical information surrounding the composition process of *A Love Supreme* as being a product of Coltrane's experience of God.

King's description of his conversion follows a similar structure. In his "Autobiography of Religious Development" King frames his first conversion as a result of "the gradual intaking of the noble ideals set forth in [his] family and environment."[16] Like Augustine, King describes his second conversion, what King labeled his "kitchen conversion," as a seismic shift marked by the deepening of his faith by orders of magnitude. This second conversion occurred during King's experiences leading the Montgomery bus boycott, where he was forced to grapple with the personal sacrifices such leadership would entail, the danger that engulfed his family, as well as a new recognition of his own mortality brought by mounting death threats.

Like King, Coltrane was also raised in a Christian family, and his second conversion experience likewise signified a more radical personal transformation. Perhaps even more prolific in the public imaginary following the Civil Rights era, Malcolm X's transformation from a street hustler to a firebrand public intellectual was also due to a conversion experience, to Islam, while he was imprisoned. In his autobiography, he rendered his transformation as being "struck numb," like the Christian apostle Paul on the road to Damascus. Malcolm remarked of Paul, "I was so smitten that he was knocked off of his horse, in a daze. I do not now, and I did not then, liken myself to Paul. But I do understand his experience."[17] However, Malcolm X's religious conversion to Islam, through the Nation of Islam and its leader Elijah Muhammad, was also the awakening of an anti-integrationist, political, Black consciousness. Malcolm X would later undergo a second conversion, to mainstream Islam, and develop a prointegration stance, as a consequence of his pilgrimage to Mecca. Thus for both King and Malcolm X, their religious conversions were directly related to their political conversions. *A Love Supreme* manifests, for Coltrane, this same duality of spiritual sincerity bearing political consequences. Although Coltrane's liner notes lack any explicit political appeal, it is his combination of genres and his stylistic take on them that provides the album's political edge.

Supreme features an array of genres—spirituals, blues, hard bop, and free jazz. Free jazz, led by artists such as Ornette Coleman, Cecil Taylor, Sun Ra, Archie Shepp, Sonny Rollins, as well as Coltrane, was regarded as a highly experimental form that had strong ties to African American spirituals and mystical or religious thought. This genre of music included more growls, screams, hollers, and other unorthodox sounds to express more vocality and a wider range of emotions (see figure 13). These ornamentations were intentional maneuvers to reframe the temporal and spectral profile of the music as Afrocentric, even to the extent of the music's amplitude and distribution of frequencies. The use of drums to articulate pitches is a stylistic quality of free jazz that represents a quest to "re-Africanize" the approach to the instrument. Thus free jazz presented an ethos and expectation of an authentic African American sound and rejected common harmonic and rhythmic conventions. Its critique of European systems of harmony and rhythm correlated with Black Nationalist rejections of Eurocentrism in American aesthetics and politics. Imitating the human voice is another central characteristic of free jazz and a feature that Coltrane excels at on *Supreme*. His shouts and growls create textures or "sound pictures" of the agony and euphoria of

Figure 13. This excerpt presents Coltrane's iconic introduction to part one of the *A Love Supreme* suite, "Acknowledgement." It has a transcendental, chant-like quality due to the use of gongs and symbols and Coltrane's vocal imitations.

the human experience and a burgeoning Black consciousness that sonically translates the social turbulence of the time.[18]

Amiri Baraka's *Blues People* (1963) and *Black Music* (1967) were among the first monographs to discuss jazz in relation to the political climate of the 1960s. Baraka argued the merit of free jazz in relation to the music of previous generations. Commenting on the centrality of Black music to the American landscape, Baraka wrote: "Blues was the initial Afro-American music, and bebop the reemphasis of the non-western tradition. And if the latter saved us from the vapid wastes of swing, singlehandedly, the new avant-garde (and John Coltrane) are saving us from the comparatively vapid 50's."[19] Along with Baraka, other Black intellectuals, such as Larry Neal, A. B. Spellman, James T. Stewart, Ron Welburn, and Holly West, saw Black music as an important part of the social and political fabric of the Black experience in America. For example, in his *Four Lives in the Bebop Business* (1966), Spellman explored the lives of Cecil Taylor, Ornette Coleman, Herbie Nichols, and Jackie McLean as a way of framing a conversation about the social, political, and economic dimensions of jazz.[20] Spellman then argued that the indifference paid to aspects of African American culture that are not "entertaining" is a feature of the "blind adulation of European culture" in America. He also used his exploration of music and musicians as a way to understand and address larger issues facing Black America. In his critique of the racism embedded in the music industry, Spellman declared: "That a Dave Brubeck can be approaching millionaire status while Cecil Taylor, Jackie McLean, and Ornette Coleman are relative paupers is, from my perspective, outrageous; but why be naïve? Has it ever been different? Did not the Original Dixieland Jazz Band make many times the money of Jelly Roll Morton's Red Hot Peppers?"[21] Spellman's work became an important part of the larger public dialogue about the economy of jazz and the cultural bias facing Black art. In an article written in direct response to Spellman's book, Larry Neal's "The Black Musician in White America" argued that the "history of the jazz musician in America is the history of the worst kind of oppression ever perpetrated" and that the experiences of Black musicians served as a "microcosm of the experience of Black America in general."[22] Despite the fact that their work made millions of dollars for others, their obvious talents could not save them from economic hardship. According to Neal, the two important issues at stake were business and aesthetics. Black musicians were always seen as less than classical performers by white America and, as a result, would never receive the recognition they deserved, even as white musicians were influenced by Blacks' musical innovations.[23] Additionally, music critics were approaching the music with "white Western prejudices," and most cases of financial success were obtained at the expense of cultural and artistic integrity.

In response to Spellman's discussion of the declining Black audience for musicians like Ornette Coleman, Neal argued in 1967 that most Black communities lacked the cultural institutions (Black equivalents to the Metropolitan Opera or the New York Philharmonic, for example) that could sustain the kind of artistic expression offered by Coleman, which was experimental in nature and unaccommodating to the demands of popular music. Neal laid part of the blame for this state of affairs at the feet of the "Negro bourgeoisie," which was "not persistent enough in turning inward on some of its own problems."[24] More important, Neal broke from musicians and writers like Amiri Baraka by urging his readers to use caution when deploying the term "revolutionary music" to describe the music produced by Archie Shepp and Coleman. Neal claimed that music worthy of that name would need to "extend itself into the Black community in a manner which it has failed to do" and that it must "mean to the community what the Supremes, the Impressions, and James Brown now mean" by having a more direct impact on the political and social life of the community.[25] For Neal, technical innovations were not enough. However, Coltrane is noticeably left unmentioned in this critique.

In a later article, "Any Day Now" (1969), Neal provided a robust definition and program for the role of the arts in the Black Power movement. While proclaiming that Black music "represents the highest artistic achievement of the race," Neal argued that Black arts are "primarily concerned with the cultural and spiritual liberation of America" by linking art and politics with an "Afro-American and Third World historical and cultural sensibility."[26] The attempt was to fashion "a total vision of ourselves" as a response to the split vision that W. E. B. Du Bois referred to as double consciousness.[27] To Neal, Coltrane and other select musical artists transcended the world of entertainment.[28] Rather, they were the "poets and philosophers of Black America" and "keepers of our memory, tribal historians, and soothsayers."[29] Demonstrating his awareness of the rhetorical value of Black music, he argued: "The feeling of a James Brown or an Aretha Franklin. That is the feeling that unites us and makes it more possible for us to move and groove together, to do whatever is necessary to liberate ourselves. John Coltrane's music must unquestionably be a part of any future revolutionary society, or something is diabolically wrong with the fools who make the revolution."[30] Furthermore, Neal saw musician-activists as critical to the project of Black liberation. In "Black Boogaloo" he issued a challenge: "Stop bitching. Take care of business. All get together all over America and play at the same time. Combine energy. Combine energy. Play together. Wild screaming sounds. Wailing women. Slaves moan in slave ships. Cut America into tiny strips. Blow. Walk into the columbia and blue note studios, take them over. Kick rudy van gelder in his ass, take his equipment. Get yourself some tape recorders Cecil. Get back what they stole, Archie."[31]

Neal, as well as other African American writers, sought to provide an alternate mode of analysis for Black music while advancing a new Black aesthetic that was grounded in the empowerment of Black musicians, their music, and the Black community. Combined with the distinctive musical qualities of jazz, explicit arguments from critics and scholars about the cultural context of jazz posed questions of cultural authenticity and political agency amid a rising wave of Black Nationalist discourse.

These ideas met resistance from many white jazz critics and journalists, such as Martin Williams, Gunther Schuller, Leonard Feather, and John Tynan. These critics often used their positions to attack musicians such as Coltrane, Max Roach, and Charles Mingus concerning both politics and art. For example, in one of the most infamous critiques of Coltrane's music, Tynan of *DownBeat* magazine used terms like "anti-jazz" and "anarchistic" to describe one of Coltrane's performances:

> Go ahead, call me reactionary. I happen to object to the musical nonsense currently being peddled in the name of jazz by John Coltrane and his acolyte, Eric Dolphy. At Hollywood's Renaissance Club recently, I listened to a horrifying demonstration of what appears to be a growing anti-jazz trend exemplified by these foremost proponents of what is termed avant garde music. I heard a good rhythm section . . . go to waste behind the nihilistic exercises of the two horns. . . . Coltrane and Dolphy seem intent on

deliberately destroying [swing]. They seem bent on pursuing an anarchistic course in their music that can but be termed anti-jazz. Melodically and harmonically their improvisations struck my ear as gobbledegook.[32]

This article launched a controversial series of discussions about avant-garde music and race that eventually caught the attention of Coltrane, who decided to respond publicly to his critics. In a feature titled "John Coltrane and Eric Dolphy Answer the Jazz Critics," Coltrane remarked—via an interview with *DownBeat*'s editorial board—that his performances were long because "all the soloists try to explore all the avenues that the tune offers. They try to use all their resources in their solos."[33] Regarding questions about the purpose of his music, Coltrane added: "What we know we feel we'd like to convey to the listener.... That's what music is to me—it's just another way of saying this is a big, beautiful universe we live in, that's been given to us, and here's an example of just how magnificent and encompassing it is.... But I think it really ends up with the listener. You know, you hear different people say, 'Man I felt this while he was playing', or 'I thought about this'."[34] Coltrane's discussion of beauty, universalism, and his desire to impact his listeners in positive ways contradicted the mounting criticism that his music was mostly about anger, discord, or anarchy. The public dispute between Coltrane and his critics in part mirrored the overall rhetorical combat between voices of African American protest and adversaries who dismissed militant rhetorical performances as "angry" or "too emotional." Such tactics amounted to appeals to respectability politics.

Moreover, the musical emphasis of Afrocentrism and collectivity in jazz referenced the oppression of African Americans in ways that clashed with industry expectations. This new, forceful political awareness was regarded as racially separatist and exclusionary.[35] The debates surrounding free jazz became intertwined with questions of the cultural and aesthetic differences between Black and white Americans, and the arguments involved, as Neal indicated, issues of white control and Black economic and creative empowerment.[36]

In response to charges of appropriating African American culture and aesthetics, many white critics argued that the standards of jazz, such as swing, the blues, and melodic expression were "colorless." But

Coltrane's music, despite his verbal embrace of universalism, spoke to Black pride and assertion in the public sphere, combining artistic genius with the politics of outspoken racial consciousness.[37] His artistry, and that of his peers, upset much of the white-dominated critical and commercial establishment. For example, consider critic Ira Gitler's review of Abby Lincoln's *Straight Ahead* (1961). Gitler referred to Lincoln's album as racial propaganda and saw jazz as an inappropriate place for political statements. He stated that "pride in one's heritage is one thing, but we don't need the Elijah Muhammad type thinking in jazz."[38] Some critics, such as Nat Hentoff, sometimes sided with the artists, though Hentoff was still criticized for being close to the circle of writers who were critical of artists like Lincoln and Coltrane.[39]

As part of a challenge to conventions of the music industry and normative practices of jazz performance, some free jazz musicians sought venues besides the traditional jazz clubs, and they rejected contracts with record labels. Instead, they formed their own organizations, such as the Chicago-based Association for the Advancement of Creative Musicians (AACM). AACM wanted to be acknowledged both for its Afrocentrism and its contribution to the world of experimental music at large. In George Lewis's exceptional historical study of this collective, he argues that AACM developed strategies for collective self-production and promotion that reframed the artist/business relationship and challenged racialized limitations on venues and infrastructure.[40]

Animating all of this activity, as much as any album could, was *A Love Supreme*. The resistant dissonance, the tracings of African American spirituals and folk songs merging with postmodern experimentalism and Black popular music: all these spoke energetically to diverse legions of artists, activists, and, later, scholars. In his novel *Bedouin Hornbook*, writer and scholar Nathaniel Mackey connects dissonance (or what he calls dissonance in dissidence) to improvisation as the sonic residue of the Black experience. To him, dissonance represents more than the clash of a diverse array of diatonic tones. It is also the intentional space caused by delayed resolution. As Eddie Prevost has argued, one musician's dissonance is another's jazz, and a "dissonant form may become quietly soothing."[41] Dissonance functions as the continuous negotiation between cohesion, alienation, and constructions of the self in relation to community. Coltrane's style of improvisation, compositional structures, harmonic and textual colors, and the contributions by the other musicians in response to his musical ideas create messages that engage listeners. According to Kenneth Burke, aesthetic form is located in the experience, not the artifact, provided to the listener or viewer.[42] One's selection of the appropriate verb to describe that experience, whether it envisions, transports, summons, calls into being, remembers, or prophesizes, has much to do with the relationship between the broader rhetorical situation and the composition of, in this case, the music itself. Coltrane's blending of Eastern and Western tonalities and textures, epistemic sonic schemas, becomes rhetorical when viewed as intentional, transformative juxtapositions of spirituals, bebop, and free jazz that signify on a broader canon of Black musical traditions. It is a presentation of the kind of unity rare in the broader public sphere yet essential to advancing a collective social and political vision of democratic transformation.

The rhetorical function of Coltrane's music was aided by the public perception of his personal life. His victory over drugs and alcohol, alluded to in the spiritual narrative of his liner notes, signified a very strong theme of redemption and spiritual devotion in the vein of Malcolm X.[43] His personal life amplified the poignancy of his music as a redemptive force in jazz, serving as an escape from the growing materialism and secularism in American culture. This particular spirituality has been described by scholars Davis W. Houck and David E. Dixon as a "Divine Call to personhood, faithful enactment of God's Plan, and a fulfillment of a uniquely American promise."[44] This is how Coltrane connected love to justice and why Cornel West linked Coltrane to King. *Supreme*'s texture and aural qualities invoke the ideas of universal brotherhood, spiritual solidarity, and a shared destiny governed by the will of God. These ideas are what Kenneth Burke called "consubstantial" in his reference to the shared values and beliefs that contribute to the moments when people experience themselves as unified within a particular group identity.[45] Whatever its appeal to a broader public, *Supreme* was consubstantial with a burgeoning Black spirituality and identity situated in relation to the events of the 1960s.

Recalling his initial encounter with *Supreme* in the spring of 1969, poet, musician, and novelist Gil Scott-Heron expressed: "The first time I heard the [*Love Supreme*] chant, the spirituality, the mix of instruments, the way the solos were set up, the way the tune was done and the length of it at almost 20 minutes long—I got lost in it. I was literally taken aback."[46] Scott-Heron and likeminded artists, inspired by Coltrane and in the manner of Larry Neal, viewed their art as a weapon to be used to destroy white supremacy and conquer the legacy of minstrelsy devaluing Black culture.[47] One need not look any further than the "Coltrane Poem," which became a distinct genre in African American poetry. Poems such as "Ode to John Coltrane" by Quincy Troupe, "How Long Has Trane Been Gone" by Jayne Cortez, "a/Coltrane/poem" by Sonia Sanchez, "Don't Cry, Scream" by Haki Madhubuti, and "Dear John, Dear Coltrane" and "Here Where Coltrane Is" by Michael Harper indicate the important impact Coltrane made on African American writers. Scott-Heron created his own version of the Coltrane poem with the lyrics to "Lady Day and John Coltrane." Coltrane's resonance with artists reflected his ability to transfigure their ideals regarding the potential of human expressive power.

Of the many contemporary authors whose work is influenced by avant-garde jazz, few have generated the sustained inquiry of Nathaniel Mackey, whose work foregrounds musical themes. Mackey has described how an interaction with Coltrane as a youth served as an inspiration for his work, and he reimagines this experience in his poem "Ohnedaruth's Day Begun," which envisions Coltrane's performance at the Village Gate in 1965.[48] (*Ohnedaruth* means *compassion* in Sanskrit and is the spiritual name that Coltrane adopted.) Mackey's approach to writing, even in fiction, is "musical deployment of language," and he seeks to create "language bordering on song."[49] His epistolary novels, which include *Bedouin Hornbook*, *Djbot Baghostus's Run*, *Atet A. D.*, *Bass Cathedral*, and *Late Arcade*, trace the experiences of an unnamed narrator (referred to as "N.") who is a musician and composer in a band known as Molimo m'Atet. Similar to James Weldon Johnson's unnamed narrator and his discussion of ragtime in *The Autobiography of an Ex-Colored Man*, Mackey uses N. (a reference to his own name) to engage the meanings and implications of Black music, especially jazz and improvisation. As Johnson's unnamed narrator is based, in part, on Johnson's own experiences as a ragtime composer, Mackey's narrator is based on his dreams of playing with the greats of jazz music, such as Coltrane, Ornette Coleman, Thelonious Monk, and others.[50]

Coltrane's music expresses what Mackey refers to as "telling inarticulacy," which communicates substance or carries content by approaching the "unsayable."[51] Mackey uses this concept to expand the notion of speech to include what Dawn Lundy Martin terms the "stutter, the guttural, the moan, the cracking of the throat, a cold sweat, [or] a hoarse drunkenness."[52] In *Bedouin Hornbook*, N. describes "graspability" as utterances that express emotions and experiences in ways that may lack a precise language but "grasp" at intelligibility in some way.[53] These notions also apply to Black music and harmonic structure. In this conception, experimental harmonies, melodies, and graspability are cognates. Although for Burke aesthetic form is found in the audience's experience, the stakes of rhetorical discourse in jazz are not just located in audience expectations. Rather, such discourses also include the performer's self-discovery and self-expression. Improvisation carries the expectation of individual expression; communal solidarity is conducive to individuality, not contradictory to it. Moreover, the concept of music as language (including its anecdotal references) signals a long history of wrestling with the limits of intelligible communication. Mackey's theory of telling inarticulacy resists this binary, as does the rhetorical function of Black music. Meditating on Dizzy Gillespie's scat singing, N. writes: "Trademark visuality, it seems to me, wants to domesticate or mask an acoustic risk the music otherwise runs, the risk of acousticality itself. I've touched on something like this before, I realize, but bear with me long enough to consider Dizzy's recourse to scat and his affection for 'oo' . . . his love affair, more generally speaking, with the vocable, as an explicit, so to speak, vocalization if not verbalization of the occult clamor whose risk he runs on the horn."[54]

In this passage, N. discusses the subversive nature of "acousticality," reasoning that the visual realm is much easier to consume and commodify. The risk of acousticality lies in the challenge of engaging speech that is foreign, seemingly devoid of logic, or lacking clear signals and receivers. Therefore, these instances of inarticulacy carry such risks; they also contain revelatory and transformative potential for both the speaker and listener. Thus Mackey's texts explain how music functions rhetorically by reconciling experiences with both sound and language. For example, when N. discusses the music of Al Green in relation to Anthony Heilbut's *The Gospel Sound*, he utilizes Heilbut's description of the gospel sound as "a wordless moan" capable of rendering the indescribable in ways that words can't begin to tell.[55] He reasons that Green's moaning signifies that "the falsetto explores a redemptive, unworded realm—a meta-word, if you will—where the implied critique or the momentary eclipse of the word curiously rescues, restores and renews it: new word, new world."[56] Mackey's positing of an "unworded realm" and "meta-word" gestures toward a deeper notion of how forms of seemingly unintelligible communication, like music at times, are actually critical to expressing the surplus of human emotion.

Bass Cathedral features instances where words and sentences literally float out of the musicians' instruments as ghost-like figures in moments of sonic apparition. The first appearance of these musical phantasms comes from the band's bass player, Aunt Nancy, during one of her solos at a concert as "time-lapse translations of thoughts and feelings."[57] The appearance of this musical-ghost-text is Mackey's way of transcribing how music is rhetorical. Music causes its performers and listeners to grapple with emotions and experiences in profound and unexpected ways. Within these episodes of musical performance, Aunt Nancy attempts to find resolution with the events from her past by reexamining them through music and reorienting herself to these events through improvisation; this includes improvising her sense of being in the world.

Everything about jazz, including its structure, style, performance, and culture, engenders a radical practice of imagination and creativity. Coltrane's, with *Supreme* as the apex, rearticulates pain, anguish, joy, love, and salvation in experimental, intellectual, and mystical registers. The most radical art is not protest art but works that take us to another place and envision a different way of seeing and feeling.[58] Coltrane's freedom in sound provides another way of conceptualizing freedom itself. Additionally, his work reveals a continual attempt to reinvent his sound and, consequently, himself.[59]

Another way of accounting for the impact of major musicians like Coltrane is through comparison with other musicians similarly praised for their virtuosity, such as nineteenth-century violinist Niccolò Paganini. Virtuosity itself functions as a performance that transfigures cultural ideals.[60] Paganini's violin playing personified the Romantic ideals of artistry and human agency, and his "expressive force" was integral

A (Rhetorical) Love Supreme 119

to creating a unique sense of "communitas," whereby audiences became unified in the celebration of the performance and, vicariously, realized heroic achievement during a period of great political unrest.[61] Granting that instrumental music has propositional dimensions and embedded commentary on social issues, the "musical enthymeme" is an implied argument encoded in the tonal structure of a piece. However, implicit musical claims can become explicit when heard within the sonic milieu of a particular community.

Coltrane's *Supreme* also created a sense of "communitas" upon its release, and his virtuosic display of improvisation functioned as a particular kind of ethos. He had the credibility to unify disparate sensibilities in the African American community during a period of great social upheaval. Although scholars like Herman Gray urge caution when making Coltrane an emblem of political radicalism and modern Black collective consciousness, Coltrane's lack of explicit political affiliation does not make his work less political.[62] On the contrary, it allowed for broader appeal and unifying power. While interviewing him in 1966, Frank Kofsky mentioned that a friend of his saw Coltrane at one of Malcolm X's speeches. Coltrane responded by stating that he was quite impressed with the speech. When Kofsky asked Coltrane if the issues voiced by Malcolm X were related to the new developments in jazz, Coltrane replied that the music was "an expression of the human heart" and that it "does express just what is happening."[63] Kofsky then asked Coltrane directly about the term "new Black music" and its appropriateness for describing his music. Coltrane, as with many other jazz artists, rejected the use of that label for his music or that of his peers. Kofsky then pressed Coltrane further on this point by referencing other musicians who were clear about their intentions to use music to engage the political and social issues raised by Malcom X. When asked if those ideas were important to him, Coltrane replied, "They're definitely important." However, when Kofsky attempted to make direct connections between these issues and Coltrane's music, Coltrane remarked:

> I make a conscious attempt, I think I could say truthfully that in music I make, or I have tried to make, consciously, an attempt to change . . . to change what I've found in music, you see. And, in other words, I tried to say, "Well, *this*, I feel, could be better, you

see, in my opinion, so I will try to do this to make it better." And this is what I feel that we feel in any situation that we find in our lives—when there's something we feel should be better, we exert an effort to try and make it better. So it's the same socially, musically, politically, in any department of your life.[64]

When Kofsky once again referred to other musicians who saw their music as a tool to change society, Coltrane suggested that music "can create the initial thought patterns that create the changes in the thinking of the people."[65] Additionally, Coltrane saw jazz as the expression of "higher ideals" and "brotherhood," which, when embraced, would solve the problems of war and poverty. Asked about the influence of Africa and Asia on jazz, Coltrane revealed that he intended to make a trip to Africa to "gather whatever I can find, particularly the musical sources."[66] Later on in the interview, Kofsky asked Coltrane if he were willing to begin engaging audiences directly, outside of his music. Coltrane acknowledged this desire and replied: "you can't ram philosophies down anybody's throat—and the music is enough! You know, and that's philosophy. But I think the best thing I can do at this time is to try to get myself in shape, you know, and know myself. If I can do that, then I'll just play, you see, and leave it at that. . . . And I think they'll get it, because music goes a long way—and it really is—it can influence."[67]

Despite Coltrane's avoidance of political affiliations, he was clear, as his comments indicate, about his intentions to use his music to influence people. Although he attended, as far as we know, only one speech by Malcolm X, he played benefit concerts for both Civil Rights and Black Nationalist organizations.[68] He composed the song "Alabama"—as "talking" an instrumental piece as there is—in response to the bombing of the Sixteenth Street Baptist Church in Birmingham by white supremacists. The song was modeled after the speech given by Dr. Martin Luther King Jr. at one of the funerals for the young girls killed in the blast. Coltrane took his appreciation for Dr. King a step further with his album *Cosmic Music* (1968), which he dedicated to him. Additionally, Coltrane composed or performed a variety of songs, such as "Dahomey Dance," "Ogunde," "Dakar," "India," and "Brazilia," that incorporate non-Western themes and ideas into his artistry and reveal sympathy for the conditions of those in other countries.

A Love Supreme gave Coltrane the status to continue extending jazz into America's discourses of race, ethnicity, multiculturalism, and internationalism with particular inflections of racial pride, resistance to oppression, and global harmony. Amiri Baraka made one of the most succinct yet pertinent remarks about Coltrane's influence: "If you can hear, this music will make you think of a lot of weird and wonderful things. You might even become one of them."[69]

5
Move On Up

The Rhetorical Mastery of Mahalia Jackson

Martin Luther King Jr.'s speech at the March on Washington in 1963, one of the most iconic moments of African American rhetoric, could have turned out much differently without the assistance of Mahalia Jackson, the "Queen of Gospel Music," and her earnest plea, in the course of it, to "Tell them about the dream, Martin!" However, her value to the development of African American rhetoric extends beyond this exceptional moment. In fact, her performance of the songs "How I Got Over" and "I've Been Buked and I've Been Scorned," contributed on their own to the emotional and spiritual energy buzzing in the atmosphere that day. In addition to her activism during the Civil Rights movement, Jackson's mastery of the gospel sound became a critical element of the Black freedom struggle. This chapter examines the rhetoric of Jackson and the larger role of gospel music in public discourse. Jackson's unique sound became an ideological and religious site of consensus, as well as a sonic commonplace, between various strands of Black music. Jackson's virtuosic performances combined the most central characteristics of Black music (melodic and rhythmic improvisation, blues tonalities, musical narrative, and highly expressive vocal timbres) with socially conscious spirituality and powerful acts of personal testimony. Thus in addition to her worldwide renown as the Queen of Gospel Music, and one of the most admired women of her generation, Jackson should also be recognized, as I hope to show, as a superior rhetorician, equal to King, of the African American rhetorical tradition.[1]

Jackson's oeuvre brings to the surface myriad tensions permeating African American culture over class, gender, and the sacred and secular. Her work also outlines the contentious struggle within the Black church between a focus on individual salvation versus the collective liberatory struggle against racial oppression. Although King is usually considered the figure through which such fracturing was made whole, I argue that Jackson's music was just as critical to imagining this duality as a complete praxis. Jackson's style of performance bridges the sanctified and Holy Ghost–filled tradition of Black gospel singing and the blues idiom found in the tradition of blues women such as Bessie Smith and Ma Rainey. Although Jackson never sacrificed her religious devotion, her work reflects the fluidity of sacred and secular performance found elsewhere in the African diaspora and combines it with the kind of soul-stirring power that caused Mary Lou Williams to say, "that woman makes cold chills run up and down my spine," an experience no doubt shared by many of her listeners.[2] Jackson's music embodies the fusion of these two musical traditions and functions as a sonic corollary to the social consolidation and political activation of the Black church of the 1950s and 1960s.

There are six dimensions of Jackson's artistry and rhetorical practice that combine to make a complex, career-spanning rhetorical strategy, and these will structure my argument. The first dimension is Jackson's personal background and musical roots. Beyond biography I provide a specific description of Jackson's style of performance and offer some context for her first successful recording, "Move On Up a Little Higher." The second dimension is Jackson's interactions with the Black church and Black audiences. The third dimension of Jackson's rhetorical practice has to do with the complicated dynamics of her gender and personal relationships and their interaction with Black church cultures. The fourth dimension involves Jackson's international audience reception; I pay particular attention to the impact of her music on audiences who were mostly non–English speaking and unfamiliar with African American culture and history but no less intrigued by her artistry. The fifth dimension has to do with how Jackson harnessed the power of cultural and spiritual authenticity—her ethos. This part of the discussion will explore Jackson's delicate balance of audience expectations and authenticity as well as her fluid movement between sacred and secular culture and her relationship with blues and gospel music. Jackson also navigated competing, and sometimes contradictory, interests of the music industry while maintaining her reputation as a pious and devout servant of the church. The final dimension is Jackson's direct civil rights activism, a product of both her political commitments and her personal experiences of racism. These experiences, as I will show, were inseparable from her success with white audiences. I conclude the chapter by emphasizing Jackson's ability to theorize an explicit rhetorical project for her artistry that reflects considerable critical and theological innovation.

Origins and Musical Roots

Raised in New Orleans, the birthplace of jazz and blues, Jackson could not escape being inundated with musical influences as diverse as Ma Rainey and Joe King Oliver. Funerals, picnics, fish fries, and lodge parties incorporated the rich sounds of brass bands while artists such as Jelly Roll Morton performed in local cafés and cabarets. No area of her community went untouched by some sort of musical accompaniment. Jackson described it as almost inescapable: "You couldn't help but hear blues—all through the thin partitions of the houses, through the open windows, up and down the street. I don't sing the blues myself—and I don't sing in night clubs or places where blues are played—but you've got to know what the blues meant to all of us then. The Negroes all over the South kept these blues playing to take our minds off our burdens."[3] Immersion in the blues was not merely a matter of cultural surroundings but was, in fact, equivalent to a sustained study of a secular musical form. These experiences were critical to the mastery demonstrated in her performances, which we can thus understand as a product of rigorous study and practice in addition to natural talent. Although Jackson often sought to downplay this dimension of her craft, which I will discuss later, conceptualizing Black music as a discipline worthy of deep study was, and remains, a critical component of the political and social context of the music's production and consumption by Black audiences.

Jackson's performance style presents a unique fusion of the musical influences of her youth. Elliott Beal, a childhood friend and fellow performer in the children's choir that served as the genesis of Jackson's career, described an extremely active musical life for children in their neighborhood, as it was common to perform outside of church services for other communal events. Although church elders publicly frowned upon the blues and jazz, a strict prohibition was almost impossible considering that in New Orleans even the most mundane activities, such as buying fruits and vegetables, could be accompanied by musical performances by the salesmen. Beal further explained that as children they "couldn't help but get caught up in that Ragtime Jazz" and that they would "listen behind [their] parents' back if [they] could get away with it, and sometimes [they sang] jazz at birthday parties."[4] Beal's account of his youthful experiences with Jackson provides an important counter-narrative to Jackson's many attempts to downplay the complex musical experiences that became the foundation of her artistry, with lines such as "I just took what I'd heard all my life, and sang it."[5]

Jackson sought solace in her family's church at a young age, and her level of devotion and sacrifice to the cause of advancing the word of God quickly earned the respect of her local community in New Orleans. Additionally, Jackson's adolescence was shaped by racial segregation, extreme poverty, and the loss of her mother around the age of five. Although she was adopted by her aunt and namesake, Mahala Clark ("Aunt Duke"), when Jackson sang songs such as "Sometimes I Feel Like a Motherless Child," her voice resonated with the power of her own personal experiences as well as the pain and sorrow of the Black experience. Her ability to imbue her artistry with the weight of such experiences, empowered by her faith in the Holy Ghost, led to the kinds of performances that would leave audiences in trancelike states of euphoria.[6] Jackson once remarked, "Sometimes when I am singing, I become a complete instrument to be used. I reach a higher realm and something divine, a spirit, takes possession of my body."[7]

Like many other African Americans during the era of the Great Migration, Jackson left the south for Chicago in search of better opportunities during the 1920s as a teenager. Her desire to become a nurse was quickly put on hold by the realities of harsh economic conditions. When Jackson joined a choir after arriving in Chicago, Greater Salem Baptist, she was quickly promoted to lead soloist as word of her talent began to spread. Jackson's first professional exposure began as a member of one of the first gospel groups, the Johnson Brothers. As Jackson described it, many churches were reeling from the effects of the Great Depression and looked to performance groups like theirs as a means to raise church revenue. These conditions created an opportunity for the group to travel widely across the region and perform for a range of churches belonging to a variety of denominations. As this pattern was duplicated by other rising gospel acts, the music became a powerful force of consensus by elevating shared worship practices and beliefs over denominational differences. Moreover, the compositional and sonic advances of gospel music awakened a new generation of listeners to the kinetic energy and innovation in Black sacred music. In this way the continuity of the sonic Black lexicon enabled the interplay between gospel music and the blues to be immensely generative for artists on both sides of the aisle.

Eventually breaking with the Johnson Brothers and performing on her own, the next evolution in Jackson's career came when she began her collaboration with musician and composer Thomas Dorsey. Regarded as the father of gospel music for genre-defining compositions such as "Precious Lord, Take My Hand" and "Peace in the Valley," Dorsey began his career as "Georgia Tom," the pianist and leader of Ma Rainey's blues band. Following the death of his wife and son, Dorsey devoted his craft solely to gospel music and brought the blues idiom to bear on the sacred music of the Black church. Given Jackson's talent and familiar blues impulse, their collaborations, which included Dorsey's business partner, vocalist Sallie Martin, proved to be paradigm-shifting.

"Gospel with a Bounce"

Jackson's vocal style can be described as the modernization of Black "surge singing," but this style has also been referred to as "lining-out," "long-meter," or "Dr. Watts," in reference to Dr. Isaac Watts (1674–1748) and his widely popular hymns. Ethnomusicologists began paying explicit attention to this style of singing for its similarities to a style of congregational singing that began in Scotland during the seventeenth century, which featured "lining," the singing of each line of a psalm before it is sung by the larger congregation or choir. This method of singing aided congregations where literacy was scarce and is purported to have been introduced to African Americans sometime around 1750. Because of its similarities with the African tradition of call and response and vocal ornamentation, this style offered a vehicle for the larger task of merging African diasporic traditions with Western Christian hymns and liturgy.[8] As this style took root in African American congregations, the lining-out practice diminished in service of a focus on ornamentation and rhythmic flair, or "surging."

128 Chapter 5

The melodic and tonal inflections performed by Jackson reflect the kinds of modernizations that made Black gospel music stand out from any other kind of American sacred music. When ethnomusicologist William Tallmadge interviewed Jackson about her style of singing and her knowledge of the lining-out tradition in Black congregations, Jackson confirmed that prior to more modernized stylings of Black gospel music, she had sung in the style of "Dr. Watts." Tallmadge includes the following transcription of Jackson's modern stylistic fusion (see figure 14):

Figure 14. "Amazing Grace" transcribed by William H. Tallmadge (1961), *Mahalia Jackson* (Apollo, LP201). Thirty seconds singing time.

As one of the earliest transcriptions of Jackson's style of singing, Tallmadge isolates many of the qualities of Jackson's style of performance that made her sound distinctive: rhythmic phrasing, dynamics, note selection, and style. More important, it is a transcription of Jackson performing for a live audience: a setting that would prompt a much more expressive performance than the constraints of a recording session allowed and would be more reflective of the Mahalia Jackson her audiences most often experienced. The rhythmic phrasing, ornamentation, vibrato, pitch, and timbre were communicative both musically and symbolically. African American listeners, particularly those within Black church communities, were able to interpret the simultaneous musical innovation and a bold embrace of what felt like a truly authentic approach to Black sacred musical performance. It was precisely this mixture of characteristics that led to Jackson's popularity.

Jackson began recording solo records for Decca in 1937 but, due to poor sales and promotion outside of Chicago, she did not record again for almost a decade. Yet Jackson's profile continued to rise as a highly sought-after artist and headliner at Black Baptist conventions. Jackson began recording with Apollo Records in 1947, and her recording of W. Herbert Brewster's "Move On Up a Little Higher," released as a double-sided single by Apollo Records in 1948, became the first chart-topping song for the genre of gospel music (see figure 15).[9]

Figure 15. Excerpt from "Move On Up a Little Higher." Rev. W. Herbert Brewster. Alfred Publishing Company (1946).

The political impulse of "Move On Up" would not go unnoticed by a Black America bracing itself for a new generation of freedom struggles. However, it was Jackson's interpretation of the song and her style of vocal performance that led to its improbable success. The degree of improvisation and ornamentation can be seen by comparing Brewster's version to a transcription of Jackson's interpretation (see figure 16).

"Move On Up" features a rhythmic, New Orleans–flavored improvisatory impulse of melodies that became symbolic of the power and force Mahalia brought to her vocal performances. (Even the musicians backing her up on the recording, pianist James Lee and organist "Blind" James Francis, were New Orleans natives.) Figure 16 features a transcription of Jackson at around the timestamp of 1:46. At this point in the song, Jackson starts heading toward the climax of the vamp section (repeated chord progression). The abundance of dotted eighth notes marks the heightened rhythmic feel of the song. What makes this part distinctive is

Figure 16. Excerpt from transcription of Mahalia Jackson's recording of "Move On Up a Little Higher." Pt. 2. *The Original Apollo Sessions.* Couch and Madison Partners, 2006.

the improvisatory elements as well as the emotional force Jackson brings to the recording. There's a growling and bluesy edge to her delivery that stands out in addition to a skillful use of dynamics.

"Move On Up" became the first Black gospel song to reach a million sales, outselling all the other genres of music produced on the Apollo label, which included jazz, pop, and rhythm and blues.[10] This song is important not only for its financial and cultural success but also because it marks the moment when Jackson "moved on up" from a regional singing sensation to an artist leading the entire genre of gospel music. Emblematic of Jackson's distinctive style, "Move On Up a Little Higher" would become somewhat of a calling card throughout the rest of her career, cementing her status as a gospel artist and forever linking her to a rising political consciousness of the Black masses. The song imagines the joy of reaching the heavenly hereafter and relishes the anticipation of finally marching "all around God's altar." In the tradition of the jazz funeral and second-line parades, it reframes death as a celebratory homecoming while simultaneously pointing to a sociopolitical telos of liberation through its not-so-subtle reliance on the African American rhetorical tradition of signification, which associates movement or ascension of some kind with escaping oppression and racial uplift:

> I'm gonna move up a little higher
> Gonna meet ol' man Daniel
> I'm gonna move up a little higher
> Gonna meet the Hebrew Children
> I'm gonna move up a little higher
> Gonna meet Paul and Silas
> I'm gonna move on up a little higher
> Gonna meet my friends and kindred
> I'm gonna move on up a little higher
> Gonna meet my loving mother
> I'm gonna move on up a little higher
> Gonna meet that Lily of the Valley
> I'm gonna feast with the Rose of Sharon[11]

Jackson often described her experiences in church as the source of her artistic style, especially her rhythmic innovation, which she would commonly refer to as her "bounce."[12] In fact, "gospel with a bounce," an early phrase used to describe Jackson's unique approach to vocal performance and gospel music, became the title of a series of articles celebrating her success on radio. These articles were also keen to note the improvisatory nature of her performances, noting that when performing the same song twice, Jackson's versions could vary between forty and fifty seconds in length.[13] Similar to Mary Lou Williams, Jackson explained her improvisatory inclinations as an extension of a long tradition of Black music:

> I know now that another great influence in my life was the Sanctified, or Holiness, churches the Negroes had in the South. Right next door to our house there was a Sanctified church, and everybody in there sang and clapped and stomped their feet. They gave

> their songs a real powerful beat, a rhythm that came from way back in slavery times and probably before that from Africa. We Baptists sang real sweet and we did beautiful things with our hymns and anthems; but when those Sanctified people lit into "I'm So Glad Jesus Lifted Me" they sang out with a real jubilant expression. I believe the blues and that rock-and-roll stuff, all of them got their beat from the Sanctified-church people.[14]

From Jackson's statements, we can extrapolate her theorizing of the Black sonic lexicon, including the performative techniques for its operationalization. For example, Jackson explained the selection of certain songs over others for her performances as a process of structural and communicative alignment: "I say this out of my heart. A song must do something for me as well as for the audience that hears it. If a song doesn't have a message for me in it, I can't make myself get the sense of it."[15] When expounding on her highly expressive physical movements and style of performance, Jackson once asked, "How can you sing prayerfully of heaven and earth and all God's wonders without using your hands? I want my hands, my feet, my whole body to say all this is in me. The Lord doesn't like us to act dead. If you feel it, pat your feet a little—dance to the glory of the Lord!"[16] Jackson understood that production and consumption of her music constituted what scholars in sonic studies have referred to as an embodied sonic experience.[17] Jackson's body-centric musical practices troubled the boundaries of gendered performance expectations and in turn performance conventions within the Black church. Robert Anderson, one of Jackson's pianists and leader of the celebrated gospel group the Caravans, spoke explicitly about this dimension of Jackson's innovation: "Mahalia had a beautiful shape, and with her style of singing she was more or less a sexy singer of the gospel because Mahaila would move her body . . . and this would intrigue the people. Mahalia was the first one to bring in the beat and bounce in gospel music. . . . She was the first person to bring in the rhythm and the beat and the feel of gospel music."[18]

Jackson's artistry highlighted what theologian James Cone described as the rejection of Western cultures' distinction between the spirit and body by Black people who embraced the "spiritual function of the human body," for whom a history of physical oppression summons "inherent power in bodily expressions of love."[19] Although the politics of respectability often led more conservative wings of the Black church to resist such expression—more so rhetorically than in actual practice—Jackson offered her own interpretation of biblical scripture as a defense: "I don't think that people dancing and having a nice time, and going to the theatre are sinning. What I think is a sin is going against the commandment to love thy God with all your heart and love thy neighbor as thyself."[20]

Jackson theorized the communicative power of her music and worked intentionally to leverage that power for the causes of spiritual and social freedom, later stating that "it all depends upon what condition or frame of mind I'm in. Songs fit my occasion"—a clear indication of rhetorical savvy.[21] Her commitment to sonic persuasion remained tethered to a faith-driven, social optimism despite her awareness of this modality's limits. Further elaborating the purpose of her music in an interview with the *Ladies' Home Journal* in 1963, Jackson reasoned, "It's not that you're lifted out of segregation or poverty or sickness, but [music] lifts your mind above, that you can endure things. It gives hope that whatever may betide, whatever is wrong in the neighborhood or the world, tomorrow will be better."[22] In a later statement of her rhetorical intentions, Jackson remarked in the *Himmat, Bombay Weekly* that, "a song must do something for me as well as for the people that hear it. I can't sing a song that doesn't have a message. If it doesn't have the strength, it can't lift you."[23]

If Black preaching is one of the foundations of African American rhetorical traditions, Jackson understood her music as participating in this tradition, stating, "the basic way that I sing today [is] from hearing the way the preacher would preach in a cry, in a moan, [or] would shout sort of like in a chant . . . a groaning sound which would penetrate my heart."[24] Jackson's conception of a sound that "penetrates the soul" holds potential for expanding theoretical constructs of listening.[25] The Black sonic lexicon is responsive to how "dominant listening practices accrue—and change—over time, as well . . . as how the . . . culture exerts pressure on individual listening practices."[26] This idea conjoins with a notion of Jackson's artistry wherein Black music and its attendant listening practices, in this case the sacred music of the Black church, works as a countercultural listening practice for liberatory ends via sounds that challenge social hierarchies. Although her dream of opening a music school never materialized during her lifetime, these ideas would undoubtedly have been at the center of her pedagogy.[27]

Black Church Cultures and Black Audiences

It wasn't just Jackson's vocal talents that made her so popular in the Black church community. Jackson forged a style of performance that embraced African American vernacular expression. However, Jackson met considerable resistance to this style early in her career. Throughout the myriad interviews Jackson gave during her career, including those for her biographies, she only describes a single instance of seeking out vocal lessons for traditional, classical concert singing. Jackson recounts that the instructor ended the lesson immediately, claiming, "white people would never understand you." While Jackson describes this incident with evident irony due to her eventual success, it stands out as emblematic of a particular kind of sonic disciplining that she repeatedly resisted.[28] Jennifer Stoever refers to this kind of disciplining as a product of what she terms "the sonic color line," the dominant listening practices that normalize certain associations between race and sound that lead to a distinct racial hierarchy of correctness.[29] Thus whiteness, and the variety of sounds that become coded as white, within the context of music and performance could only be a product of "cultivation" and study. Jackson rejected such standards, including the normative rules for breathing, dynamics, vibrato, and pronunciation. A failure to acquiesce to such requirements prohibited performers from accessing the respectability and social capital that would allow their virtuosity to be respected as acts of brilliance instead of mere "natural ability," another code word for Blackness. This resistance was not lost on Jackson's listeners, as it functioned as a signifier of her cultural authenticity.

The contrast between "I'm gonna move up" and "I'm going to move up" represented one of many shifts in style away from traditional Western choral performance for which she faced a great deal of criticism during the early stages of her career. In fact, the onslaught of such criticism led to Jackson's robust defense of her accent, speech patterns, and use of African American vernacular terms. Just as scholars in sociolinguistics, such as Geneva Smitherman, were beginning to publish spirited defenses of African American language practices, Jackson took part in a rich tradition of defending African American vernacular expression, sometimes from other segments of the Black community who were leery of reinforcing negative stereotypes, particularly those that equated African American vernacular with inferior intelligence.[30] In one instance, she remarked, "I believe in being completely natural. I don't ever polish things up. That's why I sing spirituals in dialect. That's the way they originated. We should be proud of our dialect, not ashamed. It's all the more to be proud that we came from such humble beginnings."[31] Biographer Laurraine Goreau noted that Jackson encountered a great deal of ridicule from "Society Negros" who made fun of her because of the way she talked following her move to Chicago. Jackson recounted, "I did have that New Orleans brogue—and I still have it. Back home, people didn't worry about their diction, or their words. They just went on and sang. If you understood it, you understood it; and if you didn't, well, they had felt it, you see."[32]

The rhetorical and cultural implication of Jackson's stylistic choices caught the attention of other authoritative voices within the Black community. In one of the many columns he wrote for the *Chicago Defender*, Langston Hughes explored the intersection of music and vernacular expression with the help of his fictitious friend "Simple." Hughes specifically refers to Jackson in addition to providing his own humorous and spirited defense of "Music He Can Understand." Proclaiming his disdain for "concert singers," or vocal performers who adopt the style of traditional Western classical music, Simple remarks, "I will take a good old group of gospel singers for mine any time. Gimme Mahalia Jackson singing 'Even Me' or the righteous Martin Singers . . . and I will plank down my dollar-ten anytime."[33] Hughes then counters in his own voice taking up the opposing argument on behalf of concert singers. After Hughes asks Simple about the source of his displeasure, he further explains his reasoning: "'They say "haw-ve" instead of "have," and "hawnd" instead of "hand,"' said Simple. 'When Mahalia sings "hand" she sings "hand"—not "hawnd." And she can really sing, "Precious Lord, Take My Hand," too—not "hawnd."'"[34] Simple then goes on to offer a recounting of his last attendance at a concert filled with complaints about his troubles understanding classical music performed in European languages ("I swear she was singing as if she had mush in her mouth") as well as the organization of the program ("Why couldn't she put some colored songs at the front of the program instead of them foreign things not a human soul can understand?"). However, even the spirituals on the program disappoint Simple because "they were nothing like Mahalia's 'Move On Up a Little Higher.'"

Unfortunately, not all segments of the Black church community were as accepting of Jackson's style of performance during the early part of her career as Hughes. Prior to Jackson's mainstreaming of her vernacular expressions and such highly rhythmic and physically expressive styles of worship, such performances received harsh criticism from more conservative, middle-class sectors of the Black church community. This criticism was a reflection of the many denominational and sociocultural divides Jackson's artistry would eventually traverse.[35] Differences in worship style were more than a matter of aesthetics, indexing sharp theological and cultural disagreements.[36] Jackson's presence challenged the traditionally marginalized role of women in the church as well as the church's ongoing negotiation of its relationship with its secular community. For example, in one instance Jackson was rebuked from the pulpit by a minister for bringing what he labeled "jazz" into the church. Jackson responded by confronting the minister in front of the congregation, exclaiming, "I had been reading the Bible everyday most of my life, and there was a Psalm that said, 'Oh clap your hands, all ye people! Shout unto the Lord with the voice of triumph!' It was what the Bible told me to do."[37] Despite serious objections from various seats of power within the Black church, particularly from Baptists, the denomination of Jackson's church in Chicago, Jackson's style of praise was consistent with the traditions of African diasporic religious practices in New Orleans.[38] Jackson's unwillingness to compromise her style of performance or speech resonated deeply with listeners who felt similarly restricted.

Conservative sectors of the Black church understood the performance of religious piety and devotion as precious cultural capital. Even the slightest deviation from the worship practices of white churches could be interpreted as theological incompetence amongst Black clergy, or, worse, proof of primitivism in the congregations. Therefore, the double consciousness of this portion of Black church saw protecting its image and reputation as critical to a particular program of racial uplift, a view that linked model citizenship with performing model discipleship, a means of securing spiritual salvation as well as gaining acceptance from white communities. Ironically, it would be Jackson's performances that ultimately legitimatized the ethos of Black Christians at home and abroad due to their authenticity and devout spirituality, introducing audiences around the world to the sonic wonders of the Black church. However, the shaming of Black cultural religious practices within Black churches had much to do with the politics of respectability and internalized shame, one more iteration of Geneva Smitherman's discussion of the "push-pull" pendulum of African American culture affecting rhetorical expression. There is a constant tension between the pull of integration and assimilation and the push toward Black nationalism and Afrocentrism. This pendulum explains the instances in which Black communities either pull closer to Eurocentric sensibilities and aesthetics in order to gain acceptance in America or push away those characteristics in favor of greater communal solidarity, Afrocentric sensibilities, and Black aesthetics.[39] Jackson addressed this idea specifically in an interview with her friend, radio personality, and music promoter Studs Terkel:

> When it comes to singing anthems, that's something else. Like the Hallelujah chorus from *The Messiah*. But you have to have the right voices, good strong young voices. Our older people used to sing them in churches when I first came up to Chicago. They seemed uncomfortable. I know they'd have felt a lot better with spirituals or gospel songs or just plain hymns. They seemed so stiff, not free. No matter what kind of songs people sing, it must come natural to them. They shouldn't just try to sing something just because they feel it's the proper thing to do. Then the real person gets lost. He's away from his roots.[40]

Jackson followed this explanation by commenting on the Fisk Jubilee Singers, crediting them with popularizing the spirituals despite the alterations they made to their performance. According to Jackson, "They took out the beat that the Holiness people gave them and cultivated it. They concertized them, prettied them up. Not much feeling, but, oh, it sounded so sweet!"[41] Jackson's shift in style represented a conscious return to the roots of Black performance and the refusal to conform to Eurocentric stylistic preferences.

However, the intensity of the rebuke aimed at Jackson was much more than a product of bruised Black, middle-class sensibilities. Jackson's performances brought to the surface a deeper identity crisis within the Black church caused by conflicting demands from both whites and Blacks. The desire to protect the image and purity of the Black church was not only a product of religious orthodoxy but also a reaction to a long history of defending the church against conflicting claims from whites. On one hand, Black churches were viewed as primitive, profane, and overly emotional at the expense of true biblical devotion. Such views were forged during the history of slavery, where African diasporic religions and worship styles were castigated by white clergymen and slave owners as blasphemous and contrary to Christian doctrine. On the other hand, there was the idea that African Americans possess an innate, superior spirituality. This idea of "innate spirituality," a product of the Romantic racism found in works such as Harriet Beecher Stowe's *Uncle Tom's Cabin*, was often juxtaposed as the antithesis to that of colder, materialistic, and rationalistic whites who were anxious about the future of American morality and virtues, particularly after the Second World War. The subtext of such racist claims was that what Blacks supposedly lacked in intelligence they gained in spirituality and emotional conviction.

Given the historical tradition of framing religion as the crucial common ground between Black and white communities, protecting the image of the Black church and the legitimacy of Black religious expression has always had high stakes. Scholars such as Curtis J. Evans have argued that this history has burdened Black religion with a delicate balancing act performed under the white gaze, a performance that Jackson's artistry began to transfigure.[42] Jackson's ability to establish a core audience of Black congregants ushered in a new wave of cross-denominational identification with the Black church as a cultural and historical site of political and theological consensus. This coalition was fortified early in her career by a shared enthusiasm for gospel music as a unifying discourse that spoke to the essence of Black religion itself.

The Performance of Gender and Personal Relationships

The controversy surrounding Jackson's style of performance was also shaped by her appearance, marital status, and gender, which was frequently discussed in the Black, white, and international press. Jackson's physical appearance was often used to gauge her religious devotion. For example, many reviews of her performances in mainstream, white publications took considerable interest in her "homely face," like this one in the *Saturday Evening Post*:

> This woman, with the wonderfully homely face that gives you an occasional glimpse of her soul, packed the auditorium to near capacity, it was one of the largest crowds I've seen at the school. And when you see this woman perform, you can easily understand why great crowds gather at her feet. She radiates a perfect faith and shouts her gospel singing with the glad heart of an old-time Baptist evangelist. Her voice is impressive as it is; but that expressive face is quite a thing to behold. Some fundamentalist Protestants may question her treatment of sacred music, which carries a strong hint of Jazz, or even the blues. But she is not a blues singer. The blues are for the sad and the lost. Mahalia has given religion and hope to the blues.[43]

It was also common for media commentary to introduce Jackson as divorced, childless, and lonely while noting that she was an excellent cook and performed her own cleaning and domestic duties.[44] Additionally, her appearance and personal life were leveraged against the tension surrounding the "strong hint of jazz or even the blues" in her style of performance. Jackson was often confronted with a considerable amount of pressure to discuss her romantic life in the press because her status as a single woman performing Christian music drew continued scrutiny. In a 1959 interview entitled "I Can't Stop Singing," Jackson was candid about both the class and gender dynamics involved in the dissolution of her first marriage and the challenges confronting her choice of vocation:

> Isaac loved me, but he didn't like my songs. He thought gospel singing wasn't educated. He wanted me to take voice training to

become a concert singer. He'd say, "Why do you want to waste your wonderful voice on that stuff! It's not art!" We finally came apart over it. A man who marries a woman doesn't want her running around all over the country either—even for the Lord. But sometimes you feel something deep down inside you that has to come out—that was the way my gospel singing was for me. I felt I had to express it or be torn apart by it; and finally, this feeling ended my marriage.[45]

Jackson's status as a single woman without children, combined with the confidence and strength she was able to project with her music, struck a powerful chord with women who took notice of the inherent challenges of her racial and gendered subjectivity. A previously untranslated fan letter within a trove of archival materials related to Jackson's international tours offers concrete evidence of the kinds of emotional connections Jackson was able to forge with her listeners abroad. A woman from Austria, Herta Dimmer, wrote Jackson about her sympathetic understanding of Jackson's loneliness as a divorced woman. Dimmer begins her letter stating, "You have taken on a very beautiful and humane task; you are needed by thousands and mean much to these people. And yet, you feel lonely."[46] While detailing a litany of abuse she endured from her husband and surrounding family, Dimmer remarks, "My family demands everything from me and I am not in the position to pump even more out of myself."[47] Dimmer constructs this comparison in an attempt to express that the domestic freedom Jackson enjoys is worthy of envy. Dimmer then writes, "I have written all this just to tell you, that one can have a family and yet be without a home and all alone. For me there is no independence—freedom, and if one knows this, then one also knows it is a sad and hard fate."[48]

International Sensation

When President Richard Nixon called Jackson "a magnetic ambassador," he was acknowledging her infectious charisma on the international stage as an ambassador of goodwill for the United States during her tours abroad.[49] Jackson's reception by international audiences forms an important chapter in the much-discussed history of African American artists abroad. The worldwide embrace of Black music helped to bring much needed attention to the plight of African Americans and, as was the case for Duke Ellington, Louis Armstrong, and Dizzy Gillespie, Jackson's performances overseas expanded the reach of her music as well as her rhetorical project. Jackson strategically avoided criticizing racial oppression in the international press and instead relied on her sense of the universal language of musical expression to express her faith as well as truths of the Black experience in America. Pressed by an American interviewer about her experiences in other countries, Jackson admitted: "I'm a little ashamed of some of the things that happened in America. . . . I couldn't answer a lot of questions truthfully that people in Europe asked me because I feel a house divided cannot stand. . . . I haven't met any Negro yet who wants to leave America. We love America. We've been here too long to feel any other way."[50]

However, this commitment did not preclude international audiences from understanding the social importance of her artistry. For example, an unnamed critic in the Tokyo-based *Mainichi Daily News* stated that Jackson "exists not only for music lovers but for the people of the world at large. She is like the sun, giving spiritual comfort to the audience."[51] In fact, Jackson's reception went so well in some countries that there were demonstrable diplomatic impacts, such as her performance for the Empress of Japan in 1971.[52] Further, during her 1971 tour in India, which included several encore performances for the prime minister of India, Indira Gandhi, Ambassador K. B. Keating compared Jackson to Indian artists Ravi Shankar and Ali Akbar Khan, stating, "There is a remarkable emotional parallel between a sitar concert by maestro [Ravi] Shankar, which I have found to be an exquisite experience, and the singing of Miss Jackson."[53] Laurraine Goreau's coverage of Jackson's performance for the empress of Japan (which also occurred in 1971) included her observation that "Mahalia turned into a national phenomenon among people who rarely understood a word." Jackson remarked, "Music helps the spirit to speak. You don't need language."[54] Proof of the diplomatic power of Jackson's performances occurred, as Goreau noted, when U.S. Ambassador Armin Meyer and his wife were invited to the palace after more than two years of seeking access. Music critics took notice of Jackson's international appeal, and many agreed with voices such as Carlton Brown, who stated that Jackson had the largest audience of any religious singer in the world. Such listeners were not hindered by a language barrier but drawn to the "purely musical quality of her performances" and the "driving, rocking, exultant style of her first Columbia album and several of her later ones—performances that rank with the greatest vocal or instrumental ones in jazz."[55]

Jackson's Strategies of Ethos Construction

Jackson's music gave her the ability to operate as an unofficial clergywoman who could speak authoritatively on spiritually. Her growing popularity combined with her facility wielding social and political power challenged patriarchal traditions of church leadership and was viewed by some as theological heterodoxy. However, such authority was not just a consequence of her success. Around the age of fourteen, Jackson was considered to have "the gift" by her community.[56] This "gift," recognized as spiritual awareness and prophetic insight, became an important component of Jackson's identity due to the sense of responsibility it implied, no doubt furthered by the biblical teaching "to whom much is given, much is required."[57] This belief culminated in an encounter in which, at the age of seventeen, Jackson's performance during a church revival service inspired a man with a life-threatening illness who was walking by on the street to be drawn into the church and receive salvation.[58] The fact that the man asked for Jackson, and not the minister, to pray with him was transformative for Jackson's sense of agency and leadership within her church community. While there may be little evidence available to validate such claims, Jackson's commitment to its veracity is important to understanding her rhetorical practices. Whether or not Jackson possessed "the gift," she operated as if it were so, and members of her audience took it to be so. Her intense, personal devotion to her faith was pivotal to her acceptance and success as a gospel artist. Jackson came to believe that she possessed a special talent for converting others, be they potential Christians or potential political allies.

Jackson's early rhetorical education also had much to do with her aunt, Mahala Clark ("Aunt Duke"). Clark belonged to several "colored women's societies" in New Orleans, and she required that Jackson serve as the secretary of each group. Jackson remarked she would "sit there and simmer and make notes while the old ladies made their motions and speeches."⁵⁹ While Jackson may have only referred to this personal history as one of the many grueling chores she was assigned as a youth, scholarship informs us that the Black women's club movement was instrumental to the political and social organizing of Black communities.⁶⁰ These organizations, such as the National Association of Colored Women, were vehicles for some of Black America's most iconic rhetoricians, such as Ida B. Wells and Mary Church Terrell. Scholars have pointed to these societies as critical sites of rhetorical education and literacy acquisition.⁶¹ Jackson spent countless hours in meetings where she would have been privy to the social and political discourses surging through the Black community as interpreted by some of the community's leading women. Additionally, biographer Mark Buford uncovered Jackson's close relationship with one of her elementary school teachers, O. C. W. Taylor, who became a prominent voice for Black liberation as the editor of the *Louisiana Weekly*, one of the first Black newspapers in the region.⁶² Therefore, it's safe to say that Jackson would have been introduced to sophisticated rhetorical practices as well as critical conversations about the role and function of media within the Black community and its potential for liberatory struggle well before her eventual migration to Chicago as a teenager.

Deborah Atwater's exploration of African American women's rhetorical practices describes the prevailing rhetorical constraint that unites Black women, despite differences in space and time, as the "driving need to establish personhood, dignity, and respect not only for themselves, but also for the men and children that they [are] close to" in an often hostile and degrading society.⁶³ Ethos, a complex term explored by scores of rhetoricians as far back as Aristotle and Isocrates, can be invoked here to name this most central problem: the way forms of gendered and racial oppression manifest themselves as barriers to women of the African diaspora being accurately seen and heard within any particular public sphere. Ethos generally refers to one's reputation, credibility, and character and the role they play in the process of persuasion. Aristotle places specific emphasis on ethos as "the most effective means of persuasion" one may possess.⁶⁴ There is no exception to Atwater's argument when it comes to Jackson, and I argue that Jackson was so aware of the importance of her ethos that she devised a complex strategy that wove together her performance practice and use of media coverage. To explain her strategy, I will show how Jackson took considerable measures to distance herself from secular music, especially the blues, in order to protect the reputation of gospel music. These measures included strict rules regarding which venues, events, and audiences were appropriate for her performances. She also used the media to advertise turning down large sums of money offered for performing blues, jazz, or Broadway music. Her highly publicized refusals were another way Jackson established her credibility and validated her spirituality and piety.

When discussing her background, Jackson often crafted a narrative to aid the construction of her ethos, which contributed significantly to the reception of her music. This narrative concerned her lack of formal musical training; she once declared, for example, "I never had a music lesson and I still can't read music. I don't know anything about chord structures; I just sing it. I never sing the same song the same way twice. I have to get my own little way in there somehow."[65] Such statements were Jackson's attempts to downplay her musical talents and minimize her facility with the Black sonic lexicon. As previously mentioned, Jackson would describe her vocal prowess as a gift from God rather than the product of years of immersion in Black musical traditions and rigorous practice. This narrative shifted the focus to her love for singing to God as the primary reason for her success and the foundation of her artistry. Framing her success this way disarmed critics who, if she claimed her talent, might suspect her of pride, or others who might want to focus their attention on her appearance or personal life. At the same time it diffused tensions surrounding her identity as a Black woman speaking authoritatively about Christianity during an era in which few Black women inside or outside of the church had access to mainstream cultural outlets.

This kind of rhetorical sophistication, a shrewd unpretentiousness cloaked in folksy humility, wasn't uncommon for Black performers of Jackson's era. As a matter of professional and personal survival, it was imperative to avoid offending white, patriarchal sensibilities. Jackson understood how her identity could, at times, place her in a perilous, rhetorical position. She often made statements exclaiming, "The Lord took me, and I was nothing, and He put me up. It can happen to you too. If the Lord can bring me this far—take me out of the washtubs and off my knees scrubbing other people's floors—then He can do as much and more for others."[66] Jackson consistently juxtaposed what she characterized as an unremarkable background against her exceptional God-given gift as both a gesture of sincere religious piety and a savvy form of engaging her listeners. However, Jackson's ability to combine such rhetorical moves with her virtuosic and genre-bending artistry were uniquely powerful.

When Jackson began to receive national acclaim as a gospel singer, her coverage in the press paid considerable attention to her refusal to leave her exclusive regimen of religious performances for more lucrative offers to join blues and swing bands. Jackson decided to contribute to this narrative with an article entitled "Why I Turned Down a Million Dollars," which was written by Jackson and published in *Tone* magazine in 1960. The article features Jackson's characterizations of such offers, including a Greenwich Village club owner's offer of five thousand dollars per week and a Broadway producer's offer of a quarter of a million dollars and her own stage show. While such accounts on their surface appear to be the normal coverage of daily celebrity activity, for Jackson they were powerful moments of ethos construction.[67] While rejecting a million-dollar offer still raises eyebrows in a twenty-first century economy, Jackson's public refusals were critical to sanctifying her public image, as they added to the sincerity and gravity of her performances. Further, the article contains several critical rhetorical maneuvers that Jackson would come to rely on as her career continued its ascendence. She begins by dramatizing the lucrative offers, stating, "I'm not going to pretend that the offers haven't excited and tempted me. After all, I came from a poverty-stricken New Orleans water-front family. During my childhood, I never had a doll or a toy."[68] Jackson then pivots to framing her desire to sing as a devotional act to God and not an attempt to "make money [her] idol." Jackson then offers a lengthy description of the lucrative offers she rejected before claiming, "I am not bragging about these offers. I simply want to point out that you can achieve success and financial independence and still keep your word to God in the face of temptation."[69] Jackson then admits to her own weakness as a child in New Orleans enticed by the blues:

> I gave in to temptation when I was a child. My parents loved God dearly. They wanted me to hear no music but his. All around me in New Orleans were the deep moving hymns—the swelling, rocking spiritual and gospel songs. I loved the hymns and gospel songs but I disobeyed my parents and listened to the blues, the sorrow songs

of my people. I heard the rich, throbbing voices of Ma Rainey, Ethel Waters, and Bessie Smith.

There was other music—the haunting rhythms of the work songs chanted by the Negro men as they sweated and strained, laying the railroad ties. The inspiration of the church songs, the haunting quality of the work songs and the wail of the blues all got mixed up together in my brain.[70]

Jackson's subtle apology works as a line of defense for other religious figures who were critical of her genre-bending performances.

However, she goes on to claim that, "I don't believe I could sing the blues." Jackson defines the blues as containing only despair, loneliness, and unhappiness, as against gospel music with its emphasis on hope and consolation. I argue that her statements had more to do with protecting herself, and the genre of gospel music, from criticism than expressing her actual beliefs. Although her "internal emphasis" was always sacred, at this time neither the Black church nor American mass media were completely ready to accept the duality of Black music, or, at the very least, make such admissions in public. Jackson frames blues and gospel as a dichotomy by narrowing the essence of the blues to despair. However, the extensive body of scholarship and discourse on the blues immediately contests this characterization and no doubt she was sensitive, on some level, to the blues' true complexity. Scholars such as Albert Murray have utilized the blues as a major thematic and hermeneutic tool to express the complexity of the Black experience in postbellum America. In Murray's *Stomping the Blues* (1976), he excoriates narrow definitions of the blues as "a type of song written in a characteristic key with melancholy lyrics and syncopated rhythms."[71] He reveals a more nuanced operation of the music as capable of expressing multiple moods such as joy and determination. He argues that "instead of melancholy and longing there is low, gravy mellowness."[72] Murray uses the examples of W. C. Handy's "The Memphis Blues," Louis Armstrong's renditions of "Memphis Blues" and "Beale Street Blues," and Count Basie's "Sent for You Yesterday" to explain the central role of dancing in blues music and to argue that the blues is neither constrained to slower tempos nor is it primarily a vocal tradition. He argues further that blues instrumentation often operates in direct contrast to the lyrics: "[what] blues instrumentation in fact does, often in direct contrast to the words, is define the nature of the response to the blues situation at hand, whatever the source. Accordingly, more often than not even as the words of the lyrics recount a tale of woe, the instrumentation may mock, shout defiance, or voice resolution and determination."[73]

Additionally, James Cone explains the symbiotic relationship between the spirituals and the blues as a product of their shared origin in West African music and its predominant characteristic of "functionality." By functionality Cone is suggesting that Black music operates at "the core of daily life," which is an Africanism that "distinguishes it from Western music and connects it with its African heritage."[74] This explanation buttresses Cone's wider theological and cultural analysis of the blues. Cone states: "The blues are 'secular spirituals'. They are secular in the sense that they confine their attention solely to the immediate and affirm the bodily expression of Black soul, including its sexual manifestations. They are spirituals because they are impelled by the same search for the truth of Black experience."[75]

Given Jackson's admitted immersion in blues music during her youth, it is safe to assume that she understood the nuances that Murray and Cone describe. Nonetheless, she repeatedly took rhetorical measures to distance gospel music from the blues. Considering the often crude characterizations of Black artists in the press during this period, the abundance of caution was to be expected. However, Cone's emphasis of the theological link between the blues and the spirituals as the "affirmation of self" and the "somebodiness of Black people" helps to ground a conception of gospel music as an interconnected genre that also seeks to preserve "the work of Black humanity through ritual and drama." The purpose of this genre is to "create the emotional forms of reference for endurance and esthetic appreciation" that, in tandem with the blues, "recognizes the painfulness of the present but refuses to surrender to its historical contradictions."[76]

While Jackson always remained true to the religious sincerity of gospel music and its teleological focus on spiritual salvation, the blues was always there lurking beneath her rich vocal vibrato, between her improvisatory phrasings, and behind her lived experiences. Although the blues contains the same musical material as gospel music in terms of melodic and rhythmic phrasing, its secular orientation has always remained an important criterion of difference. Jackson strove to maintain, and often police, the boundaries between these consanguineous genres: "The blues taught me all I know, and I respect it deeply, but too often gospels are confused with blues or jazz. They are not the same. They are from the same source, but the tempo, and even more important, the internal emphasis is quite different."[77] Jackson's use of the phrase "internal emphasis" was important to her efforts to find language that could explain how the continuity of Black music did not disturb the sacred-secular dichotomy, despite its permeable nature within the African diaspora. When questioned about this complexity, Jackson often admitted that there was much in common between the two genres musically, but there was always a caveat: "The songs I sing . . . help rekindle the faith."[78]

Jackson was also wary of the appropriation of gospel aesthetics by a cottage industry of secular entertainment venues and rhythm and blues artists seeking to capitalize on the wide popularity and financial success of gospel music through crude imitation.[79] For the press, Jackson strove to maintain a stark contrast between her work and that of secular artists in order to shift attention back to her efforts to promote gospel music.

The next rhetorical maneuver Jackson undertakes in "Why I Turned Down a Million Dollars" is to introduce a second reason why she refuses to leave gospel music by describing the "bitter fight" it took to win acceptance in the Black church. Jackson explains the resistance she and Dorsey encountered when they began performing and how lonely it was to be "pioneering" the "new" gospel music: "Gospel music—the way we sang it—was the same old church music—but with a little bounce. Sunday after Sunday, the finest preachers in the connection railed and stormed at us from their pulpits, accusing us of bringing jazz into the church. What they didn't realize—but they do now—is that gospel music isn't new. It is as old as the birth of the Savior. When Christ was born, people went forth and sang in joy."[80]

Jackson expounds on the rhetoric of gospel music while providing a theological defense of the "new" gospel through a counterlinguistic interpretation of biblical scripture that reclaims Black joy and suffering as legitimate expressions of faith. She concludes the article by stating that "the banner of Gospel singing has at last been planted solidly in the hearts and minds of the world," a treasure "which cannot be measured in dollars and cents." Yet paradoxically, her work did lead to abundant financial success.[81] It would be reasonable to conclude that such statements reveal a third layer of rhetorical calculation on Jackson's part. She understood that too much attention to material gain could be interpreted as a mark of religious insincerity. Jackson was rhetorically savvy enough to forge her own version of Christian entrepreneurism, a mixture of branding and marketing that foregrounded Christian beliefs and commitments. Jackson's career emerged during the depths of the Great Depression, a period in which the Black church increasingly relied on musical groups like the Johnson Brothers to raise capital. The financial straits of these institutions impacted how congregants thought about the intersections of capitalism and Christianity. Finding creative ways to draw potential congregants to the church, especially the youth, became imperative. At least part of the financial astuteness found in many of Jackson's financial decisions can be attributed to this wider context.[82] Jackson negotiated this fraught territory with rhetorical nuance:

> Gospel singing doesn't need any artificial phony sounds.... Gospel singing is commercial—but in its own way. If a man can till the earth to bring up vegetables and sell them and live off what he earns, it's all right. If a man can make gospel records and sell them that's all right too, but the records should be real gospel singing and real gospel singing is uplifting. I do believe gospel singing can be commercial and holy at the same time. God is that wide, that broad, he supplies all our needs.[83]

In addition to speaking frequently about gospel music and her style of singing, Jackson was often queried about the details of her personal life, including her health. Jackson was placed in the position of divulging sensitive details about her medical condition as well as the kinds of treatments she was receiving. More than providing reassurance to her fans about her well-being, Jackson turned these occasions into opportunities to display her mastery of the African American rhetorical tradition of testifying. Jackson habitually found ways to tie discussions of her health to her artistry, sometimes in unexpected ways. On September 11, 1954, Jackson authored a front-page article in the *Chicago Defender* entitled "God Spared Me to Sing," detailing the trials surrounding her ill health. Jackson begins the article describing the gravity of her experiences through biblical allegory. Jackson situates her achievement as the product of God's divine provision and then describes her harrowing journey from collapsing on stage while performing in London to being rushed back to the United States to undergo an operation for a "malignant growth." Jackson then states: "Lying on a pain-racked bed, I asked God to spare my life. But I didn't ask for selfish reasons alone. For he had shown me such wonderful grace that I wanted my life for more important reasons than just living to gratify myself. I wanted to serve Him in bigger and better ways. I wanted to rededicate myself in His army."[84]

In addition to addressing the controversy surrounding her health, the article also displays a deft packaging maneuver in the announcement of the *Mahalia Jackson Show*, a national Sunday-night radio broadcast on CBS affiliates. Jackson's appearances on the radio would "expand the advertising campaign which Christians must wage to publicize God's message."[85] Intuiting the possibility that members of her audience would view this as selling out, Jackson quickly admits that like the "concert singer who pleas with her audience to try a new cold cream" she is indeed sponsored. However, she counters that she is "sponsored by God's message" and needs her listeners' support.[86] Jackson's healing narrative anticipated negative criticism by using the theme of redemption to frame her artistry as a product of her piety and suffering. Rather than celebrating or boasting, Jackson described her radio program—a groundbreaking achievement for gospel music and one of the first of its kind for any Black woman in America—as a challenge she would accept with humility. Those resistant to hearing a Black woman with her own radio show would have to take up their grievances with the God who spared her to sing.

The Challenges of Navigating White America

Historical accounts of Jackson's relationship to other civil rights leaders, especially Martin Luther King Jr., discuss her dogged commitment to holding rallies and fundraisers to support the efforts of protesters, including raising bail money for those who were incarcerated.[87] She arguably deserves, in fact, to be recognized as a leading figure in the Civil Rights movement rather than a mere supporter, and, but for her gender, she might well be. In addition to Jackson's commitment to the collective struggle of Black communities, her efforts were, in part, a response to her own repeated experiences of racism.[88] Among the innumerable instances in which racism impacted her life, her work as a traveling performer led to dangerous interactions with police. It would be improbable that such experiences had no role in the urgency and potency of her political endeavors.[89] They also offer important context to her interactions with white audiences.

For example, in one traumatic encounter with the Louisiana State Police, Jackson was stopped in the middle of the night while she was searching for a place to sleep that would serve African Americans. As a small group of police officers surrounded her vehicle, Mahalia's attempt to perform diplomacy was met with suspicion. The officers did not believe a Black woman in the South could afford her own lavender Cadillac, therefore, it must be stolen—never mind the valid license and registration. Jackson sought to diffuse the situation quickly and put her improvisational prowess to work concocting a story that she was just returning the car to New Orleans for her "madam," Ms. Dorsey, who was currently flying home from Chicago. However, Jackson's alibi would not prevent the police from taking five hundred dollars out of her purse and arresting her anyway. She was released the next day but not without paying an additional $250 for a bogus speeding charge. Jackson left the police station grateful that she survived, as such dangerous encounters were quite common for African Americans, especially in the South.[90] Working and traveling as a Black entertainer was exceedingly hazardous, not only because of the limited number of hotels, restaurants, and gas stations restricted by Jim Crow segregation but also due to their vulnerability once removed from the protection of Black enclaves.

In many instances, Jackson was the first African American to perform in venues that were reserved for whites, and her refusal to perform for racially segregated crowds led to some of the first integrated gospel concerts in cities across the nation. Jackson understood the gravity of her position as well as the rhetorical possibilities accruing with each publicized instance of racial integration. One such occasion was captured by the press in 1961. After Jackson performed to a racially mixed crowd in Knoxville, Tennessee, making her the first African American to perform in the town's civic auditorium, she also became the first person of color allowed to sleep in a downtown hotel. The hotel initially sought to cancel the reservation when it discovered Jackson would be their guest.[91] In addition to capturing the financial and racial stakes surrounding Jackson's performance, the way in which the Knoxville *Times-Herald* covered the story reveals that there was an effort to construct a secondary performance of racial integration and reconciliation. While celebrating Jackson's recent concert as powerful enough to make one "forget all worldly troubles when listening to her singing" in a "sermon in songs," the article includes a large photograph of Jackson sleeping in the hotel that sought to refuse service.[92] The public shaming of the hotel's discrimination is highlighted by the photo; it is notable that, on closer scrutiny—considering her perfectly coiffed hair and subtle smile—Jackson is clearly posing for the picture and not actually sleeping (see figure 17). This article participated in a wider discourse

Figure 17. "Mahalia Rocks and Rolls," *Times-Herald* [Knoxville, TN], December 24, 1961.

sensationalizing racial integration, and it suggests that the arguments for viewing Jackson's virtuosity as racially transcendent and those that framed Jackson as (Black but) an ideal candidate for white acceptance are not mutually exclusive. Once Jackson became a celebrity, this tension would play a large role in constructing her performances, rhetorical choices, and political activity.

Aside from her experiences of racism on the road, when Jackson bought a home in a white, affluent neighborhood outside of Chicago, not only did the white residents begin moving out in droves, but gun shots were frequently fired at her house and a bombing was attempted. The harassment and terrorism were so severe that police had to be posted outside of her home. These events occurred simultaneously with an onslaught of daily microaggressions, which Jackson continued to experience well after her celebrity had risen to international acclaim. When such events were documented in the press, such as an instance when a flight stewardess refused to seat Jackson in first class, there was little room to express her frustration. In fact, press coverage appeared to celebrate her lack of anger regarding all manner of mistreatment: "'You know, we got to Chicago, where all the whites said "Hi, Mahalia," and that white stewardess was just as sweet as she could be,' she tells you, face creasing in a wide smile. 'I just felt sorry for her that she couldn't realize that someone who isn't Mahalia Jackson needs the same Christianity and kindness as somebody who is not.'"[93]

Jackson's transition to national and international celebrity beyond the Black community had much to do with her success with white audiences. This transition was aided by a steady stream of support from white male liberals such as Studs Terkel, John Hammond, Marshall Stearns, and Mitch Miller, who were, in various capacities, staunch supporters of African American expressive culture. Such support not only validated the virtuosity of Jackson's performances but also led to her ascendancy within the music industry, which included recording contracts with top companies such as Columbia Records and extensive and highly profitable touring contracts that included prestigious international venues. These acts of validation were critical for helping to create an interpretive lens for listeners with little or no affiliation or familiarity with the Black church and its sonic traditions.

One of the most critical points of validation was heavily documented: Jackson's participation in an elite, invitation-only scholarly retreat for musicologists and jazz aficionados called Definitions in Jazz in 1951. Held at the Music Inn in Lenox, Massachusetts, the retreat's theme was concerned with solidifying the origins of jazz at a time when tensions were rising over conflicting historical accounts and a growing awareness of the tremendous social capital at stake with the worldwide validation of Black music. As Mark Buford argues, the retreats were the birth of jazz studies in academia. These retreats were led and organized by Marshall Stearns and his circle of interlocuters, which included scholars such as anthropologist Richard Waterman and folklorist Willis James.[94] Jackson was recruited to demonstrate "blue tonality," the term that academics were then using to label the sound and texture of Black music. In addition to providing a series of performances, Jackson was heavily questioned about her influences, technique, and stylistic choices by this cadre of progressive liberals she labeled the "great wise men."

This pivotal moment in Jackson's career was remarkably similar to the circumstances in which Phillis Wheatley, the first African American woman to publish a book of poetry, found herself confronted by a panel of eighteen white men who, like the scholars at Definitions in Jazz, were seeking to authenticate her artistry in 1772. Referring to themselves as "the most respectable characters in Boston," they felt compelled by Wheatley's work to confront the question of whether or not a Negro was capable of producing literature. Of course, these two panels were starkly different in terms of the content and historical context surrounding them. Wheatley confronted a board of men who were most likely slave owners, and her achievements threatened the very foundation of their oppressive regime: the belief in the inferiority of Africa and its diasporic descendants was untrue. In contrast, Jackson's invitation was honorific, and she was treated more like an esteemed guest than a potential threat to their livelihood. While Wheatley was questioned in order to ascertain if it was in fact her actual writing or a clever trick for publicity, Jackson was grilled on her relationship to blues music, as the similarities between the blues and gospel music seemed to vex white scholars who were insistent on determining linear, compartmentalized origins for specific components of jazz music. However, what joins these two historical events is that these panels effectively validated the artistry of these women for white audiences during critical moments of their burgeoning careers. Jackson's own description of the event is informative:

After supper the professors got me into a kind of lounge in the carriage house and asked me to give them a song. I leaned up against the piano and sang "Didn't It Rain, Lord!" and "Jesus, Savior, Pilot Me" and "Movin' On Up." As soon as I finished, a great big fuss busted loose. The professors started arguing with one another and asking me where I had learned to sing that way. Who had taught me? Where had I learned such tonal shading and rhythm? After they quieted down a bit, I told them I'd been singing around Baptist churches and gospel tents and at prayer meetings all my life. I didn't learn to sing any special way, I just found myself doing it.[95]

Another pivotal moment of Jackson's transition to the national stage was her first appearance on *The Ed Sullivan Show* on January 20, 1952. Although she was not the first African American to appear on the show (that honor went to Billy Kenny and the Ink Spots), Jackson was the first gospel artist, and, from all accounts, she was received well and would later return several times for other performances. Receiving an invitation to perform on the *Ed Sullivan Show* meant that a Black artist held crossover appeal for white audiences, and given the show's emerging role as a standard-bearer for American popular music, an appearance symbolized a tacit level of acceptance from white America. Journalist Laurraine Goreau's archival materials contain a recorded interview with Ed Sullivan that was used in preparation of her biography on Jackson. Sullivan was asked about the circumstances that led to inviting Jackson to perform on the show, his general impressions of Jackson, as well as if there had ever been any negative reactions to her appearances. Sullivan's answers are useful for understanding how Jackson was perceived by white audiences. For example, Sullivan stated that what prompted Jackson's invitation to appear on the show was the amount of discussion Jackson was generating among white, music-industry insiders combined with the pressure exerted by the Black community for better representation:

> We always tried to make sure that we'd have Negro representation on the show because at that time the Negros were in an uproar and they said that the whites were monopolizing T.V. and that the producers of T.V. were apparently scared to put a Negro on because of the Southern reaction . . . they were scared of the

southern reaction. Well, the southern reaction was as great as the northern reaction for her and the other ones.[96]

Goreau was aware of the discrimination Jackson encountered during her time appearing on Chicago's local CBS affiliate station WBBM-TV and pressed Sullivan further on whether or not there were any negative reactions to Jackson's appearance on the show. He responded, "They loved her. The people sitting at home aren't worried about your color, race, religion. They want to be entertained and she was a tremendous entertainer."[97] While comparing Jackson to Ethel Waters, Sullivan stated, "Nowadays there is so much talk about the differences between black and white and some negros would cringe because of it. Ethel and Mahalia never even . . . never even . . . I don't think the thought ever entered their mind."[98] Sullivan's comments, rife with the kinds of color-blind assumptions that disavowed the actual lived experiences of Jackson, are, in part, indicative of the cultural strategies white audiences could deploy to detach Jackson from the weighty issues of race, class, and gender for the pleasures of entertainment. When he mentioned that Jackson was someone who could be your "mother or sister," he came just short of naming the minstrel "mammy" trope operating underneath the surface of his comments, which, in addition to its symbolic link to Black servitude during slavery, functions as a space of suspended animation for those it imprisons. The figure of the mammy exists only to serve and comfort her white owners or employers through considerable domestic and emotional labor. Other aspects of her humanity, her familial, social, and political commitments, including her existence as a sexual being, are elided. The pressure to both resist and conform to this caricature required Jackson to constantly negotiate authenticity and contradictory audience expectations.[99]

Jackson spoke candidly about the challenges and opportunities surrounding performing for white audiences almost always in conciliatory tones that framed anti-Black racism as a consequence of whites and Blacks not talking to each other.[100] When queried about why white audiences attended her performances, Jackson offered responses such as "they tried drink and they tried psychoanalysis and now they're going to try to rejoice with me a bit. If more white people only dared let themselves go and show their true deep feelings maybe some good might come of it."[101] When Jackson was explicitly critical of white supremacy, she often chose to utilize the rhetorical commonplace of Christianity. In her article "I Can't Stop Singing," Jackson recounted an episode in which she was rebuffed for proposing that her television show be picked up by the CBS network to air across the nation. When she was told that she would not find a sponsor that sells a product in the South that would "take a chance on a negro," Jackson responded, "I just couldn't believe it. If they're Christians, how in the world can they object to my singing hymns?"[102]

Jackson followed these remarks with the revelation that any hopes she had for her own racial ascension due to her newfound celebrity were quickly dashed when she returned to the South. Even after taking steps to enforce integrated seating at her concerts, she characterized leaving the concert hall as feeling like she had "stepped back into the jungle." Jackson openly marveled at the contradiction between the behavior of whites at her concerts and how she was treated once she left: "There were lots of white people at those concerts, and they sat side by side with colored folks because my instructions to the ushers are for them to say, 'Come right in. Pick a seat and sit right down—anywhere'. Because if you come to hear religious music, you're not supposed to feel any bigger than anybody else. Those white people applauded just as hard as anybody, and afterward some of them came around to tell me how much they had enjoyed the evening."[103]

Jackson did not hide her frustration and bewilderment concerning whites who would clap and cheer at her concerts but then expect Jim Crow-era subservience in all other matters. Despite Jackson's limited power to impose desegregation elsewhere, these concerts were symbolic blows to the institution of white supremacy. It was hard for critics to defend segregating a religious concert. There were no readily available excuses similar to those used against other genres of music—such as the purported potential for morally questionable or socially devious consequences of jazz and blues. Jackson understood that the religiosity of her brand insulated her from such criticism, and she worked to leverage that power for both salvation and social justice. However, Jackson began to offer a much more forceful social critique following the death of Dr. King.[104] Speaking to the *Milwaukee Journal* on May 5, 1968, Jackson proclaimed: "The American white man ought to believe by now that the

Negro has been loyal. He's imitated and respected. He wants to take care of his family. A man shouldn't kill another man's pride. I tries when I goes to Europe never to say anything bad about my country. America is my home and I don't think anyone should tell destructive things about his own home. Let's iron it out ourselves. Some are losing faith that they won't get what Martin wanted."[105]

Jackson's Legacy

Although James Cone never uses the term "rhetoric" or invokes rhetorical studies, he specifically addresses both the rhetorical nature of the blues and, in turn, gospel music. Cone argues that Black music is "not an artistic creation for its own sake" but rather a statement about "the feeling and thinking of an African people," and that the blues are "not truths about the Black experience" but the "essential ingredients that define the essence of the Black experience," and a "state of mind in relation to the Truth of the Black experience."[106] The range and dexterity of Jackson's rhetorical maneuvers, her personal experiences of racism, and the contours of her improbable rise to national stardom, which I have endeavored to survey here, serve two important purposes for understanding her artistry. First, they offer important context to the rhetorical challenges surrounding her career. Second, and more important, they help make the case that Jackson brought the same level of rhetorical calculation to her music. Jackson explicitly assigned a communicative strategy to her artistry, and she believed in its success as a form of resistance to oppression and an opportunity for both national and international reconciliation. Accordingly, she once remarked, "The world is trying to get a better understanding but they haven't got the right communication."[107] Jackson's primary choice of modality, in which the sonic was predominant over the oratorical, illuminates her belief in the rhetorical power of Black music:

> I still have hopes that my singing will break down some of the hate and fear that divide the white and colored people in this country. Whenever I've sung on the TV shows of Steve Allen, Ed Sullivan, Bing Crosby and Dinah Shore, and in the motion picture, *Imitation of Life*, white people in the South as well as the North have

telephoned and written to me to tell me how much my singing has meant to them. More and more white folks are coming to my concerts. Even down South they are coming. I've seen them clap their hands and rejoice with the spirit of Jesus.[108]

Jackson believed her music could help an America awash in racist propaganda and stereotypes better understand the African American community.[109]

The combination of appearing to fight temptation while rejecting materialism became part of the branding that helped to launch Jackson's career to international heights. In fact, Jackson's evasion of the blues became so attached to the popular discourse surrounding her career that one of the musicals created about her life following her death personified the blues as a zoot-suited, male seducer that emerges from smoky Chicago jazz clubs.[110] Jackson's dogmatic policing of the boundary between gospel and the blues became a model for other gospel artists who were aware of the economic and rhetorical stakes involved for a fledgling music industry.[111] Her comments also betray a sensitivity to language that might both desacralize and depoliticize the power and meaning of her work. Although couched in religious tropes, Jackson's stated desire to "plant the banner of gospel singing solidly in the hearts and minds of the world" included planting the seeds of liberation and resistance to oppression. Although Jackson's political activity may have begun with her many performances for local political functions during her youth, she was in no way a passive observer. Jackson quickly developed a sophisticated set of political commitments that included advocacy for housing and jobs for Black communities in northern cities.[112] Thus the world that Jackson wanted to "move on up" to wasn't just a heavenly spiritual plane but also the just America that was the aim of the freedom struggle of her time.

Jackson's rich body of work justifies her status as an exemplar within the tradition of African American rhetoric, particularly the rhetorical strategies of gospel music, which include a divine love of justice that extends beyond individual conversion to a collective struggle for freedom and equality in the tradition of prophets such as Isaiah, Jeremiah, and Amos. Its modern incarnation implies a willingness to speak truth to power and confront authoritarianism and oppression, a tradition that echoes throughout Jackson's music and political activism. During Jackson's funeral service, Harry Belafonte argued that she was "the single most powerful Black woman in the United States, the womanpower for the grass roots." Belafonte wagered that "there was not a single field hand, a single Black worker, a single Black intellectual who did not respond to her Civil Rights message."[113] Close analysis of Jackson's rhetorical practices proves Belafonte's assertions more than accurate, and her reputation persists not only as an iconic figure in her own right but also as representative of a sound that combines the power of the spirituals, the impulse of the blues, and the righteous struggle of the Civil Rights generation.

Conclusion

Shout Chorus

During the summer of 2023, I was given the opportunity to work with a small group of UMBC undergraduate students on an archival project. Through a surprising turn of fortune, the UMBC Library Special Collections had come into possession of a treasure trove of documents from a grassroots, Baltimore-based, interracial and intergenerational jazz club known as the Left Bank Jazz Society. As my students and I began working with the documents, we quickly realized how important they were to the history of Baltimore and the story of Black music in America. The Left Bank Jazz Society was founded in 1964 by a group of jazz fans who were committed to providing live music concerts in Baltimore. Although the Left Bank is most often mentioned in relation to the series of albums produced from the organization's archive of rare and unheard performances from some of jazz's biggest names, equally impressive is the story of the group's longevity as an organization that operated on the principles of racial inclusion and community engagement.

When my students and I interviewed John Fowler, one of the few surviving board members of the organization, we asked him what he thought was the secret to the success and longevity of the Left Bank. Fowler first responded by explaining the advantageous logistics of the organization's concert times and location. Concerts were held on Sunday afternoons in what was then known as the Famous Ballroom in Baltimore, which was just a short walk from Penn Station for musicians commuting to Baltimore by train. Since night clubs were the dominant source of live jazz performance, Sunday afternoons presented an opportune time free from the competition of other better-paying venues. Additionally, the organization's nonprofit status meant that the primary focus was placed on compensating the musicians, which allowed the organization to pursue a wide range of artists for their concerts without the burden of turning a profit. However, most compelling was Fowler's description of the familial atmosphere the organization created for musicians and audience members alike. Fowler stated that in the entirety of the organization's existence, there was never an incident or altercation at any of the concerts, which totaled more than one thousand. Fowler remarked that members of the group did not realize that they were operating one of the few desegregated venues in the region until they saw coverage of the organization begin to appear in the press as early as 1965. "Our philosophy," Fowler explained, "was that as long as you had money to pay the admission, we didn't care who you were or what you were. We were really realizing that this wasn't happening anywhere else. The love of music brought everybody out."[1] For more than thirty years, a diverse array of Baltimore families from myriad ethnic and racial backgrounds came together to break bread and commune with one another through their passion for Black music. Among their organizational documents, concert flyers, meeting notes, and other ephemera, there are no lengthy declarations defending the value of diversity and inclusion or ruminations about the complexity and challenges of navigating a multiracial organization. Instead, there are simply photos of members laughing, eating, and enjoying music together. In many ways, the rich legacy of the Left Bank is adorned by its simplicity: they made the liberatory and affirmational dimensions of jazz their modus operandi. Black music was both their symbolic and literal soundtrack to building community. Given the organization's origin during a tumultuous time in American history, the Left Bank's unusually well-documented history stands out as a fitting concluding anecdote and a rare archival testament to the power of Black music as a force for claiming space, creating sanctuary, and composing community.

Throughout *On Rhetoric and Black Music*, I have endeavored to place Black musicians and their music at the center of public discourse. However, judging their rhetorical effectiveness, beyond the criterion of commercial success, involves listening to the cacophony of discourses surrounding the production, dissemination, and consumption of their work in both the public and private spheres. The artists explored here were all precursors to new waves of musical innovation by integrating and interrogating the genre-bending capabilities of Black popular music as a dialogic synthesis of musical influences in juxtaposition with important matters of public discourse. This book relies on a conception

Figure 18. Excerpt from *The Baltimore Jazz Scene, 1977*. The Left Bank Jazz Society published this yearbook as a way of documenting their activities and accomplishments.

of Blackness as both shaped by and through the sonic. This music, including ragtime, blues, and jazz attests to the rhetorical impact of the Black sonic lexicon. From this perspective, music is not just a model for rhetorical invention but is *itself* rhetorical practice within the medium of sound. The methods involved in this study—musical analysis, archival research, and close textual analysis—trace how these artists strategically used sound to locate an alternative register from which to reimagine liberation while diffusing negative stereotypes.

As a product and instrument of the Black public sphere, Black music has been critical to the establishment of a subaltern counterpublic for Black life and activism, a space to imagine and call into being liberatory futurities.[2] Such was Scott Joplin's motivation for *Treemonisha*, as well as James Weldon Johnson's musical and literary enterprise. Ragtime, as the site of one of America's important culture wars, and through its sheer force of popularity and musical innovation, loosened the grip of cultural tastemakers who were committed to the fiction of Black inferiority. What is both illuminated and made audible within the ex-colored man's paradoxical journey is that ragtime operationalized the "in/audibility" of Blackness.[3] Or, put another way, ragtime signifies on Du Bois's iconic symbol of the veil, which shrouds whatever Blackness may be within the polarity of visibility and invisibility, as the interiority of Black life exists simultaneously with its indecipherability for those wedded to conceptions of Blackness as the antithesis of Western modernity. The symbolic action of ragtime's sonic presence indexed a subversive, cultural noise challenging the status quo of racial oppression and exclusion.

As cultural texts, the music explored in this book stitched together communities of listeners, including the Left Bank, through the trafficking of topoi, or the ideas that serve as the basis for constructing value systems and hierarchies, and invested in the power of African American expressive culture and the commitment to the survival of Black communities. Mary Lou Williams's jazz jeremiad was a product of such commitment, as she understood Black music as an active force that anchored Black futurity to a shared history of struggle and liberation. Williams's musical innovations debunked narratives that marginalized the cultural contributions of Black women, and her dogged determination to be taken as a serious composer mirrored the efforts of Black women artists who refused to be silenced and insisted that their voices, and music, be heard as critical contributions to the Black public sphere.

Black music offers listeners a rhetorical artifact upon which to deliberate as well as an alternative form of deliberation itself, beckoning listeners into an identification with particular aesthetic cultures and political paradigms. Duke Ellington, through his exploration of sound, used works like "Black and Tan Fantasy" and *Black, Brown and Beige* to engage, and make sense of, Black history through sound. Ellington's music provided a soundtrack for grappling with the African diaspora and the Black experience in America while daring to center Black audiences. The sound of Blackness, whatever it may be, is a powerful rhetorical invention that, even when untethered from the Black body and mediated by technology, constitutes a site of spiritual, cultural, psychological, and political imagination and futurism, a world-making and world-changing resonance, and a defining characteristic of Black subjectivity.

The specific sound of Black music, its mixture of tonalities, harmonies, melodies, timbres, and other modernist musical techniques, offers a blending that eventually animated a sweeping, global, revolutionary noise.[4] Therefore, it is important to consider the relationship between not only the music and its antecedent origins but also that of a global, musical landscape responding to all manner of oppression, political mobilization, cultural upheaval, and economic uncertainty. John Coltrane's music captured and distilled this noise into a potent concoction of spiritual and political imagination through works such as *A Love Supreme*, which aided Black artists and writers in their quest to reshape Black rhetorical landscapes.

This book has also sought to explain how Black music has troubled the boundaries of sacred and secular cultures through its multiplicity of modalities. Mary Lou Williams's creation of jazz liturgy expanded the possibilities of jazz beyond the club or concert hall while reengaging the roots of Black music as a form of praise and worship. Black music, through the form of the spirituals, was a crucial vehicle for engaging the divine and linking the communal survival of slavery and Jim Crow segregation in America to God's providence. Further, Mahalia Jackson's "gospel with a bounce" became a part of the soundtrack of the Civil Rights movement. Her music embodied the generational and geographical transformations occurring in Black communities that forced a reckoning with the Black experience and soldered it to a form of Christian theology that was unwilling to turn a blind eye toward human rights abuses and racial oppression.

On Rhetoric and Black Music was written during a calamitous time in American history. A global pandemic, a racial reckoning inflamed by the death of George Floyd, heightened income inequality, extreme political polarization, and an unfolding climate crisis are just a few of the challenges that confront American citizens. Under these conditions, even a cursory observation of the role of Black music in American life reveals its continued importance, not just as form of entertainment, but as a lifeline, one still strong enough to tether its listeners to what James Weldon Johnson described in "Lift Every Voice and Sing" as the "song full of faith that the dark past has taught us." Although this book has focused on earlier forms of Black music, its conclusions are no less important to more recent developments in hip-hop and R&B, as they provide pathways for placing emerging artists in a wider panorama of Black intellectual history. Consider, for example, the layered connections between Kendrick Lamar's Pulitzer Prize for his 2017 album *Damn* and Duke Ellington's Pulitzer snub in 1965. Similar to the impact Lamar has made on the American musical landscape, Ellington's popularity and status had grown to the extent that few artists of any genre could ignore his trendsetting and boundary-pushing musical contributions. However, rather than grant Ellington the well-deserved honor of being the first African American to win the Pulitzer Prize for music (that honor would not occur until 1996 when the prize was given to composer George Walker), as was the decision of the Pulitzer juries, the Pulitzer board decided to forgo presenting the award to anyone. Lamar's award, in light of the racism involved in Ellington's rejection, represented a major step forward on the long journey for public recognition of Black music's many contributions to America. Yet the weight and significance of this journey, as well as Lamar's achievement for the genre of hip-hop and his impact on the public sphere, becomes clearer when heard through the sonic lexicon of Black music and its role in the historical struggle for Black freedom and liberation.

The evolution of Black music during the eras of Scott Joplin, Duke Ellington, John Coltrane, Mahalia Jackson, and Mary Lou Williams offers an important historical reference by which to evaluate current trends and developments in Black music. The music explored here for its rhetorical accomplishments demonstrates the central role that sonic experience has long played in African American life and its contribution to the Black liberatory struggle. Between these melodies, harmonies, and rhythms lies the resonance of resistance and frequencies of future possibilities. All we must do is listen.

Notes

Introduction

1 Kate Clifford Larson, *Bound for the Promised Land*, 214–15.
2 Emma P. Telford, *Harriet*, 42–43.
3 A wealth of scholarly investigations of African American spirituals and gospel music foregrounds this claim, including John Lovell Jr.'s *Black Song*, Anthony Heilbut's *The Gospel Sound*, Jerma A. Jackson's *Singing in My Soul*, and Robert Darden's *Nothing but Love in God's Water*.
4 "Of Our Spiritual Strivings" is the title of the first chapter of W. E. B. Du Bois's *The Souls of Black Folk*.
5 Jacques Attali, in *Noise*, explores the relationship between music, power, and politico-economic structures in Western societies. Attali states that "every major social rupture has been preceded by an essential mutation in the codes of music," and discusses an explicit connection between economic and musical evolution. He asks the question, "Can we understand music through its relations with money" to situate music as part of a social structure that generates noise? This noise works as a text that is prophetic because it can, in Attali's view, explore all the possibilities in a given code faster than material reality can, thus predicting economic development. See p. 10.
6 Houston A. Baker, *I Don't Hate the South*, 133.
7 The word "changes" is a popular way of referring to the chord structure of a song. One of the challenges a jazz soloist faces is keeping up with the pace of one chord changing to another as he or she attempts to improvise an accompanying melody.
8 Plato, *Republic*, book 3, 398–403.

Notes to Introduction

9 Aristotle, *Politics*, 26.
10 For example, see Charles Batteux's *Les beaux arts reduits à un même principe* (The fine arts reduced to one common principle), 1746.
11 For more information, see Ignaz Theodor Ferdinand Arnold's biography of Joseph Haydn and Wolfgang Amadeus Mozart (1810) where he calls Haydn a "clever orator."
12 Mark Evan Bonds, *Music as Thought*, 13.
13 Bonds, 14.
14 Bonds, 33.
15 See Kant's *Critique of Judgment* (1790), which exemplifies hurdles in analyzing music in the Western tradition. See also Christian Gottfried Korner's rebuttal in "On the Representation of Character in Music" (1795), which provides an early model of the use of traditional rhetorical theory music criticism.
16 Keith Gilyard and Adam J. Banks, *On African-American Rhetoric*, 12.
17 Molefi Asante, *Afrocentric Idea*, 72.
18 Asante, 75.
19 Asante, 80.
20 Aniruddh Patel, *Music, Language, and the Brain*, 9. Patel argues that human infants are born with both linguistic and musical sound systems that are shaped by the cultures they are immersed in. While pitch is the foundation for sound categories in music, timbre is the foundation for sound categories in speech. Both timbre and pitch play a role in the similarities between speech and music. Patel comes to these conclusions based on a survey of empirical research in cognitive neuroscience. The idea of learned sound categories comes from Stephen Handel's *Listening*. For more information on the idea that music and language share mechanisms for sound category learning, see Jenny R. Saffran, and Erin McMullen "Music and Language."
21 Patel, *Music, Language, and the Brain*, 190.
22 Patel, *Music, Language, and the Brain*, 202. Also see John Sloboda and D. H. H. Parker, "Immediate Recall of Melodies."
23 Patel, *Music, Language, and the Brain*, 114.
24 Patel, *Music, Language, and the Brain*, 105. Patel mentions a study by John Sloboda in 1983 in which behavior, perception, and brain signals were tested for their sensitivity to musical meter. See John Sloboda, "Communication of Musical Metre," 377–96.

25 Michael A. Arbib, "Five Terms in Search of Synthesis," 20. The idea of a language-music continuum was the subject of the 2009 Ernst Strüngmann Forum on science and communication, initiated by Arbib. Arbib discusses the similarities and differences between music and language with reference to cultures in which music and language are viewed as one. This includes tonal and nontonal languages and animals (such as birds, who use songlike utterances to communicate).
26 Arbib, "Five Terms in Search of Synthesis," 20.
27 Kenneth Burke, *Rhetoric of Motives*, 55.
28 Bernd Herzogenrath explains "sonic thinking" as a space where "research, art, theory, and practice are coextensive" and facilitated by sound. See Bernd Herzogenrath and Patricia Pisters's *Sonic Thinking*, 10.
29 See Ren Ellis Neyra's *Cry of the Senses*, 23. Neyra uses the term "sensorial solidarity" in his work on Caribbean and Latinx poetics that explores how sound can challenge a range of epistemologies, including racism, colonialism, and humanism.
30 W. E. B. Du Bois, *Souls of Black Folk*, v–vi.
31 Du Bois, *Souls of Black Folk*, 156.
32 Aristotle, *On Rhetoric*, 1335a.
33 Patel, *Music, Language, and the Brain*, 241. Although the term "musical syntax" has different meanings for different scholars, Patel defines it as "the principles governing the combination of discrete structural elements into sequences."
34 Du Bois, *Souls of Black Folk*, 155.
35 Du Bois, *Souls of Black Folk*, 157.
36 Anne E. Carroll, "Du Bois and Art Theory."
37 Carroll, "Du Bois and Art Theory," 243–44.
38 See Kevin Thomas Miles, "Haunting Music in the Souls of Black Folk."
39 Cited in Gerard A. Hauser, *Vernacular Voices*, 95.
40 Hauser, *Vernacular Voices*, 33, 94.
41 Andrew Ward, *Dark Midnight When I Rise*, 114–15.
42 Theodore F. Seward, Preface, 2.
43 Seward, Preface, 2.
44 Seward, Preface, 3.
45 "Amusements," *New York World*, December 29, 1871.
46 "The Jubilee Singers at the Home and Tomb of Lincoln," *People's Advocate*, July 24, 1880.

47 Quoted in "Jubilee Singers," *People's Advocate*.
48 See J. B. T. Marsh, *Story of the Jubilee Singers*, 188. Douglass identified this song as part of his inspiration to escape slavery.
49 Marian McPartland, "Mary Lou," 12.
50 Leroi Jones (Amiri Baraka), *Blues People*, x.
51 Alexander G. Weheliye, *Phonographies*, 6. Weheliye uses the term "sonic Afro-modernity" in his exploration of "the in/audibility of Blackness by a whole range of cultural, philosophical, political, social and economic discourses," 6.

Chapter 1

1 Edward A. Berlin, "Ragtime."
2 Seventeen year-old Alice Roosevelt, daughter of President Theodore Roosevelt, raised eyebrows when she requested that "Maple Leaf Rag" be played by the Marine Band at a diplomatic reception at the White House in 1905. See Berlin, *King of Ragtime*, 153.
3 See Chaïm Perelman and Lucie Olbrechts-Tyteca, *New Rhetoric*, 83–84
4 See David A. Jasen, *Ragtime*, 190–99; and Berlin, *Ragtime*.
5 Black-faced performers originated in the South during the 1820s as small parts of larger theatrical performances. The development of stand-alone minstrel shows began as early as the 1840s in New York City with the advent of Thomas Dartmouth Rice and George Washington Dixon, two figures credited with launching the popularity of the Jim Crow and Zip Coon caricatures. In addition to portraying Black Americans as unintelligent, lazy, and inferior to whites through racist stereotypes, they also portrayed them as naturally musical, creative, and unbound by proper etiquette or traditional styles of performance.
6 This is one of the central claims of Robert Toll in *Blacking Up*.
7 Eric Lott, *Love and Theft*, 25.
8 Toll, *Blacking Up*, 38.
9 See George W. Walker, "Negro on the American Stage."
10 Toll, *Blacking Up*, 201.
11 Although Black minstrel groups performed for Black audiences on occasion, the majority of performances were for white or racially

segregated audiences. With public access came a high degree of surveillance. See Walker, "Negro on the American Stage."
12. Berlin, *Ragtime*, 5.
13. See "Account of the Negroe Insurrection in South Carolina (1739)" (315–16).
14. "Account of the Negroe Insurrection" (315–16).
15. W. F. Gates, "Ethiopian Syncopation," 341.
16. The first ragtime instrumental published by an African American was "Mississippi Rag" by William Krell in 1897.
17. Rudi Blesh and Harriet Janis, *They All Played Ragtime*, 33.
18. Berlin, *King of Ragtime*, 62.
19. Berlin, *King of Ragtime*, 65.
20. Berlin, *King of Ragtime*, 57.
21. Berlin, *King of Ragtime*, 58.
22. See David A. Jasen, *Recorded Ragtime 1897–1958*, 138.
23. David Gilbert, *Product of Our Souls*, 6.
24. Lori Brooks, "Composer versus the 'Perfessor'," 174.
25. "Condemns Melodies of Ragtime," *San Jose [CA] Evening News*, October 4, 1900.
26. Shai Burstyn, "In Quest of the Period Ear."
27. Hans Robert Jauss. *Toward an Aesthetic of Reception*, 63–68.
28. Jean-Luc Nancy, *Listening*, 10.
29. Georgina Born, Introduction, 3.
30. Mendi Lewis Obadike, "Low Fidelity," 135–37.
31. Quoted in "Says Rag-Time Is Dying Out," *San Jose Evening News*, October 7, 1905.
32. See Charles Peabody, "Notes on Negro Music"; Halbert H. Britan, "Music and Morality"; Edwin L. Norton, "Selection of School Songs"; Gutzon Borglum, "Imitation the Curse of American Art."
33. Quoted in "Amusements," *New Orleans Times-Picayune*, May 22, 1902.
34. William Sanders Scarborough, "Negro in Fiction as Portrayer and Portrayed," 360.
35. Scarborough, "Negro in Fiction," 360.
36. Scarborough, "Negro in Fiction," 360.
37. See "Music, Literature, and the Drama," 361.
38. See Eileen Southern, *Music of Black Americans*, 272.
39. Theodore Drury, "Negro in Classic Music," 324.

174 Notes to Chapter 1

40 "To Play Ragtime in Europe," *St. Louis Post-Dispatch*, February 28, 1901.
41 "To Play Ragtime in Europe."
42 "To Play Ragtime in Europe."
43 "Des Moines Has a Ragtime Club and an Anti-Ragtime Club," *Omaha [NE] World-Herald*, April 18, 1906.
44 The public profile of James Weldon Johnson, J. Rosamond Johnson, and Bob Cole as a musical production team took a considerable hit when their status as African Americans became known publicly. See David Gilbert, *Product of Our Souls*, 72.
45 Monroe H. Rosenfeld, "Scott Joplin a King," *Sedalia Times*, June 13, 1903.
46 Berlin, *King of Ragtime*, 198.
47 Scott Joplin, *Treemonisha*, liner notes, unpaginated.
48 Joplin, *Treemonisha*, liner notes.
49 Joplin, *Treemonisha*, liner notes.
50 Joplin, *Treemonisha*, arrangement, 30–31.
51 See Berlin, *King of Ragtime*, 130.
52 W. E. B. Du Bois, *Talented Tenth*, 33.
53 Berlin, *King of Ragtime*, 203.
54 Susan Curtis, *Dancing to a Black Man's Tune*, 152.
55 Joplin made extensive revisions to his opera to address these issues; however, much of the revisions were lost or destroyed, including the full orchestration, by Joplin himself during periods of depression. See Berlin, *King of Ragtime*, 238.
56 "Musical Novelty."
57 Joplin promoted the opera himself in the press and performed select pieces for various audiences in hopes of securing funding for a larger production. Therefore, many artists and fans of Joplin were well aware of the opera and its contribution.
58 Bruno Nettl, "'Musical Thinking' and 'Thinking about Music'," 147.
59 James Weldon Johnson, *Autobiography of an Ex-Colored Man*, 17.
60 W. E. B. Du Bois, *Souls of Black Folk*, 2.
61 Johnson, *Autobiography of an Ex-Colored Man*, 149.
62 Johnson, *Autobiography of an Ex-Colored Man*, 8.
63 Johnson, *Autobiography of an Ex-Colored Man*, 8.
64 The narrator intentionally avoids naming specific locations out of the fear that it may lead to his identification.
65 Johnson, *Autobiography of an Ex-Colored Man*, 110.

66 Johnson, *Autobiography of an Ex-Colored Man*, 181.
67 Eric J. Sundquist, *Hammers of Creation*, 3.
68 Nick Heffernan, "'You Aint Got to Be Black to Be Black'," 21.
69 Michael Bull, *Sounding Out the City*, 24.
70 Heffernan, "'You Aint Got to Be Black to Be Black'," 33.
71 James Weldon Johnson, *Along This Way*, 153.
72 Recent examples of such tactics include the collaborations of R&B artists Usher and Justin Bieber, and hip-hop artists T. I., Iggy Azalea, Dr. Dre, and Eminem, which, in part, had the strategic goal of reaching white audiences by allowing access to Black music without the confrontation with Black bodies.
73 Johnson, *Along This Way*, 179.
74 Johnson, *Along This Way*, 196.
75 James Weldon Johnson, "Preface to the First Edition," 10.
76 Johnson, *Autobiography of an Ex-Colored Man*, 20.
77 "Ragging It," 10.
78 J. Lawrence Erb, "Where Is the American Song?"
79 See Charles Reginald Sherlock, "From Breakdown to Rag-Time"; and C. A. Browne, *Story of Our National Ballads*, 208.
80 Natalie Curtis, "Negro's Contribution to the Music of America," 660.
81 Natalie Curtis, "Negro's Contribution to the Music of America."
82 "Ragtime."
83 "General Mention," *Daily Inter Ocean* [Chicago], August 26, 1896.
84 Advertisement, *Idaho Daily Statesman*, March 26, 1905. See also Harney's description of his invention of ragtime in Louisville, Kentucky, published in "Origin Of Rag Time: One Ben Harney Said to Have Invented It and Its Name at Louisville," *Portland* [OR] *New Age*, June 21, 1902.
85 Ben Harney's 1895 composition "You've Been a Good Old Wagon but You Done Broke Down" was considered the first ragtime composition by many media outlets such as *Time* magazine. For Johnson's comment, see *Autobiography of an Ex-Colored Man*, 12.
86 Edward A. Berlin, *Ragtime*, 31, notes the intricacies surrounding Harney's ethnicity. Claims that Harney was African American were supported by notable Black musicians, including Eubie Blake and Willie "The Lion" Smith. The assertion that Harney may have passed as Black to get closer to African American musicians was suggested by William Tallmadge in "Ben Harney."

87 "Ragtime's Father."
88 "The Origin of Ragtime: Fred Stone Credits Ernest Hogan, a Negro, With Starting the Jazz Era in Music." *New York Times*, March 23, 1924.
89 Eric King Watts, *Hearing the Hurt*, 3.
90 Gilbert, *Product of Our Souls*, 5.
91 "Great, Colored Song Writers and Their Songs," *Freeman* [Indianapolis IN], December 23, 1911.
92 In "Arts of the Contact Zone," Mary Louise Pratt uses this term to describe "social spaces where cultures meet, clash, and grapple with each other, often in contexts of highly asymmetrical relations of power, such as colonialism, slavery, or their aftermaths as they are lived out in many parts of the world" (34).
93 See David Gilbert's discussion of James Reese Europe's performance at Carnegie Hall in 1912 in *Product of Our Souls*, 1.
94 Nathaniel Mackey, *Bedouin Hornbook*, 42.
95 Toni Morrison, *Playing in the Dark*.

Chapter 2

1 Duke Ellington, *Music Is My Mistress*, 175.
2 Edward Green and Evan Spring, *Cambridge Companion to Duke Ellington*, 127.
3 Maureen Anderson's rhetorical analysis of white resistance to jazz points to the bulk of criticism as "aggression by white critics against the recently emancipated Black man." See Maureen Anderson, "White Reception of Jazz in America."
4 Rollo H. Myers, *Music in the Modern World*, 122.
5 For one of the first sociological approaches to the white response to jazz, see Morroe Berger's 1947 essay "Jazz."
6 Swing rhythm utilizes a specific eighth-note rhythmic feel. It is based on triplet subdivisions of the beat rather than on dividing each beat perfectly in half in a stable, forward-leaning series of straight eighth notes.
7 Samuel A. Floyd, "Ring Shout!" 273.
8 John Pittman, "Interview in Los Angeles."
9 Pittman, "Interview in Los Angeles."

10 James P. Murray, "Duke Ellington's Legacy of . . . A Thousand Tunes and Memories: Cover Story," *New York Amsterdam News*, June 1, 1974.
11 Mutes are objects that are stuck into the bell of a trumpet to alter the sound. The use of the rubber from a toilet plunger became popular through the skilled performances of members of Ellington's orchestra, like Bubber Miley. Miley became one of the early masters of this technique, which combined the use of a straight mute, a growling sound in the throat, and a rubber plunger to shape the sound.
12 David Metzer, "Shadow Play."
13 Marshall Stearns, "Bubber Miley's Jungle Iron, Choking and Sobbing Fades Dunn," 10.
14 The difficulty of Ellington's compositions became a common point of discussion in the press. See Al Monroe, "Think Duke Ellington's Ascension and Hold on Top Due to Odd Mood," *Chicago Defender*, December 16, 1944.
15 For evidence of the kind of impact Ellington's music had on the public, see "Sepia along Broadway," *Philadelphia Tribune*, October 3, 1929; Cary B. Lewis, "7,400 Storm Savoy in Chicago to Hear Duke Ellington and His Band," *Pittsburgh Courier*, March 28, 1931. The phrase "Black and tan fantasy" came to signify various racial meanings. For example, a love triangle involving two white men and an African American woman was characterized as "a Black and tan fantasy" in "Slain in Brawl over Domestic: White Men in Tragedy over Woman's Love; Printer Is Held without Bail Pending Action of Grand Jury," *New York Amsterdam News*, September 3, 1938. An article discussing colorism and the lack of roles for dark-skinned actors used the phrase "Black and tan fantasy" in its description of the challenges dark-skinned performers faced. See Edgar Rouzeau, "Stardust: This Battle of 'Colored' Folks," *New Journal and Guide* [Norfolk VA], May 23, 1942. Another article used the phrase when discussing the practice of African American railroad porters who were complicit in directing African Americans into segregated cars even after such practices were made illegal. See "Black and Tan Fantasy," *Chicago Defender*, March 3, 1951.
16 Chadwick Jenkins, "A Question of Containment," 415–41.
17 Ellington goes into great detail about the racial dynamics of the Cotton Club and his observation of the desire for "jungle music" by white audiences. See *Music Is My Mistress*, 419–20.

Notes to Chapter 2

18 Quoted in "Ellington in Class with Music Masters," *Philadelphia Tribune*, November 3, 1938.
19 "Tibbett Thinks Well of Negro Compositions," *New York Amsterdam News*, November 17, 1934.
20 Lucius Jonesokay Realmites, "Duke Ellington Ticker-Tape," *Atlanta [GA] Daily World*, July 24, 1935.
21 Quoted in "From Cellar Cafe to Fame," *Philadelphia Tribune*, May 14, 1936.
22 Quoted in "From Cellar Cafe to Fame."
23 R. D. Darrell, "Black Beauty," 58.
24 "Duke Ellington and Orchestra to Play Here," *New Journal and Guide* [Norfolk VA], March 9, 1935.
25 Dudley Murphy is also known for directing *St. Louis Blues* in 1929, which featured Bessie Smith. *St. Louis Blues* and *Black and Tan* were the first films to portray Black culture outside of minstrelsy stereotypes.
26 Fredi Washington is best known for her role as Peola in *Imitation of Life* (1934), a film that deals with the experience of African Americans with lighter skin colors and the act of "passing" as white.
27 Metzer, "Shadow Play,'" *Black Music Research Journal*.
28 Quoted in John Edward Hasse, *Beyond Category*, 92.
29 Arbib, "Five Terms in Search of Synthesis," 20.
30 Gerhard Kubik, "The African Matrix in Jazz Harmonic Practices," 172–80.
31 For an example of his various titles that contain a reference to jungle music (e.g., "maestro of jungle music"), see "Duke Ellington to Stay in West," *Chicago Defender*. May 19, 1934; "How Ellington Evened 'Spoiler' Score with Great Glenn Miller," *Chicago Defender*, May 30, 1931; "The Camera," *Pittsburgh Courier*, June 13, 1931; "Speedy Elevator Speeds Up Appetite," *New Journal and Guide*, September 5, 1931; "Diverse Social Problems Confront World Today," *Pittsburgh Courier*, March 19, 1932.
32 "S. R. O. Signs When Duke Plays in Loop," *Chicago Defender*, February 21, 1931.
33 "Duke in National Broadcast from Temple Monday," *Pittsburgh Courier*, January 2, 1932.
34 Sterling A. Brown. "Negro Character as Seen by White Authors."

Notes to Chapter 2

35 Sterling Brown, "Negro Character as Seen by White Authors," 197.
36 Sterling Brown, "Negro Character as Seen by White Authors," 197.
37 Ellington acknowledged this idea, although he characterized it as an emergence of his interest in African American history. See *Music Is My Mistress*, 419–20.
38 Janet Mabie, "Ellington's 'Mood Indigo'," *Christian Science Monitor*, December 13, 1930, 27.
39 Florence Zunser, "'Opera Must Die', Says Galli-Curci! Long Live the Blues!" *New York Evening Graphic*, December 27, 1930, 45.
40 Graham Lock, *Blutopia*, 83.
41 Lock, *Blutopia*, 82.
42 Racquel J Gates, *Double Negative*, 6.
43 "Does African Jungle Hold the Secret of the Actual?" *Baltimore* [MD] *Afro-American*, January 10, 1931.
44 "Does African Jungle Hold the Secret of the Actual?"
45 "Does African Jungle Hold the Secret of the Actual?"
46 Alain Locke, "New Negro," 30.
47 Langston Hughes, "Afro-American Fragment."
48 Langston Hughes, "Negro Artist and the Racial Mountain," 694.
49 Countee Cullen, "Heritage," 1311.
50 See Edwin Black, *Rhetorical Criticism*, 29.
51 Floyd G. Snelson, "Duke Continues to Lead in Big Courier Contest," *Pittsburgh Courier*, September 26, 1931.
52 Isadora Smith, "Duke Ellington Rated Joe Louis of Music,'" *Pittsburgh Courier*, July 16, 1938.
53 Ellington was asked to take Langston Hughes's poem "I, Too, Sing America" as the subject for his sermon.
54 Duke Ellington, "We, Too, Sing 'America'," 146.
55 Ellington, "We, Too, Sing 'America'," 147.
56 This organization was composed of writers such as Langston Hughes, Ira Gershwin, and Sid Kuller. For more discussion about this organization's role in the production of *Jump for Joy*, see Terry Teachout, *Duke*, 225.
57 Ellington, *Music Is My Mistress*, 175.
58 Barry Ulanov, *Duke Ellington*, 240.
59 The talks leading up to the creation of *Jump for Joy* involved a host of Hollywood elites, including writer Sid Kuller and actors Mickey

Notes to Chapter 2

Rooney and Jackie Cooper. Moreover, the cast included over sixty Black entertainers. For a detailed list of the personnel involved in launching the production, see Gena Caponi-Tabery, *Jump for Joy*, 176–80.

60 Ellington, *Jump for Joy*, liner notes, 13.
61 Caponi-Tabery, *Jump for Joy*, 182.
62 Ellington, *Music Is My Mistress*, 176.
63 Teachout, *Duke*, 227.
64 Teachout, *Duke*, 227.
65 Caponi-Tabery, *Jump for Joy*, 184.
66 Harry Levette, "Gossip of the Movie Lots," *Kansas City* [KS] *Plaindealer*, September 5, 1941.
67 Quoted in Ulanov, *Duke Ellington*. 242.
68 George T. Simon, "Joe Turner Star of Duke's Revue!"
69 Alyce Key, "Key Notes by Alyce Key," *Los Angeles Tribune*, December 27, 1943.
70 Key, "Key Notes by Alyce Key."
71 Ellington, *Music Is My Mistress*, 176.
72 David Johnson, "Jump for Joy."
73 Teachout, *Duke*, 237.
74 Teachout, *Duke*, 238.
75 Teachout, *Duke*, 238.
76 A copy of the program from the Carnegie Hall concert is reprinted in Ellington, *Duke Ellington Reader*, 163.
77 Although Ellington was the first African American bandleader to perform in Carnegie Hall, the honor of the first jazz band performance went to Benny Goodman in 1938.
78 Ellington, *Music Is My Mistress*, 181.
79 Ellington, *Music Is My Mistress*, 181.
80 Quoted in Teachout, *Duke*, 240.
81 Ellington, *Music Is My Mistress*, 182.
82 Ellington, "We, Too, Sing 'America'," 147.
83 See Ulanov, *Duke Ellington*, 253.
84 Paul Bowles, "Duke Ellington in Recital for Russian War Relief," 165.
85 Bowles, "Duke Ellington in Recital for Russian War Relief," 165.
86 Bowles, "Duke Ellington in Recital for Russian War Relief," 165.

Notes to Chapter 2

87 Mike Levin, "Duke Fuses Classical and Jazz!" 12.
88 John Hammond, "Is the Duke Deserting Jazz?"
89 Leonard Feather, "Rebuttal of Hammond," 14.
90 Feather, "Rebuttal of Hammond," 20.
91 J. A. Blades, "Says Ellington Sells Himself for Pottage," *New York Amsterdam News*, May 27, 1943.
92 Blades, "Says Ellington Sells Himself for Pottage."
93 Blades, "Says Ellington Sells Himself for Pottage."
94 Blades, "Says Ellington Sells Himself for Pottage."
95 Langston Hughes, "Here to Yonder," *Chicago Defender*, February 6, 1943.
96 Hughes, "Here to Yonder."
97 Hughes. "Here to Yonder,"
98 Hughes, "Here to Yonder."
99 Hughes, "Here to Yonder." Hughes concludes the review by saluting "the great Republic of the USSR with its many varied races working and fighting together" in direct reference to the Carnegie Hall concert with its mixed audience.
100 Teachout, *Duke*, 226.
101 Teachout describes the content of Ellington's Federal Bureau of Investigation files as thirty-five pages containing lists of Ellington's known associates. Given Ellington's extremely heavy touring schedule during the 1930s, 1940s, and 1950s, he would have had little time for the kind of political activity that would have drawn the consistent attention of the FBI (Teachout, *Duke*, 226).
102 Dan Burley, "Says Duke's Concert Advanced Race 20 Years," *New York Amsterdam News*, January 30, 1943.
103 Peter Suskind, "Duke 'Terrific' as Thousands Cheer Carnegie Concert: Proves Negro's Contribution to Music Universal, Unique Distinctive Style Makes Concert Success Audience Hears Music in Quiet Dignity," *New Journal and Guide*, January 30, 1943.
104 Ellington, *Music Is My Mistress*, 183.
105 Ellington, *Music Is My Mistress*, 184.
106 For an extensive analysis of *The Liberian Suite* in relation to broader themes of Africa in Black music, see David F. Garcia's *Listening for Africa*.
107 Duke Ellington, Letter to Richard Wright.
108 George Russell introduced this concept in his 1953 book on jazz music theory titled *The Lydian Chromatic Concept of Tonal Organization*. The

term "Lydian" refers to a sequence of pitches organized as a musical scale comprising three whole tones, a semitone, two additional whole tones, and then a final semitone. Russell argued that the Lydian mode was the source of all tonal music. Russell's ideas contributed to the innovative work of trumpeter Miles Davis, who incorporated these ideas into his albums *Milestones* and *Kind of Blue*.

Chapter 3

1. Linda Faye Williams, "Black Women, Jazz, and Feminism," 126.
2. Williams recorded her own celebration of the famous subway line heading to Harlem titled "Eighth Avenue Express" in 1944, just after Duke Ellington's "Take the 'A' Train." However, these kinds of creative overlap are often left out of popular narratives about jazz history.
3. Roy Carr, Brian Case, and Fred Dellar, *Hip*, 52.
4. Cornel West, "The Prophetic Tradition in Afro-America."
5. Tammy Kernodle, *Soul on Soul*, 13.
6. Kernodle, *Soul on Soul*, 26.
7. Mary Lou Williams, unpublished memoir, 43.
8. Mary Lou Williams, unpublished memoir, 50.
9. Kernodle, *Soul on Soul*, 56.
10. Mary Lou Williams, unpublished memoir, 28.
11. Mary Lou Williams, unpublished memoir, 66.
12. "Stride piano" is a style of solo jazz piano performance that is derived from adapting ragtime's left-hand patterns. See Gary Giddins, "Modern Mary."
13. Evidence of Williams's influence can be heard in Thelonious Monk's "Rhythm-a-Ning," which utilizes the first four bars of Williams's song "Walkin' and Swingin'." See Robert L. Doerschuk, *88: The Giants of Jazz Piano*, 46.
14. Linda Dahl, "'Night Life.'"
15. Carol Bash, *Mary Lou Williams*.
16. Deborah F. Atwater, *African American Women's Rhetoric*, 1.
17. Atwater, 2.
18. See Michelle R. Scott's rigorous analysis of the Black vaudeville circuit in *T.O.B.A. Time*.
19. Kernodle, *Soul on Soul*, 103.

20 Farah Jasmine Griffin, *Harlem Nocturne*, 151.
21 Delores Calvin, "Seein' Stars," *Arkansas State Press*, May 9, 1958.
22 Kernodle, *Soul on Soul*, 96.
23 "No Kitten on the Keys."
24 Susan McClary, *Feminine Endings*, 8.
25 "Why Women Musicians Are Inferior."
26 Eric Townley, "Interview with Mary Lou," 4–5.
27 Owen Coyle, "Mary Lou Williams and Her Jazz Crusade," 6.
28 "Andy Kirk and His 12 Clouds of Joy," 19, 58.
29 John Hammond, "Count Basie's Band," 6.
30 Barry Ulanov, "Mary Lou Willliams," 13.
31 Ajay Heble, *Landing on the Wrong Note*, 151.
32 Marshall Stearns, "New Records," 5.
33 Dan Morgenstern, in liner notes to Mary Lou Williams, *Zodiac Suite*.
34 Williams noted that according to her research the only other composer to feature astrological concepts in their compositions was Robert Forsythe, an English musician. See Mary Lou Williams, "Why I Wrote the Zodiac Suite," in liner notes to Mary Lou Williams, *Zodiac Suite*.
35 Morgenstern, in liner notes to Mary Lou Williams, *Zodiac Suite*.
36 Barry Ulanov, "Concert Spree."
37 Kernodle, *Soul on Soul*, 149.
38 Friar Peter F. O'Brien, S.J., in liner notes to Mary Lou Williams, *Mary Lou Williams Presents Black Christ of the Andes*.
39 Linda Dahl, *Morning Glory*, 247.
40 Altevia "Buttercup" Edwards, interview by Rev. Peter F. O'Brien, S.J., undated, Mary Lou Williams Collection, Institute of Jazz Studies, Rutgers University.
41 Deanna Witkowski, *Mary Lou Williams*, 54.
42 Shannen Dee Williams, *Subversive Habits*, 6.
43 Shannen Dee Williams, *Subversive Habits*, 11.
44 Mary Lou Williams, *Mary Lou Williams Presents Black Christ of the Andes*, liner notes.
45 O'Brien, who was drawn to Williams through a *Time* article announcing her composition honoring "St. Martin de Porres" and her return to musical performance after an extended hiatus, described the impact of Williams's music, recalling that "my life at once took on

Notes to Chapter 3

a permanent new direction." See liner notes to Mary Lou Williams, *Mary Lou Williams Presents Black Christ of the Andes*.

46 Mary Lou Williams, *Mary Lou Williams Presents Black Christ of the Andes*, liner notes.
47 Mary Lou Williams, *Swinging the Blues*.
48 Williams once demonstrated this communicative process on the piano. See Mary Lou Williams, *Swinging the Blues*.
49 Kernodle, *Soul on Soul*, 220.
50 Mary Lou Williams, *Mary Lou's Mass*, liner notes.
51 Kernodle, *Soul on Soul*, 220.
52 In various denominations of African American churches, having had "an anointing" commonly refers to those with spiritual gifts or a strong desire to be used as a force for good in the world.
53 In folk belief, being "born with a veil" is an omen of good fortune. Additionally, children born with a veil are believed to possess extrasensory perception that may allow them to see and hear spirits or ghosts. The "veil" is a cloth-like membrane of the amniotic sack (the caul) that may partially or fully cover a newborn child.
54 Dahl, *Morning Glory*, 8.
55 Mary Lou Williams, interview by John S. Wilson, June 1973, Jazz Oral History Project, Institute of Jazz Studies, Rutgers University, p. 32, doi.org/doi:10.7282/T3JH3Q2Z.
56 Mary Lou Williams interview by John S. Wilson, 32.
57 Nabeel Zuberi, "The Transmolecularization of [Black] Folk," 78.
58 Alondra Nelson, "Introduction: Future Texts," 8.
59 David Howard-Pitney, *The African American Jeremiad*, 7.
60 Mary Lou Williams, interview by John S. Wilson, 142.
61 David Jackson, "Jazz Is Her Religion."
62 David Jackson, "Jazz Is Her Religion," 44.
63 Cornel West, *Race Matters*, 12–13.
64 Mary Lou Williams, *Mary Lou Williams Presents Black Christ of the Andes*, liner notes.
65 Mary Lou Williams and Cecil Taylor, *Embraced*.
66 Williams performed for several years on a professional level before learning to read and compose music, which came about during her time with Andy Kirk and the Dark Clouds of Joy.

67　D. Antoinette Handy and Mary Lou Williams. "First Lady of the Jazz Keyboard." 197.
68　Williams and Taylor, *Embraced*.
69　For a recording of one of Williams's jazz history lectures, see Mary Lou Williams, "Mary Lou Williams—Joanne Burke's Rough Edit."
70　Eddie S. Glaude Jr., *In a Shade of Blue*, 5.
71　Biographer Linda Dahl describes an incident in 1978 in which Williams appeared at a women's jazz festival but publicly dismissed the premise of the celebration. See *Morning Glory*, 349.
72　Extensive reviews of collegiate jazz festivals were quite common in publications like *DownBeat*. Such reviews provide insight into the nature of jazz discourse in academia. For example, see "Campus Jazz I: First Annual Oread Collegiate Festival" by Martin Williams and "Campus Jazz II: Collegiate Jazz Festival" by Don DeMichael in *DownBeat*, June 4, 1964. Notable emphasis is placed on the evolving level of competition and on refining criteria of adjudication.
73　Williams, unpublished memoir, 180.
74　Shirley Wilson Logan, *"We Are Coming,"* xiii.
75　Angela Y. Davis, *Blues Legacies and Black Feminism*, xi.
76　Angela Davis, *Blues Legacies and Black Feminism*, xvii.
77　See the score of Mary Lou Williams, "Roll 'Em."
78　Dan Morgenstern in liner notes to Mary Lou Williams, *Zodiac Suite*.
79　Tamika L. Carey, *Rhetorical Healing*, 18.
80　Logan, *"We Are Coming,"* 11.
81　Logan, *"We Are Coming,"* 22.
82　One of the most popular annual festivals is the Mary Lou Williams Jazz Festival hosted by the Kennedy Center. See www.kennedy-center.org.
83　Mary Lou Williams, interview by Fr. Peter F. O'Brien, S.J, and Joe Kennedy Jr., undated., Mary Lou Williams Collection, Institute of Jazz Studies, Rutgers University.

Chapter 4

1　Cornel West, keynote address.
2　See Frank Kofsky's *Black Nationalism and the Revolution in Music*.
3　See Bill Cole's *John Coltrane*.
4　A. B. Spellman and Murray Horwitz, "John Coltrane"

Notes to Chapter 4

5. Robert Levin in liner notes to John Coltrane, *Blue Train*.
6. Hard bop is an evolution of bebop.
7. Zita Carno, "Style of John Coltrane."
8. Ira Gitler in liner notes to John Coltrane, *Soultrane*.
9. Gitler in Coltrane, *Soultrane*.
10. Houston A. Baker Jr., *Modernism and the Harlem Renaissance*, 49.
11. Bob Dawbarn, "Coltrane Rewrites the Rules."
12. In the previous year, 1960, several African nations became independent: Cameroon, Togo, Senegal, Mali, Madagascar, Zaire, Somalia, Benin, Niger, Burkina Faso, Ivory Coast, Chad, Central African Republic, Congo, Gabon, Mauritania, and Nigeria.
13. John Coltrane, *A Love Supreme*, liner notes.
14. Augustine, *Confessions*, 123.
15. Augustine, *Confessions*, 142.
16. Martin Luther King Jr., "Autobiography of Religious Development."
17. Malcolm X, *Autobiography of Malcolm X*, 189.
18. Robert Francesconi, "Free Jazz and Black Nationalism."
19. Leroi Jones (Amiri Baraka), *Black Music*, 79.
20. Spellman considered Coltrane to be a leading voice in this conversation; however, Coltrane declined to be interviewed for the book.
21. A. B. Spellman, *Four Lives in the Bebop Business*, x.
22. Larry Neal, "Black Musician in White America," 53.
23. Neal, "Black Musician in White America," 53.
24. Neal, "Black Musician in White America," 55.
25. Neal, "Black Musician in White America," 57.
26. Larry Neal, "Any Day Now," 54.
27. Neal, "Any Day Now," 55.
28. Neal, "Any Day Now," 55.
29. Neal, "Any Day Now," 55.
30. Neal, "Any Day Now," 56.
31. Larry Neal, "Black Boogaloo."
32. Tynan, "Take 5."
33. Don DeMichael, "John Coltrane and Eric Dolphy Answer the Jazz Critics," 21.
34. DeMichael, "John Coltrane and Eric Dolphy Answer the Jazz Critics," 22.
35. Ingrid Monson, *Freedom Sounds*, 14.

36 Monson, *Freedom Sounds*, 65.
37 John Gennari, *Blowin' Hot and Cool*, 253.
38 Ira Gitler, Max Roach, and Abbey Lincoln, "Racial Prejudice in Jazz," 21.
39 Gennari, *Blowin' Hot and Cool*, 262.
40 Such efforts would predate similar tactics deployed by artists such as Ray Charles (his refusal to perform in Augusta, Georgia, due to its segregation policies), Prince (his infamous battle over control of his music with Warner Music), and Jay Z (his launch of the music streaming service TIDAL as an attempt to create a more equitable environment for artists with the onset of music streaming services such as Pandora and Spotify).
41 Eddie Prevost, "Discourse of a Dysfunctional Drummer."
42 Kenneth Burke, *Counter-Statement*, 190.
43 Gerald Early, "Ode to John Coltrane," 377.
44 Davis W. Houck and David E. Dixon, introduction, 3.
45 See Kenneth Burke, *Grammar of Motives*, ix, 57.
46 Marcus Baram, *Gil Scott-Heron*, 57.
47 Early, "Ode to John Coltrane," 381.
48 Nathaniel Mackey, *Paracritical Hinge*, 321.
49 Mackey, *Paracritical Hinge*, 321.
50 Mackey, *Paracritical Hinge*, 212.
51 Nathaniel Mackey, *Bedouin Hornbook*, 182.
52 Dawn Lundy Martin, "Rhythmic Poetry," 17.
53 Mackey, *Bedouin Hornbook*, 43.
54 Nathaniel Mackey, *Bass Cathedral*, 23.
55 The song in question is Al Green's "Love and Happiness."
56 Mackey, *Bedouin Hornbook*, 63.
57 Mackey, *Bass Cathedral*, 6.
58 Robin D. G. Kelley, *Freedom Dreams*, 11.
59 Herman S. Gray, *Cultural Moves*, 46.
60 David L. Palmer, "Virtuosity as Rhetoric."
61 Palmer, "Virtuosity as Rhetoric," 351.
62 Gray, *Cultural Moves*.
63 John Coltrane, interview by Frank Kofsky, November 1966, tape reel, Pacifica Radio Archive, 282, http://www.pacificaradioarchives.org/recording/bc1266.
64 Coltrane, interview by Kofsky, 286.

188 Notes to Chapter 5

65 Coltrane, interview by Kofsky, 287.
66 Coltrane, interview by Kofsky, 291.
67 Coltrane, interview by Kofsky, 311.
68 For example, in 1965 Coltrane performed a benefit concert for Amiri Baraka's Black Arts Repertory Theatre/School. See Frank Kofsky, *Black Nationalism and the Revolution in Music*, 142.
69 Amiri Baraka in liner notes, John Coltrane, *Coltrane Live at Birdland*.

Chapter 5

1 Laurraine Goreau, *Just Mahalia, Baby*, 289.
2 Goreau, *Just Mahalia, Baby*, 233.
3 Mahalia Jackson, "I Can't Stop Singing."
4 Laurraine Goreau, "Mahalia."
5 Goreau, "Mahalia," 45.
6 Goreau spends a considerable amount of time exploring the impact Jackson made on her audiences. For her summary of such press coverage, see her discussion of a quote from *People Today Weekly Magazine*: "When Mahalia sings, audiences do more than just listen—they undergo a profoundly moving emotional experience" (151). For similar views articulated in African American newspapers, see Michael Graham, "Mahalia Jackson Was Great as Ever at Ushers' Concert," *Washington Afro-American*, December 6, 1969. Jackson often situated her performances as instances where she experienced spirit possession: "Sometimes when I am singing, I become a complete instrument to be used. I reach a higher realm and something divine, a spirit, takes possession of my body." See "Songstress with a Divine Vision," *Indian Express*, city edition, May 8, 1971.
7 "Songstress with a Divine Vision," *Indian Express*.
8 William H. Tallmadge, "Dr. Watts and Mahalia Jackson." For a wider sampling of this style from archival recordings, Tallmadge suggests the Folkways series *Music from the South*.
9 "Move On Up a Little Higher" was written by Rev. Herbert Brewster, the pastor of East Trigg Baptist Church in Memphis. Brewster became active in the civil rights struggle in Memphis during the 1950s and, like King and Jackson, fused his theological and political inclinations in service of liberation. Brewster would go on to compose a series of gospel songs

that became anthems for the Civil Rights movement, including "How I Got Over" and "I'm Climbing Higher and Higher."
10 Article 5 [no title], *Chicago Defender*, national edition, January 3, 1948, ProQuest, http://search.proquest.com/docview/492753653/citation/BF0F8A2EAFDF46E7PQ/1.
11 Mahalia Jackson, "Move On Up a Little Higher," Genius, accessed June 8, 2020, https://genius.com/Mahalia-jackson-move-on-up-a-little-higher-lyrics.
12 "Gospel with a Bounce," *Time*, October 4, 1954.
13 "Gospel with a Bounce," *Milwaukee Journal*, November 18, 1954, sec. Radio, Mahalia Jackson Papers, Oversized Clippings, United States, 1961–1965 [sic], Chicago Museum of History.
14 Mahalia Jackson, "I Can't Stop Singing."
15 Mahalia Jackson, "I Can't Stop Singing."
16 Mahalia Jackson, "I Can't Stop Singing."
17 See Tiger C. Roholt's *Groove* and Steph Ceraso's *Sounding Composition*.
18 Sallie Martin interview / Fragment of Robert Anderson interview, by Laurraine Goreau, November 4, 1972, box 42, ID: LG001, Tulane University Special Collections, Hogan Jazz Archive Oral Histories Collection, archives.tulane.edu/search?utf8=%E2%9C%93&op%5B%5D=&q%5B%5D=%22Robert+Anderson%22+and+%22Sallie+Martin%22&limit=&field%5B%5D=&from_year%5B%5D=&to_year%5B%5D=&commit=Search.
19 James H. Cone, *Spirituals and the Blues*, loc. 1614, e-book.
20 "A Joyful Noise," *Insight*.
21 Jules Schwerin, *Got to Tell It*, 27.
22 Don Gold, "In God She Trusts."
23 "Mahalia Jackson: Songs with a Message," *Himmat, Bombay Weekly*, May 7, 1971, clippings, India, 1971, box 2, folder 2, Mahalia Jackson Papers, Chicago Museum of History.
24 Schwerin, *Got to Tell It*, 35.
25 Darlene Donloe, *Mahalia Jackson*, 155.
26 Jennifer Lynn Stoever, *Sonic Color Line*, 7.
27 Jackson often discussed her desire for a school that would train youth from all backgrounds in African American music. For Jackson, this included the entire tradition. Said Jackson: "The slave songs . . . we need to preserve that." See Jean Otto, "I Was Crying," *Milwaukee*

Journal, May 5, 1968, sec. Women's Section, oversized clippings, United States, 1966–72, Mahalia Jackson Papers, Chicago Museum of History.
28 Although the general narrative remains stable, specific details about this incident conflict with each other across various biographies of Jackson. See Jesse Jackson, *Make a Joyful Noise unto the Lord!*, 53–59; Goreau, *Just Mahalia, Baby*, 61.
29 Stoever, *Sonic Color Line*, 7.
30 Mark Burford, *Mahalia Jackson and the Black Gospel Field*, 302.
31 Goreau, "Mahalia," 48.
32 Goreau, *Just Mahalia, Baby*, 55.
33 Langston Hughes, "Simple Is No Patron of the Arts; Loves Music He Can Understand," *Chicago Defender*, national edition, December 11, 1948.
34 Hughes, "Simple Is No Patron of the Arts."
35 Jesse Jackson, *Make a Joyful Noise unto the Lord!*, 89.
36 Carlton Brown, "What's New in Records."
37 Mahalia Jackson, "I Can't Stop Singing."
38 For more discussion of Jackson's conflict with the National Baptist Convention, particularly her willingness to hold a rally for Dr. Martin Luther King Jr. against strong objections, see Donloe, *Mahalia Jackson*, 155.
39 Geneva Smitherman, *Talkin and Testifyin: The Language of Black America*, 10.
40 Studs Terkel, "Gospel of Mahalia Jackson," *DownBeat*, December 1958.
41 Terkel, "The Gospel of Mahalia Jackson."
42 Curtis J. Evans, *Burden of Black Religion*, 5.
43 Mahalia Jackson, "I Can't Stop Singing."
44 Lynn Langway, "Mahalia Makes A Sadder Sound Today," *Akron Beacon Journal*, July 8, 1968.
45 Jackson, "I Can't Stop Singing."
46 Herta Dimmer to Mahalia Jackson, n.d., Correspondence 1962–71, Mahalia Jackson Papers, Chicago Museum of History.
47 Dimmer.
48 Dimmer.
49 Norman Vincent Peale, "'Movin' On Up' Was No Dream."
50 Denise Goodman, "Songs Ease Task of Negroes' Wait," *Journal Herald* [Dayton OH], August 8, 1963.

51 "Mahalia Jackson Here for Series of Recitals," *Mainichi* [Japan] *Daily News*, April 8, 1971, clippings, Japan 1971, box 2 folder 3, Mahalia Jackson Papers, Chicago Museum of History.
52 Laurraine Goreau, "A Gift of Gospel Music from Mahalia," *States-Item* [New Orleans], September 1, 1971, sec. For and About the Family, 40. In oversized clippings, United States, 1966–72, Mahalia Jackson Papers, Chicago Museum of History.
53 K. B. Keating, "Miss Mahalia Jackson, the Gospel Singer," *Nagpur* [India] *Times*, April 25, 1971, clippings, India, 1971, box 2, folder 2, Mahalia Jackson Papers, Chicago Museum of History.
54 Goreau, "Gift of Gospel Music."
55 Carlton Brown, "What's New in Records."
56 Goreau, *Just Mahalia, Baby*, 47.
57 Luke 12:48.
58 Goreau, *Just Mahalia, Baby*, 57.
59 Mahalia Jackson and Evan McLeod Wylie, *Movin' On Up*, 37.
60 See Floris Loretta Barnett Cash's *African American Women and Social Action*; Reiland Rabaka's *Hip Hop's Amnesia*; Wanda A. Hendricks' *Gender, Race, and Politics in the Midwest*; Nina Mjagkij's *Organizing Black America*; and Gerda Lerner's "Early Community Work of Black Club Women."
61 See Shirley Wilson Logan's *"We Are Coming"* and Jacqueline Jones Royster's *Traces of a Stream*.
62 Mark Burford, *Mahalia Jackson and the Black Gospel Field*, 57.
63 Deborah F. Atwater, *African American Women's Rhetoric*, 1.
64 Aristotle, *On Rhetoric*, 31.
65 Mahalia Jackson, "I Can't Stop Singing."
66 Mahalia Jackson, "I Can't Stop Singing."
67 I argue the cultural impact was exponentially greater than Dave Chapelle's infamous rejection of a $50 million deal from Comedy Central in 2005 or, more recently, Chance the Rapper's rejection of a $10 million recording deal after winning a Grammy for best rap album in 2017. I would also be remiss not to mention Prince's epic battle to leave a $100 million contract with Warner Brothers.
68 Mahalia Jackson, "Why I Turned Down a Million Dollars."
69 Mahalia Jackson, "Why I Turned Down a Million Dollars."
70 Mahalia Jackson, "Why I Turned Down a Million Dollars."

71 Albert Murray, *Stomping the Blues*, 60.
72 Murray, *Stomping the Blues*, 57.
73 Murray, *Stomping the Blues*, 65.
74 Cone, *Spirituals and the Blues*, loc. 1461.
75 Cone, *Spirituals and the Blues*, loc. 1461.
76 Cone, *Spirituals and the Blues*, loc. 1495.
77 "Mahalia Jackson: Queen of Gospel Singers." For more examples of Jackson distancing herself from the blues, see "Mahalia Jackson," *Evening News of India*, April 4, 1971, clippings, India, 1971, box 2, folder 2, Mahalia Jackson Papers, Chicago Museum of History.
78 "Religioso Upbeat Sees More D.J.'s Hop on Spiritual-Gospel Bandwagon," *Chicago Sun-Times*, September 8, 1954, oversized scrapbook, box 3, folder 2, Mahalia Jackson Papers, Chicago Museum of History.
79 In a vociferous public condemnation of what she termed "pop gospel," Jackson sought to draw clear distinctions between authentic gospel music and its imitators: "The Devil is in those singers," said Miss Jackson. "He's making them destroy the principle of our sacred songs. They're singing songs in night clubs now just like I sang in the church when I was in my daddy's church choir . . . how can it be called gospel now? Well, they ain't out to save no one's soul. They ain't even lifting up the good thoughts to the people . . . Can't those night clubs find any entertainment? Have they got to go up and get God's books?" See Ralph Clark, "Mahalia Sings Out In Protest At 'Pop Gospel,'" *Valley Times Today*, June 12, 1963.
80 Mahalia Jackson, "Why I Turned Down a Million Dollars," 6.
81 Goreau, *Just Mahalia, Baby*, 332. Irving Townsend suspects that Mahalia's avoidance of bars was also a shrewd business decision.
82 Jackson often addressed this irony with statements such as, "I had no dreams that it would become big business, but I found that it was doing people good, doing something the psychiatrist couldn't do. It was lifting them up." See Mary Cooke, "She's Just Got To Sing Gospel," *Honolulu Advertiser*, February 20, 1963, sec. C.
83 "Joyful Noise," *Insight*.
84 Mahalia Jackson, "God Spared Me to Sing," *Chicago Defender*, September 18, 1954, 1–2, oversized scrapbook, Mahalia Jackson Papers, Chicago Museum of History.
85 Mahalia Jackson, "God Spared Me To Sing."

86 Mahalia Jackson, "God Spared Me To Sing."
87 Gold, "In God She Trusts."
88 During an interview, Jackson explained why she "rushed" to support the Montgomery, Alabama, Bus Boycott in 1955 through fundraising performances, stating, "I don't charge the good walking people. I do it for myself. I do it because I'm very glad the Reverend King came along. He's forcefully made people realize the power of nonviolence and love. Why, with dignity and strength mountains can be moved. The white man can be too." See Gold, "In God She Trusts."
89 For a detailed discussion of Jackson's early political activity, including her performances for Democrat Louis B. Anderson, an alderman of Chicago's second ward from 1917 to 1933 when she was a teenager, see Goreau, *Just Mahalia, Baby*, 58.
90 Schwerin, *Got to Tell It*, 14.
91 "Mahalia Rocks and Rolls," [Knoxville, TN] *Times-Herald*, December 24, 1961.
92 "Mahalia Rocks and Rolls."
93 Lynn Langway, "Mahalia Makes a Sadder Sound Today," *Akron Beacon Journal*, July 8, 1968.
94 Mark Burford, "Mahalia Jackson Meets the Wise Men," 431.
95 Mahalia Jackson, "I Can't Stop Singing."
96 Ed Sullivan, interview by Laurraine Goreau, November 17, 1972, folder Ed Sullivan Interview / Johnny Jackson Interview / Lindy Boggs Interview, Hogan Jazz Archive Oral Histories Collection, Tulane University Special Collections, archives.tulane.edu/repositories/3/archival_objects/202477.
97 Ed Sullivan, interview by Laurraine Goreau.
98 Ed Sullivan, interview by Laurraine Goreau.
99 Jackson's use of skin lighteners is one example of how she navigated the pressures of Eurocentric beauty standards in conjunction with balancing a range of audience expectations. Schwerin, *Got to Tell It*, 172.
100 Denise Goodman, "Songs Ease Task of Negroes' Wait," *Journal Herald* [Dayton OH], August 8, 1963.
101 Donloe, *Mahalia Jackson*, 110.
102 Mahalia Jackson, "I Can't Stop Singing."
103 Mahalia Jackson, "I Can't Stop Singing."

104 Donloe, *Mahalia Jackson*, 100.
105 Otto, "I Was Crying," *Milwaukee Journal*, May 5, 1968, sec. Women's Section, oversized clippings, United States, 1966–72, Mahalia Jackson Papers, Chicago Museum of History.
106 Cone, *Spirituals and the Blues*, loc. 1461.
107 Jean Culbertson, "Mahalia's Local Fans Register Rare Enthusiasm," *Clarion-Ledger* [Jackson MS], December 14, 1969, sec. F.
108 Jackson, "I Can't Stop Singing," 19–100.
109 Goreau, *Just Mahalia, Baby*, 252.
110 Mel Gussow, "Musical Biography of Mahalia Jackson," *New York Times*, June 6, 1978, sec. Archives, www.nytimes.com/1978/06/06/archives/musical-biography-of-mahalia-jackson-blues-and-jazz.html.
111 Jackson's message became shared by others within the gospel music community. Anna L. Murrell of The Murrell Singers of Pittsburgh, Pennsylvania offered an almost identical grievance: "Gospel was not meant to be sung in a night club nor a theatre. The drama of gospel appeals to all people; it attracts the man in the street, and eventually sends him into the church. That is the real purpose of this fiery music." Anna L. Murrell, "What Has Happened to Gospel?," n.d., clippings, United States, 1964–1965, box 2, folder 6, Mahalia Jackson Papers, Chicago Museum of History.
112 Jackson headlined a Freedom Concert sponsored by the local Congress of Racial Equality in Dayton, Ohio, in Welcome Stadium. She cited jobs and housing as the biggest racial problems in the North and told reporters of her experience in Chicago. See Goodman, "Songs Ease Task of Negroes' Wait."
113 Schwerin, *Got to Tell It*, 183.

Conclusion

1 John Fowler, telephone interview by Earl H. Brooks, June 13, 2023.
2 Daniel Robert McClure, "'Who Will Survive in America?'," 7.
3 Alexander Weheliye, *Phonographies*, 6.
4 Jonathyne Briggs, "Red Noise."

Bibliography

"An Account of the Negroe Insurrection in South Carolina (1739)." In *Slavery*, edited by Stanley L. Engerman, Seymour Drescher, and Robert L. Paquette, 314-16. Oxford: Oxford University Press, 2009.

Anderson, Maureen. "The White Reception of Jazz in America." *African American Review* 38, no. 1 (2004): 135-45. doi:10.2307/1512237.

"Andy Kirk and His 12 Clouds of Joy." *Metronome*. January 1937. RIPM Jazz Periodicals. https://ripmjazz.org/.

Arbib, Michael A. "Five Terms in Search of Synthesis." In *Language, Music, and the Brain: A Mysterious Relationship*, edited by Michael A. Arbib, 3-44. Cambridge, MA: MIT Press, 2013.

Aristotle. *On Rhetoric: A Theory of Civic Discourse*. Translated by George A. Kennedy. New York: Oxford University Press, 2006.

———. *Politics*. Translated by Benjamin Jowett. New edition. Mineola, NY: Dover, 2000.

Arnold, Ignaz Theodor Ferdinand Cajetan. *Wolfgang Amadeus Mozart und Joseph Haydn*. Vol. 1. Altenmünster, Ger.: Jazzybee Verlag, 2012. Kindle.

Asante, Molefi. *The Afrocentric Idea*. Revised edition. Philadelphia: Temple University Press, 2011.

Attali, Jacques. *Noise: The Political Economy of Music*. Translated by Brian Massumi. Vol. 16: *Theory and History of Literature*. Manchester, Eng.: Manchester University Press, 1985.

Atwater, Deborah F. *African American Women's Rhetoric: The Search for Dignity, Personhood, and Honor*. Lanham, MD: Lexington Books, 2009.

Augustine. *Confessions*. Translated by Edward B Pusey. Vol. 7. New York: P. F. Collier and Son, 1909.

Baker, Houston A., Jr. *I Don't Hate the South: Reflections on Faulkner, Family, and the South*. Oxford: Oxford University Press, 2007.

———. *Modernism and the Harlem Renaissance*. Chicago: University of Chicago Press, 1989.

Baldwin, James. "Sonny's Blues." In *The Jazz Fiction Anthology*, edited by Sascha Feinstein and David Rife, 17–48. Bloomington: Indiana University Press, 2009.

Bambara, Toni Cade. "Witchbird." In *Black-Eyed Susans / Midnight Birds*, edited by Mary Helen Washington, 375–92. New York: Anchor Books, 1977.

Baram, Marcus. *Gil Scott-Heron: Pieces of a Man*. New York: St. Martin's Press, 2014.

Barr, Marleen S. Introduction to *Afro-Future Females: Black Writers Chart Science Fiction's Newest New-Wave Trajectory*, edited by Marleen S. Barr. Columbus: Ohio State University Press, 2008.

Bash, Carol. *Mary Lou Williams: The Lady Who Swings the Band*. Documentary. New York: Paradox Films, 2015.

Batteux, Charles. *Les beaux arts reduits à un même principe*. Sydney: Wentworth Press, 2018.

Berger, Morroe. "Jazz: Resistance to the Diffusion of a Culture-Pattern." *Journal of Negro History* 32, no. 4 (1947): 461–94. doi:10.2307/2714928.

Berlin, Edward A. *King of Ragtime: Scott Joplin and His Era*. New York: Oxford University Press, 1994.

———. "Ragtime." *Oxford Music Online: Grove Music Online*. Oxford University Press. Accessed June 6, 2017. http://www.oxfordmusiconline.com/subscriber/article/grove/music/A2252241.

———. *Ragtime: A Musical and Cultural History*. Berkeley: University of California Press, 1984.

Black, Edwin. *Rhetorical Criticism: A Study in Method*. Madison: University of Wisconsin Press, 1978.

Blesh, Rudi, and Harriet Janis. *They All Played Ragtime: The True Story of an American Music*. New York: Oak Publishing, 1971.

Bonds, Mark Evan. *Music as Thought: Listening to the Symphony in the Age of Beethoven*. Princeton, NJ: Princeton University Press, 2006.

Booker, Vaughn A. *Lift Every Voice and Swing: Black Musicians and Religious Culture in the Jazz Century*. New York: NYU Press, 2020.

Borglum, Gutzon. "Imitation the Curse of American Art." *Brush and Pencil* 19, no. 2 (1907): 50–62.

Born, Georgina. Introduction to *Music, Sound and Space: Transformations of Public and Private Experience*, edited by Georgina Born, 1–69. Cambridge: Cambridge University Press, 2013.

Borschke, Margie. "Rethinking the Rhetoric of Remix." *Media International Australia* 141 (November 2011): 17–25.
Bowles, Paul. "Duke Ellington in Recital for Russian War Relief." In *The Duke Ellington Reader*, edited by Mark Tucker, 165–66. New York: Oxford University Press, 1993.
Briggs, Jonathyne. "A Red Noise: Pop and Politics in Post-1968 France." In *The Global Sixties in Sound and Vision: Media, Counterculture, Revolt*, edited by T. Brown and A. Lison, 15. London: Palgrave Macmillan U.S.A., 2014.
Britan, Halbert H. "Music and Morality." *International Journal of Ethics* 15, no. 1 (1904): 48–63.
Brooks, Lori. "The Composer versus the 'Perfessor': Writing Race and (Rag) Time." In *New Perspectives on James Weldon Johnson's "The Autobiography of an Ex-Colored Man,"* edited by Noelle Morrissette, 169–88. Athens: University of Georgia Press, 2017.
Brown, Carlton. "What's New in Records." *Redbook*, June 1963.
Brown, Sterling A. "Negro Character as Seen by White Authors." *Journal of Negro Education* 2, no. 2 (1933): 179–203. doi:10.2307/2292236.
Browne, C. A. *The Story of Our National Ballads*. New York: Thomas Y. Crowell, 1919.
Bull, Michael. *Sounding Out the City: Personal Stereos and the Management of Everyday Life*. Oxford: Berg, 2000.
Burford, Mark. *Mahalia Jackson and the Black Gospel Field*. Oxford: Oxford University Press, 2019.
———. "Mahalia Jackson Meets the Wise Men: Defining Jazz at the Music Inn." *Musical Quarterly* 97, no. 3 (2014): 429–86.
Burke, Kenneth. *Counter-Statement*. Berkeley: University of California Press, 1968.
———. *A Grammar of Motives*. Berkeley: University of California Press, 1969.
———. *A Rhetoric of Motives*. Berkeley: University of California Press, 1969.
Burstyn, Shai. "In Quest of the Period Ear." *Early Music* 25, no. 4 (November 1997): 692.
Caponi-Tabery, Gena. *Jump for Joy: Jazz, Basketball, and Black Culture in 1930s America*. Amherst: University of Massachusetts Press, 2008.
Carey, Tamika L. *Rhetorical Healing: The Reeducation of Contemporary Black Womanhood*. Albany, NY: State University of New York Press, 2017.
Carno, Zita. "The Style of John Coltrane." *Jazz Review* 2, no. 10 (November 1959): 13–15.

Carr, Roy, Brian Case, and Fred Dellar. *The Hip: Hipsters, Jazz and the Beat Generation*. London: Faber and Faber, 1987.

Carroll, Anne E. "Du Bois and Art Theory: *The Souls of Black Folk* as a 'Total Work of Art'." *Public Culture* 17, no. 2 (2005): 235–54.

Cash, Floris Loretta Barnett. *African American Women and Social Action: The Clubwomen and Volunteerism from Jim Crow to the New Deal, 1896–1936*. Westport: Greenwood Press, 2001.

Ceraso, Steph. *Sounding Composition: Multimodal Pedagogies for Embodied Listening*. Pittsburgh, PA: University of Pittsburgh Press, 2018.

Clark, Ralph. "Mahalia Sings Out in Protest at 'Pop Gospel'." *Valley Times Today* (Hollywood, CA). June 12, 1963.

Cole, Bill. *John Coltrane*. Boston: Da Capo Press, 1976.

Cole, Bob, James Weldon Johnson, and J. Rosamond Johnson. "Gimme De Leavin's." Words by James Weldon Johnson. Music by J. Rosamond Johnson and Bob Cole. New York: J. W. Stern, 1904.

———. "The Spirit of the Banjo." Words by Bob Cole and James Weldon Johnson. Music by J. Rosamond Johnson. New York: J. W. Stern, 1903.

Coltrane, John, and the John Coltrane Quartet. *Africa/Brass*. 1961. Verve/Impulse! 1748622, 2008. Compact disc.

———. *Blue Train*. 1958. Liner notes by Robert Levin. Blue Note TOCJ-9005, 2003. Compact disc.

———. *Coltrane Live at Birdland*. 1964. Liner notes by Amiri Baraka. Impulse!, 1996. Compact disc.

———. *Giant Steps*. 1960. Warner Brothers WPCR-25101, 2006. Compact disc.

———. *A Love Supreme*. 1965. Liner notes by John Coltrane. Verve 002372702, 2015. Compact disc.

———. *My Favorite Things*. 1961. Warner Brothers WPCR-25104, 2006. Compact disc.

———. *Soultrane*. 1958. Liner notes by Ira Gitler. Fantasy/Prestige 7230006, 2006. Compact disc.

Cone, James H. *The Spirituals and the Blues: An Interpretation*. 2nd revised edition. Maryknoll, NY: Orbis Books, 1992.

Coyle, Owen. "Mary Lou Williams and Her Jazz Crusade." *Mississippi Rag*. April 1976. RIPM Jazz Periodicals. https://ripmjazz.org/.

Cullen, Countee. "Heritage." In *The Columbia Anthology of American Poetry*, edited by Jay Parini. New York: Columbia University Press, 1995.

Curtis, Natalie. "The Negro's Contribution to the Music of America: The Larger Opportunity of the Colored Man of Today." *The Craftsman* 23, no. 6 (March 1, 1913): 660–69.

Curtis, Susan. *Dancing to a Black Man's Tune: A Life of Scott Joplin*. Columbia: University of Missouri Press, 2004.

Dahl, Linda, *Morning Glory: A Biography of Mary Lou Williams*. Berkeley: University of California Press, 2001.

———. "'Night Life'—Mary Lou Williams." National Registry, 2008. Accessed June 12, 2017. https://www.loc.gov/programs/static/national-recording-preservation-board/documents/mary-lou-williams.pdf.

Darden, Robert. *Nothing but Love in God's Water*. Vol. 1, *Black Sacred Music from the Civil War to the Civil Rights Movement*. University Park: Pennsylvania State Press, 2014.

Darrell, R. D. "Black Beauty." In *The Duke Ellington Reader*, edited by Mark Tucker, 57–63. New York: Oxford University Press, 1995.

Davis, Angela Y. *Blues Legacies and Black Feminism: Gertrude "Ma" Rainey, Bessie Smith, and Billie Holiday*. New York: Vintage Books, 2011.

Davis, Miles. *Kind of Blue*. 1959. Sony Music 88697883272, 2012. Compact disc.

———. *Milestones*. 1958. Sony Music 6619719, 2013. Compact disc.

Dawbarn, Bob. "Coltrane Rewrites the Rules." *Melody Maker* 37, no. 1485 (June 2, 1962): 6.

DeMichael, Don. "Campus Jazz II: Collegiate Jazz Festival." *DownBeat* 31, no. 13 (June 4, 1964).

———. "John Coltrane and Eric Dolphy Answer the Critics." *DownBeat* 29, no. 8 (April 12, 1962), 20–23.

Devoss, Danielle Nicole, and Porter, James E. "Why Napster Matters to Writing: Filesharing as a New Ethic of Digital Delivery." *Computers and Composition* 23, no. 2 (2006): 178–210. doi:10.1016/j.compcom.2006.02.001.

Doerschuk, Robert L. *88: The Giants of Jazz Piano*. San Francisco: Backbeat Books, 2001.

Donloe, Darlene. *Mahalia Jackson*. Los Angeles: Holloway House, 1992.

Drury, Theodore. "The Negro in Classic Music; Or, Leading Opera, Oratorio and Concert Singers." *Colored American Magazine*, September 1, 1902.

Du Bois, W. E. B. *The Souls of Black Folk*. Oxford: Oxford University Press, 2007.

———. *The Talented Tenth*. Scotts Valley, CA: CreateSpace Independent Publishing Platform, 2013.

200 Bibliography

Dusenberry, Lisa, et al. "Filter. Remix. Make: Cultivating Adaptability through Multimodality." *Journal of Technical Writing and Communication* 45, no. 3 (July 1, 2015): 299–322. doi:10.1177/0047281615578851.

Early, Gerald. "Ode to John Coltrane: A Jazz Musician's Influence on African American Culture." *Antioch Review* 57, no. 3 (1999): 371–85. doi:10.2307/4613886.

Ellington, Duke. "Black and Tan Fantasy." Musical score. Jazz at Lincoln Center Library. EMI Mills Music, 1934.

———. *Black, Brown and Beige*. 1958. *The Duke Ellington Carnegie Hall Concerts, January 1943*. World Records 2PCD 340042, 1999. Compact disc.

———. *The Duke Ellington Reader*, edited by Mark Tucker. New York: Oxford University Press, 1993.

———. "Jump for Joy." *The Private Collection*. Vol. 1: *Studio Sessions Chicago 1956*. Compact Disc. Kaz Records, 1996.

———. Letter to Richard Wright. June 25, 1942. Richard Wright Papers. Yale Collection of American Literature, Beinecke Rare Book and Manuscript Library, Yale University. Box 97, folder 1313.

———. *Music Is My Mistress*. Garden City, NY: Doubleday, 1973.

———. "We, Too, Sing 'America.'" In *The Duke Ellington Reader*, 146–48.

Ellington, Duke, and Billy Strayhorn. "Take the 'A' Train." 1941. *Duke Ellington 1952–1960*. Columbia 5096162, 2003. Compact disc.

Erb, J. Lawrence. "Where Is the American Song?" *Etude* 17, no. 5 (May 1, 1899): 154.

Evans, Curtis J. *The Burden of Black Religion*. Oxford: Oxford University Press, 2008.

Feather, Leonard. "A Rebuttal of Hammond." *Jazz* 1, no. 8 (May 1943): 14, 20.

Floyd, Samuel A. "Ring Shout! Literary Studies, Historical Studies, and Black Music Inquiry." *Black Music Research Journal* 11, no. 2 (1991): 265–87. doi:10.2307/779269.

Francesconi, Robert. "Free Jazz and Black Nationalism: A Rhetoric of Musical Style." *Critical Studies in Mass Communication* 3, no. 1 (March 1, 1986): 36–49. doi:10.1080/15295038609366628.

Garcia, David F. *Listening for Africa: Freedom, Modernity, and the Logic of Black Music's African Origins*. Durham, NC: Duke University Press, 2017.

Gates, Racquel J. *Double Negative: The Black Image and Popular Culture*. Durham, NC: Duke University Press, 2018.

Gates, W. F. "Ethiopian Syncopation—The Decline of Ragtime." *Musician* 7, no. 10 (October 1902): 341.

Gennari, John. *Blowin' Hot and Cool: Jazz and Its Critics*. Chicago: University of Chicago Press, 2010.

Giddins, Gary. "Modern Mary." *JazzTimes*, September 1, 2004. Accessed June 12, 2017. https://jazztimes.com/columns/cadenza/modern-mary/.

Gilbert, David. *The Product of Our Souls: Ragtime, Race, and the Birth of the Manhattan Musical Marketplace*. Chapel Hill: University of North Carolina Press, 2015.

Gilyard, Keith, and Adam J. Banks. *On African-American Rhetoric*. Milton Park, UK: Routledge, 2018.

Gitler, Ira, Max Roach, and Abbey Lincoln. "Racial Prejudice in Jazz." Part 1. *DownBeat*, March 15, 1962.

Glaude, Eddie S. Jr. *In a Shade of Blue: Pragmatism and the Politics of Black America*. Chicago: University of Chicago Press, 2010.

Gold, Don. "In God She Trusts." *Ladies' Home Journal*, November 1963.

Goreau, Laurraine. *Just Mahalia, Baby: The Mahalia Jackson Story*. Grenta, LA: Pelican, 1984.

———. "Mahalia: 'I Thought I Was the Beatles'." *Delta Review*, December 1967. Mahalia Jackson Papers. Biographical Printed Material 1964–67. Box 1, folder 2. Chicago Museum of History.

"Gospel with a Bounce." *Time*, October 4, 1954.

Gray, Herman S. *Cultural Moves: African Americans and the Politics of Representation*. Berkeley: University of California Press, 2005.

Green, Al. "Love and Happiness." 1973. *The Definitive Greatest Hits*. Capitol/EMI Records 82041, 2007. Compact disc.

Green, Edward, and Evan Spring, eds. *The Cambridge Companion to Duke Ellington*. Cambridge: Cambridge University Press, 2015.

Griffin, Farah Jasmine. *Harlem Nocturne: Women Artists and Progressive Politics during World War II*. New York: Basic Books, 2013.

Hammond, John. "Count Basie's Band and 'Boogie-Woogie' Pianists Tops." *DownBeat*, May 1936. RIPM Jazz Periodicals. https://ripmjazz.org/.

———. "Is the Duke Deserting Jazz?" *Jazz* 1, no. 8 (May 1943): 15.

Handel, Stephen. *Listening: An Introduction to the Perception of Auditory Events*. Cambridge, MA: MIT Press, 1989.

Handy, D. Antoinette, and Mary Lou Williams. "First Lady of the Jazz Keyboard." *Black Perspective in Music* 8, no. 2 (1980): 195–214. doi:10.2307/1214051.

Haraway, Donna J. *A Cyborg Manifesto: Science, Technology, and Socialist-Feminism in the Late Twentieth Century*. Minneapolis: University of Minnesota Press, 2016. http://ebookcentral.proquest.com/lib/warw/detail.action?docID=4392065.

Harney, Ben. "You've Been a Good Old Wagon but You Done Broke Down." Louisville, KY: Greenup Music, 1895.

Harper, Michael S. "Dear John, Dear Coltrane." *Dear John, Dear Coltrane: Poems*. Urbana: University of Illinois Press, 1970.

———. "Here Where Coltrane Is." *History Is Your Own Heartbeat: Poems*, 32. Urbana: University of Illinois Press, 1971.

Hasse, John Edward. *Beyond Category: The Life and Genius of Duke Ellington*. New York: Da Capo Press, 1995.

Hauser, Gerard A. *Vernacular Voices: The Rhetoric of Publics and Public Spheres*. Columbia: University of South Carolina Press, 1999.

Hayes, Eileen. M., and Linda Faye Williams. *Black Women and Music: More Than the Blues*. Urbana: University of Illinois Press, 2007.

Heble, Ajay. *Landing on the Wrong Note: Jazz, Dissonance, and Critical Practice*. New York: Routledge, 2013.

Heffernan, Nick. "'You Ain't Got to Be Black to Be Black': Music, Race, Consciousness, and Identity in *The Autobiography of an Ex-Colored Man*." In *Thriving on a Riff: Jazz and Blues Influences in African American Literature and Film*, edited by Graham Lock and David Murray, 21–39. Oxford: Oxford University Press, 2009.

Heilbut, Anthony. *The Gospel Sound: Good News and Bad Times*. New York: Simon and Schuster, 1971.

Hendricks, Wanda A. *Gender, Race, and Politics in the Midwest: Black Club Women in Illinois*. Indiana University Press, 1998.

Herzogenrath, Bernd, and Patricia Pisters, eds. *Sonic Thinking: A Media Philosophical Approach*. New York: Bloomsbury Academic, 2017.

Houck, Davis W., and David E. Dixon. Introduction to *Rhetoric, Religion, and the Civil Rights Movement, 1954–1965*, 1–18. Waco, TX: Baylor University Press, 2006.

Howard, Joseph E., and Ida Emerson. "Hello! Ma Baby." New York: T.B. Harms, 1899.

Howard-Pitney, David. *The African American Jeremiad: Appeals For Justice in America*. Philadelphia, PA: Temple University Press, 2009.

Hughes, Langston. "Afro-American Fragment." *Crisis* 37, no. 7 (July 1930): 30.

———. "I, Too, Sing America." In *The Collected Poems of Langston Hughes*, edited by Arnold Rampersad and David Ernest Roessel, 46. New York: Vintage Books, 1995.

———. "Jazz as Communication." Poetry Foundation, Jan. 5, 2021. https://www.poetryfoundation.org/articles/69394/jazz-as-communication. https://www.poetryfoundation.org/.

———. "The Negro Artist and the Racial Mountain." *Nation* 122 (June 23, 1926): 692–94.

———. "Simple Is No Patron of the Arts; Loves Music He Can Understand." *Chicago Defender*, December 11, 1948.

Jackson, David. "Jazz Is Her Religion." *Soul and Jazz Record*, September 1976. RIPM Jazz Periodicals. https://ripmjazz.org/.

Jackson, Jerma A. *Singing in My Soul: Black Gospel Music in a Secular Age*. Chapel Hill: University of North Carolina Press, 2004.

Jackson, Jesse. *Make a Joyful Noise unto the Lord! The Life of Mahalia Jackson, Queen of Gospel Singers*. New York: Crowell, 1974.

Jackson, Mahalia. "I Can't Stop Singing." *Saturday Evening Post* 232, no. 23 (December 5, 1959): 19–21, 98–100.

———. "Move On Up a Little Higher." Pt. 2. *The Original Apollo Sessions*. Couch and Madison Partners, 2006. Streaming. Spotify.

———. "Why I Turned Down a Million Dollars." *Tone*, May 1, 1960, 6.

Jackson, Mahalia, and Evan McLeod Wylie. *Movin' On Up: The Warmly Personal Story of America's Favorite Gospel Singer*. Portland, OR: Hawthorn Books, 1966.

Jasen, David A. *Ragtime: An Encyclopedia, Discography, and Sheetography*. New York: Routledge, 2014.

———. *Recorded Ragtime 1897–1958*. Hamden, CT: Archon Books, 1973.

Jauss, Hans Robert. *Toward an Aesthetic of Reception*. Minneapolis: University of Minnesota Press, 1982.

Jelks, Randal Maurice. *Faith and Struggle in the Lives of Four African Americans: Ethel Waters, Mary Lou Williams, Eldridge Cleaver, and Muhammad Ali*. Bloomsbury, 2019.

Jenkins, Chadwick. "A Question of Containment: Duke Ellington and Early Radio." *American Music* 26, no. 4 (2008): 415–41. doi:10.2307/40071718.

Johnson, David. "Jump for Joy: Duke Ellington's Celebratory Musical." *Night Lights Classic Jazz*. Indiana Public Media, February 5, 2008. http://indianapublicmedia.org/nightlights/jump-for-joy-duke-ellingtons-celebratory-musical/.

Bibliography

Johnson, James Weldon. *Along This Way: The Autobiography of James Weldon Johnson.* 1933. New York: Penguin Books, 1990.

———. *The Autobiography of an Ex-Colored Man.* 1912. New York: W. W. Norton, 2015.

Johnson, J. Rosamond, and James Weldon Johnson (lyric). "Every Woman's Eyes." New York: J. W. Stern, 1912.

———. "Roll Them Cotton Bales." New York: J. W. Stern, 1914.

Jones, Gayle. *Corregidora.* London: Serpent's Tail, 2000.

Jones, Leroi [Amiri Baraka]. *Black Music.* 1967. New York: Akashi Classics, 2010.

———. *Blues People: Negro Music in White America.* 1963. New York: Harper Collins, 1999.

Joplin, Scott. "Maple Leaf Rag." Sedalia, MO: John Stark and Son, 1899.

———. *Treemonisha.* New York: Scott Joplin, 1911.

"A Joyful Noise." *Insight: For the Best Informed Field Representatives in the Record Industry*, April 9, 1958.

Kant, Immanuel. *Critique of Judgment.* Translated by Werner S. Pluhar. Indianapolis, IN: Hackett, 1987.

Kelley, Robin D. G. *Freedom Dreams: The Black Radical Imagination.* Boston: Beacon Press, 2003.

Kernodle, Tammy. *Soul on Soul: The Life and Music of Mary Lou Williams.* Boston: Northeastern University Press, 2004.

King, Martin Luther, Jr. "An Autobiography of Religious Development." Martin Luther King, Jr., Research and Education Institute, January 23, 2015. https://okra.stanford.edu/transcription/document_images/Vol01Scans/359_12Sept-22Nov1950_An%20Autobiography%20of%20Religious%20Developme.pdf.

Kofsky, Frank. *Black Nationalism and the Revolution in Music.* College Park, GA: Pathfinder Press, 1970.

Krell, William H. "The Mississippi Rag." Chicago: S. Brainard's Sons, 1897.

Kubik, Gerhard. "The African Matrix in Jazz Harmonic Practices." *Black Music Research Journal* 25, no. 1/2 (Spring 2005): 167–222.

Lamar, Kendrick. *To Pimp a Butterfly.* Santa Monica, CA: Aftermath/Interscope Records, 2015. Compact disc.

Larson, Kate Clifford. *Bound for the Promised Land: Harriet Tubman: Portrait of an American Hero.* New York: Random House, 2009.

Lee, Harper. *To Kill a Mockingbird.* 1960. New York: HarperCollins, 2010.

Lerner, Gerda. "Early Community Work of Black Club Women." *Journal of Negro History* 59, no. 2 (1974): 158–67. https://doi.org/10.2307/2717327.

Levin, Mike. "Duke Fuses Classical and Jazz!" *DownBeat*, February 15, 1943.

Lock, Graham. *Blutopia: Visions of the Future and Revisions of the Past in the Work of Sun Ra, Duke Ellington, and Anthony Braxton*. Durham, NC: Duke University Press, 1999.

Locke, Alain. "The New Negro." In *The New Negro: An Interpretation*. Library of American Civilization. New York: A. and C. Boni, 1925.

Logan, Shirley Wilson. *"We Are Coming": The Persuasive Discourse of Nineteenth-Century Black Women*. Carbondale: Southern Illinois University Press, 1999.

Lott, Eric. *Love and Theft: Blackface Minstrelsy and the American Working Class*. New York: Oxford University Press, 2013.

Lovell, John, Jr. *Black Song: The Forge and the Flame: The Story of How the Afro-American Spiritual Was Hammered Out*. New York: Macmillan, 1972.

Mackey, Nathaniel. *Atet A. D.* San Francisco: City Lights, 2001.

———. *Bass Cathedral*. New York: New Directions, 2008.

———. *Bedouin Hornbook*. Los Angeles: Sun and Moon Press, 1997.

———. *Djbot Baghostus's Run*. Sun and Moon Press, 1993.

———. *Late Arcade*. New York: New Directions, 2017.

———. *Paracritical Hinge: Essays, Talks, Notes, Interviews*. Madison: University of Wisconsin Press, 2005.

Madhubuti, Haki. "Don't Cry, Scream." In *Don't Cry, Scream*, 27. Detroit: Broadside Press, 1969.

"Mahalia Jackson: Queen of Gospel Singers." *Calcuttan* 13, no. 4 (April 1971): 7–9.

Malcolm X, and Alex Haley. *The Autobiography of Malcolm X*. Ballantine Books, 1992.

Marsh, J. B. T. *The Story of the Jubilee Singers: With Their Songs*. Memphis, TN: General Books, 2012.

Martin, Dawn Lundy. "Rhythmic Poetry." *Black Issues Book Review*, April 2007.

McClary, Susan. *Feminine Endings: Music, Gender, and Sexuality*. Minneapolis: University of Minnesota Press, 1991.

McClure, Daniel Robert. "'Who Will Survive in America?': Gil Scott-Heron, The Black Radical Tradition and the Critique of Neoliberalism." In *Broadening the Contours in the Study of Black Politics: Citizenship and Popular Culture*, edited by Michael Mitchell and David Covin, 3–26. New Brunswick, NJ: Transaction, 2016.

McPartland, Marian. "Mary Lou: Marian McPartland Salutes One Pianist Who Remains Modern and Communicative." *DownBeat*, October 17, 1957, 12.

Metzer, David. "Shadow Play: The Spiritual in Duke Ellington's 'Black and Tan Fantasy'." *Black Music Research Journal* 17, no. 2 (1997): 137–58. doi:10.2307/779366.

Miles, Kevin Thomas. "Haunting Music in the Souls of Black Folk." *Boundary 2* 27, no. 3 (2000): 199–214.

Mjagkij, Nina. *Organizing Black America: An Encyclopedia of African American Associations*. Milton Park, UK: Routledge, 2003.

Monson, Ingrid. *Freedom Sounds: Civil Rights Call Out to Jazz and Africa*. Oxford: Oxford University Press, 2010.

Morrison, Toni. *Playing in the Dark: Whiteness and the Literary Imagination*. Cambridge, MA: Harvard University Press, 1992.

Murray, Albert. *Stomping the Blues*. New York: Da Capo Press, 1976.

"A Musical Novelty." *American Musician and Art Journal* 27 (June 24, 1911): 7.

"Music, Literature, and the Drama." *Southern Workman*, September 1, 1899, 361–62.

Myers, Rollo H. *Music in the Modern World*. London: Edward Arnold, 1943.

Nabeel, Zuberi. "The Transmolecularization of [Black] Folk." In *Off the Planet: Music, Sound and Science Fiction Cinema*, edited by Philip Hayward, 77–95. London: John Libbey, 2004.

Nancy, Jean-Luc. *Listening*. Translated by Charlotte Mandell. New York: Fordham University Press, 2007.

Neal, Larry. "Any Day Now: Black Art and Black Liberation." *Ebony*, August 1969, 54–62.

———. "Black Boogaloo." In *Black Boogaloo: Notes on Black Liberation*, 23. San Francisco: Journal of Black Poetry Press, 1969.

———. "The Black Musician in White America." *Black World / Negro Digest* 16, no. 5 (March 1967): 53–57.

———. *Hoodoo Hollerin' Bebop Ghosts*. Washington, D.C.: Howard University Press, 1974.

Nelson, Alondra. "Introduction: Future Texts." *Social Text* 20, no. 2 (2002): 1–15.

Nettl, Bruno. "'Musical Thinking' and 'Thinking about Music' in Ethnomusicology: An Essay of Personal Interpretation." *Journal of Aesthetics and Art Criticism* 52, no. 1 (1994): 139–48.

Neyra, Ren Ellis. *The Cry of the Senses: Listening to Latinx and Caribbean Poetics*. Durham, NC: Duke University Press, 2020.

"No Kitten on the Keys." *Time* 42, no. 4 (July 26, 1943), 78.

Norton, Edwin L. "The Selection of School Songs." *Elementary School Teacher* 5, no. 3 (1904): 148–58.
Obadike, Mendi Lewis. "Low Fidelity: Stereotyped Blackness in the Field of Sound." PhD diss., Duke University, 2005.
Palmer, David L. "Virtuosity as Rhetoric: Agency and Transformation in Paganini's Mastery of the Violin." *Quarterly Journal of Speech* 84, no. 3 (August 1, 1998): 341–57. doi:10.1080/00335639809384223.
Patel, Aniruddh D. *Music, Language, and the Brain*. Oxford: Oxford University Press, 2008.
Peabody, Charles. "Notes on Negro Music." *Journal of American Folklore* 16, no. 62 (1903): 148–52. doi:10.2307/533498.
Peale, Norman Vincent. "'Movin' On Up' Was No Dream." *Morning Call*, April 9, 1972, sec. B.
Perelman, Chaïm, and Lucie Olbrechts-Tyteca. *The New Rhetoric: A Treatise on Argumentation*. Notre Dame, IN: University of Notre Dame Press, 1971.
Pittman, John. "Interview in Los Angeles: On Jump for Joy, Opera, and Dissonance as a 'Way of Life' (1941)." In *The Duke Ellington Reader*, edited by Mark Tucker, 150. New York: Oxford University Press, 1995.
Plato. *The Republic*. Edited by G. R. F. Ferrari. Translated by Tom Griffith. Cambridge: Cambridge University Press, 2000.
Pratt, Mary Louise. "Arts of the Contact Zone." *Profession*, 1991: 33–40.
Prevost, Eddie. "The Discourse of a Dysfunctional Drummer." In *The Other Side of Nowhere: Jazz, Improvisation, and Communities in Dialogue*, edited by Daniel Fischlin and Ajay Heble, 353–66. Middletown, CT: Wesleyan University Press, 2004.
Rabaka, Reiland. *Hip Hop's Amnesia: From Blues and the Black Women's Club Movement to Rap and the Hip Hop Movement*. Lanham, MD: Lexington Books, 2012.
"Ragging It." *Puck*, March 27, 1912.
"Ragtime." *Outlook*, May 24, 1913.
"Ragtime's Father." *Time* 31, no. 11 (March 14, 1938), 57.
Roholt, Tiger C. *Groove: A Phenomenology of Rhythmic Nuance*. New York: Bloomsbury Academic, 2014.
Royster, Jacqueline Jones. *Traces of a Stream: Literacy and Social Change among African American Women*. Pittsburgh, PA: University of Pittsburgh Press, 2000.
Russell, George. *The Lydian Chromatic Concept of Tonal Organization*. Brookline, MA: Concept, 2001.

Saffran, Jenny R., and McMullen, Erin. "Music and Language: A Developmental Comparison." *Music Perception* 21, no. 3 (Spring 2004): 289–311.

Sanchez, Sonia. "a/Coltrane/poem." In *We a BaddDDD People*. Detroit, MI: Broadside Press, 1970.

Scarborough, William Sanders. "The Negro in Fiction as Portrayer and Portrayed." *Southern Workman*, September 1, 1899.

Schwerin, Jules. *Got to Tell It: Mahalia Jackson, Queen of Gospel*. New York: Oxford University Press, 1992.

Scott, Michelle R. *T.O.B.A. Time: Black Vaudeville and the Theater Owners' Booking Association in Jazz-Age America*. Urbana: University of Illinois Press, 2023.

Scott-Heron, Gil. "Lady Day and John Coltrane." In *Now And Then*, 46. Edinburgh: Payback Press/Brouhaha, 2000.

Seward, Theodore F. Preface to *Jubilee Songs: As Sung by the Jubilee Singers, of Fisk University (Nashville, Tenn.) under the Auspices of the American Missionary Association*, by Fisk University and Jubilee Singers. New York: Biglow and Main, 1872.

Sherlock, Charles Reginald. "From Breakdown to Rag-Time." *Cosmopolitan* 31, no. 6 (October 1901): 631.

Simon, George T. "Joe Turner Star of Duke's Revue!" *Metronome*, October 1941.

Sloboda, John. "The Communication of Musical Metre in Piano Performance." *Quarterly Journal of Experimental Psychology* 35, no. 2 (May 1, 1983): 377–96. doi:10.1080/14640748308402140.

Sloboda, John, and D. H. H. Parker. "Immediate Recall of Melodies." In *Musical Structure and Cognition*, edited by Peter Howell and Ian Cross, 143–59. Orlando, FL: Academic Press, 1985.

Smitherman, Geneva. *Talkin and Testifyin: The Language of Black America*. Detroit, MI: Wayne State University Press, 1977.

"Songstress with a Divine Vision." *The Indian Express*. May 8, 1971, City edition.

Southern, Eileen. 1971. *The Music of Black Americans: A History*. New York: W. W. Norton, 1997.

Spanos, Brittany, and Sarah Grant. "Songs of Black Lives Matter." *Rolling Stone*, July 13, 2016. Accessed June 12, 2017. http://www.rollingstone.com/music/pictures/songs-of-Black-lives-matter-22-new-protest-anthems-20160713/common-feat-john-legend-glory-20160713.

Spellman, A. B. *Four Lives in the Bebop Business*. New York: Pantheon, 1966.

Spellman, A. B., and Horwitz, Murray. "John Coltrane: 'Blue Train'." National Public Radio, August 1, 2001. http://www.npr.org/2011/06/17/4555740/john-coltrane-blue-train.

Stearns, Marshall. "Bubber Miley's Jungle Iron, Choking and Sobbing Fades Dunn." *DownBeat* 4 (June 1937), 10.

———. "New Records." *Tempo*, June 1936. RIPM Jazz Periodicals. https://ripmjazz.org/.

Stoever, Jennifer Lynn. *The Sonic Color Line: Race and the Cultural Politics of Listening*. New York: NYU Press, 2016.

Sundquist, Eric J. *The Hammers of Creation: Folk Culture in Modern African-American Fiction*. Athens: University of Georgia Press, 2006.

Tallmadge, William H. "Ben Harney: White? Black? Mulatto." *Sonneck Society Newsletter* 5, no. 3 (Fall 1979): n.p.

———. "Dr. Watts and Mahalia Jackson: The Development, Decline, and Survival of a Folk Style in America." *Ethnomusicology* 5, no. 2 (May 1961): 95. https://doi.org/10.2307/924323.

Teachout, Terry. *Duke: A Life of Duke Ellington*. New York: Penguin, 2013.

Telford, Emma P. *Harriet: The Modern Moses of Heroism and Visions*. Auburn, NY: Cayuga County Museum, 1905.

Terkel, Studs. "The Gospel of Mahalia Jackson." *DownBeat*, December 1958.

Toll, Robert. *Blacking Up: The Minstrel Show in Nineteenth Century America*. London: Oxford University Press, 1974.

Townley, Eric. "An Interview with Mary Lou." *Mississippi Rag*, January 1980. RIPM Jazz Periodicals. https://ripmjazz.org/.

Troupe, Quincy. "Ode to John Coltrane." In *Transcircularities: New and Selected Poems*, 3. Minneapolis, MN: Coffee House Press, 2002.

Tynan, John. "Take 5." *DownBeat* 28, no. 24 (November 23, 1961), 40.

Ulanov, Barry. "Concert Spree," *Metronome*, February 1946. RIPM Jazz Periodicals. https://ripmjazz.org/.

———. *Duke Ellington*. New York: Da Capo Press, 1975.

———. "Mary Lou Williams." *Metronome*, July 1949. RIPM Jazz Periodicals. https://ripmjazz.org/.

Walker, Alice. *The Color Purple*. New York: Harcourt Brace Jovanovich, 1982.

Walker, George W. "The Negro on the American Stage." *Colored American Magazine*, October 1, 1906.

Ward, Andrew. *Dark Midnight When I Rise: The Story of the Jubilee Singers*. New York: HarperCollins, 2001.

Bibliography

Watts, Eric King. *Hearing the Hurt: Rhetoric, Aesthetics, and Politics of the New Negro Movement.* Tuscaloosa: University of Alabama Press, 2012.

Weheliye, Alexander G. *Phonographies: Grooves in Sonic Afro-Modernity.* Durham, NC: Duke University Press, 2005.

West, Cornel. Keynote address, Martin Luther King Jr. Celebration, Pennsylvania State University, January 20, 2017.

———. "The Prophetic Tradition in Afro-America." *The Drew Gateway* 55, no. 2–3 (Winter/Spring 1984–85): 97–113.

———. *Race Matters.* Boston, MA: Beacon Press, 1993.

"Why Women Musicians Are Inferior." *DownBeat*, February 1938, 31.

Williams, Linda Faye. "Black Women, Jazz, and Feminism." In *Black Women and Music: More Than the Blues*, edited by Eileen M. Hayes and Linda Faye Williams, 119–33. Urbana: University of Illinois Press, 2007.

Willliams, Martin. "Campus Jazz I: First Annual Oread Collegiate Festival." *DownBeat*, June 4, 1964.

Williams, Mary Lou. "Drag Em." 1931. On *The Chronological Mary Lou Williams (1927–1940)*, Classics, 1996. Compact disc.

———. "Eighth Avenue Express." 1944. On *Masters of Classic Jazz: The Piano.* Soundies, 2000. Compact disc.

———. *Mary Lou's Mass.* Smithsonian Folkways Recordings SFWCD 40815, 2005. Compact disc.

———. "Mary Lou Williams—Joanne Burke's Rough Edit of Documentary." Mary Lou Williams Collection. Institute of Jazz Studies, Rutgers University.

———. *Mary Lou Williams Presents Black Christ of the Andes.* Liner notes by Mary Lou Williams, Eddie Meadows, and Fr. Peter F. O'Brien, S.J. Smithsonian Folkways Recordings 40816, 2004. Compact disc.

———. "Night Life." 1931. On *Queen of Jazz Piano.* Acrobat AM00232, 2008. Compact disc.

———. "Roll 'Em." 1937. On *Live At the Keystone Korner.* High Note HCD 7097, 2002. Compact disc.

———. *Swinging the Blues.* Part 2: Mary Lou Williams interview. Nebraska TV. Lincoln, Nebraska, n.d. VHS. Mary Lou Williams Collection. Institute of Jazz Studies, Rutgers University.

———. Unpublished memoir. Jazz Oral History Project, the National Endowment of the Arts/Institute of Jazz Studies, Rutgers Institute of Jazz Studies, Archival Collections.

———. "Walkin' and Swingin'." 1936. On *Queen of Jazz Piano*. Acrobat AM00232, 2008. Compact disc.

———. *Zodiac Suite*. Liner notes by Mary Lou Williams and Dan Morgenstern. Smithsonian Folkways Recordings SFWCD 40810, 1995. Compact disc.

Williams, Mary Lou, and Cecil Taylor. *Embraced*. 1977. Pablo Records / Pablo 2620108, 1995. Compact disc.

Williams, Shannen Dee. *Subversive Habits: Black Catholic Nuns in the Long African American Freedom Struggle*. Durham, NC: Duke University Press, 2022.

Witkowski, Deanna. *Mary Lou Williams: Music for the Soul*. Collegeville, MN: Liturgical Press, 2021.

Index

absolute music, 5
Adam, Stephen: "Holy City," 44
African (Black) diaspora, 1, 5–6, 22, 50, 86, 93–94, 124, 165
African American jeremiad, 71
African American literature, 116, 154
African American Vernacular English (AAVE), 7
African American vernacular expression, 134–35
African drums, 22
African musical traditions, 1, 104, 106, 109, 147
Afrocentrism, 16, 17, 67, 100, 106, 109, 113–14, 137
Afrofuturism, 86, 165
Alexander, Weheliye, 16, 172n51
Allen, Red, Sr., 50
American Musician and Art Journal, 33
amplitude, 7
Amsterdam Star-News (New York), 65
Anderson, Ivy, 57
Anderson, Marian, 61
Anderson, Maureen, 176n3
Anderson, Robert, 132
anticolonialism, 105
Apollo Records, 129
Arbib, Michael, 7, 171n25
Arendt, Hannah: representative thinking, 12
Aristotle, 4, 143
Armstrong, Lil Hardin, 74
Armstrong, Louis, 141, 146
Arnold, Ignaz Theodor Ferdinand, 170n11
assimilation, 34, 137
Association for the Advancement of Creative Musicians (AACM), 114
Astaire, Fred, 102
Attali, Jacques, 169n5
Atwater, Deborah, 75, 143
audience, 5–6
Augustine, 107–8
Austin, Lovie, 74
avant-garde, 109–14, 116
Azalea, Iggy, 175n72

Bach, J. S., 51, 101
Baker, Houston, 103
Baltimore, 161
Baltimore Afro-American, 51–52
Banks, Adam J., 170n16
Baraka, Amiri (LeRoi Jones), 15–16, 110, 111, 121, 188n68
Basie, Count, 70, 146
"Beale Street Blues," 146
Beethoven, 51
Belafonte, Harry, 160
Berger, Morroe, 176n5
Berlin, Edward A., 175n86
Bethune, Mary McLeod, 71
Bieber, Justin, 175n72
big-band era, 44
binary thinking, 5

Black (or African American) rhetorical traditions, 123; constituted African and Western traditions, 5–6; listening practices, 133; multiple levels of meaning, 100; preaching, 133; prophetic tradition, 159; rhetoricians, 143; signification, 131; testifying, 151

Black achievement, 26

Black Arts movement, 2

Black church, 124, 132, 136–38, 153; Black Baptist conventions, 128; and racial uplift, 136–37; racist views about, 138

Black culture: authenticity, 33, 51, 59, 109, 134, 156; Black/African American expressive culture, 3, 25–26, 164; as challenge to segregation, 42; and public sphere, 46, 92, 114, 162–67

Black feminism, 94–97

Black genius, 15, 28, 102

Black history, 2, 165

Black intelligence, 138. *See also* Black genius

Black liberation, 111–12, 131, 167

Black life in America, 60, 71, 88–89, 92

Black lived experience, 2, 5, 39, 99, 104, 110, 114, 126; Black joy, 148

Black music, 117, 123; authenticity, 59, 96; without Black bodies, 175n72; call-and-response, 2, 7, 44, 57, 127; canon of traditions, 115; creating community, 162; cultural contribution, 62; as discipline worthy of deep study, 125; and healing, 94–95; improvisation, 2, 62, 101, 114, 129, 130, 131–32; and liberatory futurities, 164, 166; lining-out, 127–28; sonic lexicon of, 7, 62, 100, 132, 144; spirituals, 1–2, 7, 9–15, 59; and subaltern counterpublic, 164; surging, 127; validation by whites, 153–54; white usurpation of, 113; work songs, 59; as world-making and world-changing, 165

Black musicians: exploited in music business, 110; jazz musicians judged less than classical, 111; as public intellectuals, 3

Black Nationalism, 17, 67, 100, 109, 111–12, 120, 137

Black Power, 82, 111

Black pragmatism, 71

Black sonic lexicon, 7, 62, 84, 95, 127, 132, 133, 144; epistemic sonic schema, 100–101, 105, 106

Black spirituality, 15

Black women: and Black public sphere, 165; musicians, 96; objectification of, 96. *See also* Jackson, Mahalia; Williams, Mary Lou

Blades, J. A., 63

Blake, Eubie, 74, 175n86

Bland, James, 42

Blesh, Rudi, 67

blue notes, 2

blues, 2, 45, 66, 69, 74, 93–95, 102, 106, 109, 110, 113, 123, 125, 130, 145–47, 160, 164

blues women, 93–97, 102

Bok, Edward, 38

boogie-woogie, 66, 69

Boola, 59

Bowles, Paul, 61–62

Brewster, W. Herbert, 129, 188n9

Brooke, Thomas Preston, 26

Brown, Carlton, 141–42

Brown, James, 91, 111

Brown, Sterling: "Negro Characters as Seen by White Authors," 50

Brubeck, Dave, 110

Buford, Mark, 143, 154

Burke, Kenneth, 115, 117; commonplaces, 8; consubstantiality, 116; perspective by incongruity, 100

Burley, Dan, 65

Burstyn, Shai, 24

Café Society, 75, 79

cakewalk, 39

call-and-response, 2, 7, 44, 57, 127

Index 215

Calloway, Cab, 61
Caravans, the, 132
Carey, Tamika, 96
Carnegie Hall, 43, 59, 65, 79, 176n93, 180n76, 181n99
Carno, Zita, 102
Carroll, Anne, 11
Chambers, Paul, 101
Chance the Rapper, 191n67
Chapelle, Dave, 191n67
Charles, Ray, 187n40
Chesnutt, Charles, 27
Chicago, 126, 128, 153
Chicago Defender, 63, 135, 149–50
Chopin, Frédéric, 34, 45
Christian hymns, 6, 127
Christianity, 6, 149, 166
Christian Science Monitor, 50
chromaticism, 23
civil rights, 64
Civil Rights movement, 2, 59, 100, 106, 108, 120, 123, 150–58, 160, 166
Civil War (American), 60
climate crisis, 166
Coleman, Ornette, 109, 110, 111, 116
colorblindness, 156
Colored Vaudeville Benevolent Association, 32
colorism, 59
color line, 59
Coltrane, John, 17, 67, 83, 90, 99–121, 188n66; *Africa/Brass*, 101, 105–6; bebop, 115; *Blue Train*, 101, 106; Coltrane (chord) changes, 102; Coltrane poems, 116; conceptualizing freedom, 118; and democratic transformation, 115; Eastern and Western tonalities, 115; epistemic sonic schemas, 115; free jazz, 115; *Giant Steps*, 99, 101, 102–3, 106; Martin Luther King Jr., 119; *A Love Supreme*, 99, 100, 101, 106–21, 165; Malcolm X, 119–20; *My Favorite Things*, 101, 103–5, 106; Ohnedaruth (Coltrane's spiritual name), 116; political nature of *oeuvre*, 119; scholarly disagreement about, 100; spiritual narrative, 115; virtuosity, 118–19
Columbia Records, 153
Combahee River, 1–2
communism, 64
Communist Party, 64
Cone, James, 132, 147, 158
Congo, 52
Congress of Racial Equality (CORE), 194n112
Cook, William Marion, 27–28, 33
Cooper, Anna Julia, 93
Cooper, Jackie, 180n59
Copland, Aaron, 61
Cortez, Jayne, 116
Cotton Club, 43, 48, 50, 75, 177n17
counterpoint, 23
COVID-19 pandemic, 166
Cullen, Countee, 44, 52–54; "Heritage," 53–54
cultural hegemony, white, 63
Curtis, Natalie, 39–40

Dahl, Linda, 74, 185n71
Dandridge, Dorothy, 55
Darrell, R. D., 47
Davis, Almena, 58
Davis, Angela, 94
Davis, Benjamin J., 64, 75
Davis, Gussie L., 42
Davis, Miles, 70, 101, 104, 182n108
Decca Records, 128
deconstruction, 5
Definitions of Jazz retreat, 153–54
Dillard, J. L., 7
dissonance, 23, 44, 114
diversity and inclusion, 162
Dixon, David E., 115
Dixon, George Washington, 172n5
Dolphy, Eric, 112–13
Dorsey, Thomas, 127
Douglas, Aaron, 44; *Into Bondage*, 54
Douglass, Frederick, 15, 71, 172n48
DownBeat magazine, 62, 77, 112, 113, 185n72
Drew, Kenny, 101

Du Bois, W. E. B., 9–12, 15, 32, 61, 71; double consciousness, 111; *The Souls of Black Folk*, 9, 169n4; the veil, 164
Dunbar, Paul Laurence, 27
Dunn, Johnny, 45

Eastern musical traditions, 115
Ebo, Sister Mary Antona, 82
Ed Sullivan, 155–56
Ed Sullivan Show, The, 155–56
Ellington, Duke, 16, 70, 75, 83, 86, 141, 166, 179n37, 179n53; and authenticity, 51, 59; *Black and Tan* (movie), 47–48; "Black and Tan Fantasy," 43, 44–50, 67, 165; *Black, Brown and Beige*, 43, 59–65, 79, 165; and Black identity, 43, 67; call-and-response, 57; "conversation music," 44; critique of colorism, 59; *Deep South Suite*, 65–66; diasporic frame of reference, 50, 51, 54; dissonance, 44; genealogy of jazz, 51; and hot/sweet dichotomy, 45–46, 49; and Langston Hughes, 66, 179n53, 181n99; *Jump for Joy*, 43, 55–59, 66, 179n56; and "jungle music," 43, 46, 47, 48, 50–52, 177n17; *The Liberian Suite*, 66; and modernism, 43; and modernity, 57; "Mood Indigo," 47; *My People*, 66; *New World a-Comin'*, 65; and primitivism, 48; radio broadcasts, 46; reception, 46–55; *Sacred Concerts*, 85; swing, 44, 57; "Take the 'A' Train," 57, 182n2; and Western/African dichotomy, 49; and Richard Wright, 66–67
Ellington, Mercer, 59
Emancipation, 60
embodied sonic experience, 132
Emerson, Ida, 21
Eminem, 175n72
endoxa, 9
Enlightenment, 4
Enna Conservatory of Music, 29
enslaved people. *See* slavery
equality, 60
Erb, J. Lawrence, 39

Eurocentrism, 28, 104, 109; beauty standards, 96, 193n99; and Black aesthetics, 137
Evans, Curtis J., 138
exoticism, 46
expressive timing, 7

Feather, Leonard, 62, 112
Federal Bureau of Investigation, 64, 181n101
Fisk Jubilee Singers, 13–15, 137
Floyd, George, 166
Forsythe, Robert, 183n34
Foster, Stephen, 56
Fowler, John, 161–62
Francis, "Blind" James, 129
Franklin, Aretha, 91
Freud, Sigmund, 50
Fuller, Curtis, 101

Gandhi, Indira, 141
Garfield, John, 55
Garrison, Jimmy, 104
Gates, Racquel, 51
gender and jazz, 15, 17, 69–70. *See also* Williams, Mary Lou
gender transgression, 25
Gershwin, George: *Porgy and Bess*, 55
Gershwin, Ira, 179n56
Gilbert, David, 41–42, 176n93
Gillespie, Dizzy, 67, 118, 141
Gitler, Ira, 102, 114
Goodman, Benny, 61, 75, 94, 180n77
Goreau, Laurraine, 135, 141, 155–56, 188n6
gospel music, 17, 118, 123, 129
Grainger, Percy, 47
Grammy (award), 106
Gramsci, Antonio, 99
Gray, Herman, 119
Great Depression, 126
Great Migration, 126
Green, Al, 117–18
Griffin, Farah Jasmine, 75
groove, the, 2

Haiti, 60
Hammond, John, 62, 78, 153

Index 217

Hampton Conference, 26–28, 34
Hancock, Herbie, 88
Handy, D. Antoinette, 90
Handy, W. C., 146
Harlem, 43, 60–61, 80–81; exoticized, 50
Harlem Renaissance, 2, 41, 44, 48, 54
harmony, 6–7, 44, 117, 165, 166
Harney, Ben, 40–42, 175nn84–86
Harper, Frances Ellen Watkins, 93
Harper, Michael, 116
Hauser, Gerard, 12
Haydn, Joseph, 4, 170n11
Hayes, Frank, 25
Hayworth, Rita, 102
Hentoff, Nat, 114
Heilbut, Anthony, 117–18
Herskovits, Melville J., 67
Herzogenrath, Bernd, 171n28
Hindemith, Paul, 79
Hines, Earl, 61, 74, 78
hip-hop, 166, 175n72
Hodges, Johnny, 60
Holiday, Billie, 94
Hollywood Theatre Alliance, 55, 64
horizon of expectations, 25
Houck, Davis W., 115
Howard, Joseph, 21
Howard-Pitney, David, 71
Hughes, Langston, 44, 52–53, 55, 63–64, 66, 135–36, 179n56; "Afro-American Fragment," 53; "I, Too, Sing America," 179n53; "The Negro Artist and the Racial Mountain," 53

"I Can't Get Started," 69
idealism, 4–5
"I'm Old Fashioned," 102
Impressions, the, 111
income inequality, 166
inferiority, fiction of Black, 164
integration, 151–53, 162
integrationism, 100, 109, 137, 151–53
intellectual ability, 19
iTunes, 106

Jackson, Jerma A., 169n3
Jackson, Jesse, 190n28, 190n35

Jackson, Mahalia, 17, 123–60; African American vernacular expression, 124, 134–35; blues, 144, 145–47, 159; bounce (rhythmic innovation), 131; as Civil Rights movement leader, 150–58, 160, 166; collaboration with Johnson Brothers, 126–27, 149; ethos, 142–50; experiences of and responses to racism, 150–53, 156–58; improvisation, 131–32; international reception, 140–42; jazz, 144; *Mahalia Jackson Show*, 150; "Move On Up a Little Higher," 124, 129–31, 188n9; performance of gender, 132, 139–40; as rhetorician, 133, 158–60; and sonic color line, 134
James, Willis, 154
Jay Z, 187n40
jazz, 2, 125, 130, 164; and Africa, 50–52, 67, 105–6, 109, 120; and Afro-Cuban music, 67, 106; bebop, 3, 102; big-band, 15; free jazz, 17, 90, 101, 109–14 (*see also* Coltrane, John); as gendered, 70, 72; genealogy of, 51; genius, 79; hard bop, 102, 109, 186n6; history of, 69, 95; jazz studies, 154; and public sphere, 70, 114; racist criticism of, 43; sexual politics of, 77; and slavery, 69, 97; swing, 59–60, 94; and Western classical music, 61–62, 65, 79; white audience, 58
Jazz (magazine), 62
jeremiad, African American, 71, 86–97, 164–65. *See also* Williams, Mary Lou
Jim Crow, 56–57, 151, 166
Johnson, Edward, 61
Johnson, James Weldon, 16, 19, 33–39, 42, 63; *Anthology of Negro Poetry*, 39; *Autobiography of an Ex-Colored Man*, 19, 33–36, 63, 116, 164, 174n64; collaboration with J. Rosamond Johnson and Bob Cole, 36–38, 174n44; "Lift Every Voice and Sing," 166; and NAACP, 36; and Tin Pan Alley, 36
Jones, Elvin, 104, 106

Jones, Philly Joe, 101
Joplin, Scott, 12, 16, 19, 41, 164; as composer of genius, 28; and education, 31–32; endorsement by white critics and musicians, 28–29; and European classical tradition, 28–29; formal innovations, 22; "Maple Leaf Rag," 19, 22–29, 172n2; "Paragon Rag," 32; profitability as composer, 23; and racial uplift, 20, 27; as rhetorical figure, 28; technical difficulty of compositions, 23; in Texarkana Minstrels, 20; *Treemonisha*, 19, 30–33, 164, 174n57; use of AAVE, 30–31; and Wagnerian opera, 32; and Booker T. Washington, 31–32
Jordon, Joe, 42
Josephson, Barney, 79

Kansas City, 74, 77, 94
Kant, Immanuel, 170n15
Kapp, Jack, 73
Kennedy, Joe, Jr., 96
Kernodle, Tammy, 80
Key, Alyce, 58
Khan, Ali Akbar, 141
King, Martin Luther, Jr., 71, 99, 109, 115, 120, 123, 150, 186n16, 190n38
Kirk, Andy, 72, 76, 78, 184n66
Knoxville, Tennessee, 151–53
Kofsky, Frank, 119–20
Krell, William, 173n16
Kubik, Gerhard, 49
Ku Klux Klan, 56–57
Kuller, Sid, 179n56, 179n59

Labov, William, 7
Lamar, Kendrick, 166
language: instability of, 5
language-music continuum, 7
Lee, James, 129
Left Bank Jazz Society, 161–62, 164
leitmotifs, 11
Lenox, Massachusetts, 154
Levin, Mike, 62
Lewis, George, 114

Liberia, 66
Lincoln, Abby, 114
literacy, 2, 3
Locke, Alain: *The New Negro*, 52
Logan, Shirley Wilson, 93
Los Angeles Tribune, 58
Louisiana Weekly, 143
Lovell, John, Jr., 169n3
Lucas, Sam, 42

Mackey, Nathaniel, 114, 116–18; acousticality, 117; *Bass Cathedral*, 118; *Bedouin Hornbook*, 117; graspability, 117; "Ohnedaruth's Day Begun," 116; telling inarticulacy, 117
Madagascar, 52
Madhubuti, Haki, 116
Malcolm X, 71, 106, 108, 119
Marsalis, Wynton, 88
Martin, David Stone, 88
Martin, Dawn Lundy, 117
Martin, Sallie, 127
materialism, 96, 112, 159
Mbadiwe, Kingsley O., 67; African Academy of Arts and Research, 67
McClary, Susan, 77
McLean, Jackie, 110
Medi ll, 69
melody, 6–7, 117, 165, 166
"Memphis Blues," 146
Metronome, 58
Metropolitan Opera, 61, 111
Metz, Theodore, 21
Meyer, Armin, 141
Mickey Mouse, 47
microaggressions, 77, 153
Middle Passage, 5
Miley, Bubber, 177n11
Miller, Mitch, 153
Mingus, Charles, 112
minstrelsy, 12, 15, 16, 36, 41, 48, 116, 172n5, 172n11, 178n25; and "coon songs," 20; ideological functions, 20; "mammy" trope, 156; minstrel groups, 21
modal compositions, 104
modernism, 17, 43, 165

Monk, Thelonious, 3, 70, 74, 101, 116, 182n13
Montgomery bus boycott, 108, 193n88
Morgan, Lee, 101
Morrison, Toni, 42
Morton, Jelly Roll, 74, 125
Motown, 100
Muhammad, Elijah, 108
Murphy, Dudley, 47
Murray, Albert, 146–47
Murrell, Anna L., 194n111
Murrell Singers, The, 194n111
musical enthymeme, 118
musical idioms, 2
musical syntax, 11, 171n33
music: analogy with speech, 4; as communicative act, 4
Muzak, 6
"My Blue Heaven," 69
Myers, Rollo H., 43

Nancy, Jean-Luc, 25
National Association for the Advancement of Colored People (NAACP), 36
National Association of Colored Women, 143
National Black Sisters' Conference, 82
National League of Musicians, 24
National Music Teachers Association, 24
Nation of Islam, 108
Native American musical traditions, 39
Native Son (Richard Wright), 66
native sonic milieu, 6–7, 119
naturalism, 4
Nazis, Nazism, 64
Neal, Larry, 110–12, 116
Nettl, Bruno, 33
New Negro, 41
New Orleans, 125, 129, 151
New York Amsterdam News, 63
New York Herald-Tribune, 61–62
New York Philharmonic, 111
New York Times, 41
New York World, 171n45
Neyra, Ren Ellis, 171n29

Nixon, Richard, 141
nommo, 5
note selection, 128

Obadike, Mendi, 25
Oliver, Joe King, 50, 125
"On Green Dolphin Street," 69
oppression, 164, 166
Original Dixieland Jazz Band, 110
ornamentation, 128, 129
Ottley, Roi: *New World a-Comin'*, 65
"Over the Rainbow," 69

Paganini, Niccolò, 118
Pandora, 187n40
Parker, Charlie, 70, 80
passing, 34, 35, 178n26
Pasternak, Joseph, 55
Patel, Aniruddh, 6, 170n20, 170n24, 171n33
Patterson, Louise Thompson, 64
Pennsylvania State University, 99
perception, 6–7
pitch, 128
Pittsburgh, 71
Pittsburgh Courier, 50, 54
Plato, 4
political polarization, 166
pop, 130
Popular Front, 55
Porres, St. Martin de, 83
Port Royal, South Carolina, 1
Powell, Adam Clayton, Jr., 61, 64
Powell, Adam Clayton, Sr., 80
Powell, Bud, 70
Pozo, Chano, 67
Pratt, Mary Louise, 176n92
Prevost, Eddie, 114
primitivism, 43, 48, 136
Prince, 187n40, 191n67
progress, 102
public intellectuals, 3, 108
public sphere, 3, 27, 46, 70, 114; Black public sphere, 162–67
Pulitzer Prize, 166
Puritanism, 50, 71, 86

Ra, Sun, 109
race, 8; discourses of, 12; racial essentialism, 35, 36; racial pride, 67, 114, 121
racialized listening practices, 23
racial reckoning, 166
racial uplift, 17, 27, 31–32, 131, 136–37
racism (anti-Black), 11, 20, 34, 39, 125, 138, 150–53, 156–58, 159, 166; of music industry, 110–11; Romantic racism, 138
radio, 79, 150; NBC broadcast, 46; as racialized, 46
ragtime, 12, 69, 73–74, 164; classical music vs. Black music, 29; and "coon songs" or minstrelsy, 21, 24–25; defined, 19; and racial uplift, 27; reception, 24–30; and Spanish-American War, 39; and syncopation, 21. *See also* Joplin, Scott
Rainey, Gertrude "Ma," 94, 124, 125, 127
Red Hot Peppers (Jelly Roll Morton), 110
resolution, 23
resonance, 8, 166
respectability, 27, 113, 133, 134
Revolutionary War (American), 60
rhetoric: Black diasporic and Western traditions, 5–6; of Black women, 93–97; ethos, 2, 15, 75, 101, 143; *kairotic* moment, 99–100, 106; musical enthymeme, 119; rhetorical situation, 115; strategies, 3. *See also* Black rhetorical traditions
rhythm, 7
rhythm and blues (R&B), 88, 96, 130, 166, 175n72
Rice, Thomas Dartmouth, 172n5
Rickford, John R., 7
Rimsky-Korsakov, Nikolai, 47
Roach, Max, 112, 187n38
Robeson, Paul, 61, 64
Roché, Betty, 60
Rodgers and Hammerstein, 103
Rolling Stone, 107
Rollins, Sonny, 109
Romanticism, 4, 118

Rooney, Mickey, 179n59
Roosevelt, Alice, 172n2
Roosevelt, Franklin Delano, 75
Roosevelt, Theodore, 172n2
Rosenfeld, Monroe H., 174n45
Royalties, 23–24
Russell, George, 67, 181n108
Russia, 64
Russian War Relief Effort, 59

sacred/secular binary, 45, 84, 85, 123, 147–48
Sanchez, Sonia, 116
Scarborough, William Sanders, 26–27, 34
Schuller, Gunther, 112
Scott, Hazel, 76, 79
Scott-Heron, Gil, 116–17
secularism, 115
Sedalia, Missouri, 24, 32
Selma to Montgomery march, 106
Senegal, 52
Seward, Theodore, 13, 43–44
Shankar, Ravi, 141
Shaw, Artie, 61
Shepp, Archie, 109, 111
Sheppard, Ella, 13
signifying, 100, 115
Simon, George T., 58
Slave Code of 1740 (South Carolina), 22
slavery, 1–2, 7, 138, 154
Sloboda, John, 170n24
Smith, Bessie, 94, 124, 178n25
Smith, Willie "The Lion," 175n86
Smith, Wonderful, 55
Smitherman, Geneva, 8, 134, 137
social ascension, 59
sonic Blackness, 23, 35, 36, 134, 164, 165, 172n51
sonic Black subjects, 3, 105, 165
sonic color line, 134
sonic studies, 6, 132
Soul Train, 102
Sound of Music, The, 103
Spanish-American War, 60
Spellman, A. B., 101, 110, 186n20

Index

spirituals, 30, 39, 45, 59–60, 66, 109, 114, 115, 160, 166; and the blues, 147; "Go Down, Moses," 35; relationship to Western classical music, 7, 28, 35; rhetoric of, 1–2; as Sorrow Songs (W. E. B. Du Bois), 9–15
Spotify, 187n40
Stark, John, 24
"Star-Spangled Banner, The," 39
Stearns, Marshall, 153–54
stereotypes, 12, 164, 178n25; exoticism/primitivism, 50; gender, 69–70; "mammy" trope, 156; racist, 33, 34, 50, 82, 159, 172n5
Stewart, James T., 110
Stewart, Maria W., 93
Stewart, Rex, 63
stigmatization, 22
Strauss, Richard, 47
Strayhorn, Billy, 55
Still, William Grant, 61
St. Louis Blues (film), 178n25
"St. Louis Blues," 69
Stoever, Jennifer, 134
Stone, Fred, 41
Stono Rebellion, 22
Stowe, Harriet Beecher: *Uncle Tom's Cabin*, 138
Stravinsky, Igor, 79
stride piano, 45, 73–74, 182n12
Sugar Hill (Harlem), 61
Supremes, the, 111
"Surrey with a Fringe on Top," 69
Suskind, Peter, 65
swing, 2, 44, 57, 59–60, 94, 113; defined, 176n6
syncopation, 21–22, 52

"Take the 'A' Train," 57
Tallmadge, William, 128, 175n86
Tatum, Art, 74
Taylor, Cecil, 109
Teachout, Terry, 181n101
Terkel, Studs, 137, 153
Terrell, Mary Church, 143
Texarkana, Texas, 19, 32
T. I., 175n72

Tibbett, Lawrence, 46
timbre, 7, 128, 165
Time magazine, 41, 76, 175n85, 183n45
Tin Pan Alley, 36
Toll, Robert, 172n6
tonalities, 115, 165
Tone magazine, 145
tone modification techniques, 44, 45; mutes, 177n11
topoi, 164
total art, 11
Townley, Eric, 183n26
Townsend, Irving, 192n81
Troupe, Quincy, 116
Truth, Sojourner, 93
Tubman, Harriet, 1–2, 4, 15
Turner, Big Joe, 55
Turner, Lorenzo, 7
Twelve Clouds of Joy, 72, 75, 184n66
Tynan, John, 112
Tyner, McCoy, 104–5

Ulanov, Barry, 78, 79–80
Uncle Remus stories, 39
University of Maryland, Baltimore County (UMBC), 161
upward mobility, 57, 60–61
Usher, 175n72

Vallée, Rudy, 47
vibrato, 128, 134, 147
Viscount François de Fontanges Legion, 60
voice leading, 22

Wagner, Richard, 11, 32, 51
Walker, George, 166
Waller, Fats, 74
waltz, 60
Washington, Booker T., 31–32, 71
Washington, Fredi, 47, 178n26
Washington, Grover, 88
Waterman, Richard, 154
Waters, Ethel, 156
Watts, Eric King, 41
Watts, Isaac, 127
Weheliye, Alexander, 16, 172n51

Welburn, Ron, 110
Wells, Ida B., 71, 96, 143
West, Cornel, 88, 99, 115
West, Holly, 110
Western: canon of music, 26; modernity, 164; musical traditions, 1, 104; musicology, 5; philosophy, 5
Western classical music, 13, 15, 21, 28, 44, 45, 65, 170n15
Wheatley, Phillis, 154
White, George L., 13
White, Paul, 56
Whiteman, Paul, 45, 61
whiteness, 134
white supremacy, 116
Williams, Martin, 112
Williams, Mary Lou, 15, 17, 124, 131; and African American jeremiad, 17, 71, 86–97, 164–65; and Afrofuturism, 86; and Black history, 69; and Black pragmatism, 70, 91–94; and Black prophetic tradition, 70 (*see also* African American jeremiad); and classical music, 79–80; and Miles Davis, 70; "Drag 'Em," 74; "Eighth Avenue Express," 182n2; *Embraced*, 90, 91, 184n65; ethos, 75; gender constraints, 69–70, 72–73; influence and mentorship, 70; jazz and slavery, 69; jazz, history of, 69; jazz liturgy, 165; *Mary Lou's Mass*, 69, 85; Mary Lou Williams Jazz Festival, 185n82; *The Mary Lou Williams Piano Workshop*, 79; *Mary Lou Williams Presents Black Christ of the Andes*, 83; *Mass for Lenten Season*, 85; on meritocracy, 92; misogynistic criticisms of, 76–79; and Thelonious Monk, 70, 74, 182n13; "Night Life," 73–75; and Father Peter O'Brien, 81–82, 91, 96, 183n45; "Old Time Spiritual" (check), 69; and Charlie Parker, 70; *Pittsburgh Mass*, 84–85; political involvement, 75–76; and Bud Powell, 70; as professor of jazz, 90; rhetoric of, 75, 84; "Roll 'Em," 94–95; social services ministry, 81–82; spirituality, 69, 70, 79, 80–81; "St. Martin de Porres," 83, 183n45; trauma, 74–75, 80; and Twelve Clouds of Joy, 72, 75, 76; *Zodiac Suite*, 79–80
Williams, Robert L., 7
Wilson, Garland, 80
world view, 5
World War II, 61, 138
Wright, Richard, 66–67

You Were Never Lovelier, 102